Tradition, Innovation,
Conflict

Jewishness and Judaism in Contemporary Israel

Edited by
Zvi Sobel
and
Benjamin Beit-Hallahmi

STATE UNIVERSITY OF NEW YORK PRESS

Production by Ruth East
Marketing by Fran Keneston

Published by
State University of New York Press, Albany

For information, address State University of New York
Press, State University Plaza, Albany, N.Y. 12246

Library of Congress Cataloging-in-Publication Data

Tradition, innovation, conflict : Jewishness and Judaism in contemporary
    Israel / edited by Zvi Sobel and Benjamin Beit-Hallahmi.
        P. cm. — (SUNY series in Israeli studies)
    Includes bibliographical references.
    ISBN 0-7914-0554-0 (alk. paper). — ISBN 0-7914-0555-9 (pbk. :
alk. paper)
        1. Judaism—Israel. 2. Zionism and Judaism. I. Sobel, Zvi.
    II. Beit-Hallahmi, Benjamin. III. Series.
    BM390T73   1991
    306.6′095694—dc20   90-35232
                                                                                    CIP

10 9 8 7 6 5 4 3 2 1

Contents

Part II.   Dissent and Religious Alternatives

Part III.   The Religiosity Factor

Preface

With the passage of time it becomes more and more evident that religion as an institution and as a force plays an increasingly central role in Israeli society. In the course of the governmental crisis which shook the country in the spring of 1990 a number of "truths" about the workings of the Israeli polity were revealed in stark relief. Two of these are of particular interest in the context of the present volume and they are the extent to which parties whose raison d'être is the protection and extension of the perceived interests of religious orthodoxy in the society hold the balance of power though representing only a small minority of the population and, of no less interest, the seeming willingness of the majority of non-orthodox citizens to accept this state of affairs as perhaps onerous but nonetheless legitimate. It would appear that the majority of Israelis are either remarkably passive, or perhaps, less overwhelmingly "secular" than many observers have claimed. It might also, however, suggest that in dealing with religion in Israeli society we are dealing with a highly complex phenomenon which cannot be understood through resort to clearly demarcated categories or labels such as "secular", "religious", or even the ultimately flexible catch-all "traditional".

The essays and research reports in the present volume are an effort to deal with what Isrealis believe and how they behave in the religious context. The collection was organized from the ground up, or from the field up, so to speak. Contributors were asked to write pieces reflecting the state of *their* knowledge and *their* interests rather than to follow preconceived notions of the editors about where the research should lead. The final version, presented here, is the outcome of a collaborative process between contributors and editors where the attempt has been made to always give priority to the realities of the field and the research process. The result, we believe, reflects the current religious situation in Israel in its complexity and richness. It also reflects a variety of theoretical and research disciplines, ranging from the phenomenological to the large-scale population survey.

Clearly, however, not every aspect or dimension of religion or religious life in Israel is treated in the present volume. The very attempt would be presumptuous. This is a beginning which of necessity remains partial and unfinished but will, we hope, result in the publication of follow-up works explicating this very central concern of Israeli society.

In carrying out our task as editors, we have enjoyed the invaluable help of the Research Authority at our home institution, the University of Haifa. Betty Rozen, who teaches English here, applied some polish to our English style, and was most helpful in other ways. Danielle Friedlander has served as an untiring and unflapable typist helping to save the integrity of the text from the ravages of an unpredictable computer system. We are thankful.

Introduction

BENJAMIN BEIT-HALLAHMI AND ZVI SOBEL

From the beginning of the Zionist enterprise in the nineteenth century, the role of religion and the place of religion in a Jewish polity has persisted as a central question and continues to elude easy definition, to say nothing of resolution. Most Zionist thinkers of the "classical" period at the turn of the century and in the early decades of the present century at least in some measure viewed Zionism as an escape from the dead hand of religious obscurantism and as a way of easing the Jewish masses into the mainstream of Western civilization. In some sense, and with respect to the Jewish masses of Eastern Europe, Zionism was a kind of nondeistic reform movement that some observers viewed as an effort to keep the bath water and throw out the baby. Be that as it may, the major thrust—both ideological and practical (in its settlement expression)—was of a secularizing character, but with a strong buttressing of the enterprise by traditions, acts, and rituals drawn from the religious context. These served a twofold function: they provided a web of familiarity, a skein of continuity to ease passage into an uncharted and indeed revolutionary situation, while providing a baseline or at least vocabulary for the evolvement of new societal forms; and secondly, they provided a matrix of legitimation for a possibly illegitimate act—the displacement of the native Arab population. (This second factor is only now beginning to function in a heightened fashion.)

Thus we confront an interesting and rather confusing situation in contemporary Israel where to all intents and purposes—ideationally, behaviorally, even electorally—the majority of the population is nonobservant if not fully secular, while the national symbols, rhetoric, framework are all heavily influenced and interlaced by traditional

Jewish (European) religion. Even though Israel cannot be said to be a particularly "religious" country, it tends to be seen as such by outsiders and, we would aver, increasingly by Israelis themselves. Furthermore, and to add to the seeming contradiction, while basically nonobservant, it tends to be "Orthodox" in this nonobservance, rather than tied to or tending to any of the less taxing, less rigid forms prevalent, let us say, in the largest Jewish Diaspora of our times, the United States of America. Thus those who see a possibly rosy future for the Reform or Conservative movements transplanted to Israel are, we feel, bound to be disappointed.

Insofar as a religious system took root in Israel, it was that system that emerged from the Eastern European context even to the point where in its more extreme manifestations it has overtaken and absorbed similarly inclined groupings coming from a totally different environment—the Sepharadim of the Middle East and North Africa. In effect, both ideological systems undergirding Israeli society—the religious and the secular—are overwhelmingly Eastern European in derivation.

Until the 1967 Six-Day War, the relationship between the secular majority and the religiously observant minority stayed on a more or less even keel symbolized by what has come to be called the "status quo agreement". Basic religious needs would be respected and indeed supported by the state—a sort of a minimalist agreement from the viewpoint of the religious—while loyalty to the Zionist state—also rather minimalist—would be returned by the religious. Religion would supply a sort of ceremonial continuity to the enterprise while recognizing that its "divisions" and "armor" were thin and unlikely to carry the day. At the same time, the state would make it possible for at least basic identification on the part of the observant with a broader societal consensus.

Since 1967, the status quo has been violated by both camps. Inroads into public religious observances have been made by the nonreligious majority, and increasing demands for financial support and stricter observance in the public and even personal arena have been made by segments of the religious minority. The battle has increasingly been joined with the additional complication of the "national" element, which is associated more and more with a religious stance, playing a role. Although the country's political and intellectual elite is overwhelmingly secular or nonobservant, one sees signs of religious symbols being increasingly used for the purposes of political legitimation and as a unifying theme. One reason for this utilization of religious themes is that of all the ideological camps for prestate and early state Israel—the socialist, the militantly secular, the general Zionist—

only the religious sector appears to retain a sense of continuing dynamism and commitment. Thus at the same time as every life in Israel is marked increasingly by a secular encasement, the religious context enjoys (paradoxically) greater and greater "respect" and legitimacy. Numerically, the relationship between secular and religious has not significantly changed, but the dymanic interplay has undergone change in the direction of greater intrusiveness of religion at least symbolically and politically than in the past.

Now, while the issue of religion and state and of religion and politics has been widely if only sometimes adequately dealt with in the literature, the *nature* and *functioning* of religion among Israelis and in the society at large has not enjoyed much serious treatment. In effect, this book will be the first to set forth a more basic picture of how and what Israelis believe, and how they act or do not act upon those beliefs. It is our contention that knowledge of these elements of any society, and perhaps especially Israeli society, is of more than passing importance

THE BACKGROUND

In Israel, religion can be viewed as a source of unity, but in reality it is often a source of division and tension. To say that the religious situation in Israel is unique and complex is a platitude that is still worth keeping in mind as one approaches the subject.

There are several working hypotheses with which scholars approach the current religious situation in Israel. The simplest and most common notion is that of continuity with Jewish traditions of the past wherein the question of specific traditions must be raised. If Israel is indeed reflective of Diaspora religious traditions, then which Diaspora do we have in mind? Currently, Diaspora seems to mean the English-speaking world, in which more than 50 percent of world Jewry resides. Very often one encounters wholesale projections of the Jewish religious situation from there on to the Israeli scene (that is, the division into Reform and Conservative majority, and an Orthodox minority). Such projections are absurd and totally divorced from reality because they fail to note the most important facts about the history of Israeli Judaism: first its continuity with the Diaspora of Eastern Europe, and then its continuity with the Diaspora of Arab countries, whose descendents currently comprise the majority of Israel's citizens.

Like many countries in Central and Eastern Europe, Israel has a Ministry of Religious Affairs that recognizes certain religious communities and gives them government support and supervision. These include the Druze (who for the first time in history are separate from Islam and Arabs), Catholics, Bahais, Samaritans, various Christian groups, and Jews. Religious judges in all communities are paid by the state, and the jurisdiction of religious courts is limited to personal matters, marriage, divorce, and sometimes inheritance. The Ministry of Religious Affairs is normally held by one of the religious parties and serves as a source of patronage and political influence. Most of the budget is devoted to Jewish religious services.

Of the four religious movements among Jews in the United States —Reform, Conservative, Orthodox, and Reconstructionist—only the third has a significant presence in Israel. When we speak of religious groups in Israel, we mean Orthodoxy. The other movements are totally unknown to most Israelis and are generally regarded with as much empathy as Rev. Moon's Unification Church or Confucianism. While Reform Judaism in the United States claims more than a million ad- herents, in Israel it might claim a few thousand at most.

The historical connections between political Zionism in its cur- rent forms and Judaism have to be examined to understand recent developments in Israeli politics, especially since 1967 and 1973. Zion- ism has always been a secular movement, not only because its leaders were secular in their life-style and beliefs, but because they did not base any of their thinking on religious traditions. The mere creation of Zionism, which defined Jews as a nation and developed a secular nationalism, was an active rejection of Jewish religious traditions. Zionism is "the transformation of the concept of Jewry from a divine pilot project into a human problem soluble through human devices" (Marmorstein 1969, 57). The secular character of political Zionism, and its rebellion against Jewish tradition, caused the opposition shown by Orthodox Jewry in Eastern Europe and Palestine.

What makes the religious situation in Israel so complex and unique are two factors. First, the majority of Israelis are nonobservant, constituting a majority subculture that is distinctly secular in its life-style. This majority is referred to in everyday Hebrew as *hilonim*. A minority subculture, making up about 20 percent of the population, contains Orthodox Jews of all varieties and is referred to as *datiim*. Within the *dati* subculture, one can distinguish further between the Zionist-Orthodox and the non-Zionist.

Second, compared to any Diaspora community today, Israel has a larger percentage of Orthodox Jews, and it has a far higher percent- age of Jews whose ancestors lived in Arab countries. The last demographic factor is historically not only unique but revolutionary, and this for a number of reasons, such as the relative newness of the modernization dimension and the much higher rate of religious traditionalism among Sepharadim.

Throughout modern Jewish history, non-European Jews, known as Sepharadim, were a small minority of the world Jewish population, as they are today. If one takes the best estimates for the number of Jews in the world today (around 12 million), only about 15 percent are of Sephardic origin, but the majority of this minority now live in Israel and in fact are a majority of the population! This segment of reality, often forgotten, has been shaping Israeli culture and has begun to critically influence the Israeli religious situation.

Orthodoxy Faces Modernization and Zionism

The process of leaving the ghetto and gaining formal equality between 1770 and 1870 in Europe is regarded today by some Orthodox Jews as a major disaster because it destroyed the traditional Jewish community. While secularization posed the question of defining individual and collective Jewish identity, those who avoided it found themselves in a defensive position against the whole modernizing world. Since the eighteenth century, Orthodox Judaism has been in retreat, and on the defensive, in the face of modernization.

Orthodox Jewish leadership reacted with a total rejection of modernity. It attempted complete separatism, not willing to risk any contacts. Quite soon it was clear that such a complete ghettoization was impossible in the modern world. The solution has been a selective, tactical involvement in modern culture. Separatism was reinforced by strict ritualism and regimentation, continuing the historic Jewish option of maintaining barriers between the Jewish community and outsiders, who in the modern world include both non-Orthodox Jews and non-Jews. Contact with the outside world is allowed for economic survival, and it is limited to occupations that would not entail an intense commitment to modern values. The war on modernity is waged by keeping the tradition to the fullest, resisting change, and acting confidently. Thus, Orthodox Jews might be found in some kinds of retail trade, but only rarely in science and the professions. Secular work might be necessary for survival, but it is never comparable to the higher calling of Talmudic studies and the jealous keeping of the 613 commandments that guide the life of the observant Jew.

Orthodox Reactions to Zionism

For the Orthodox, Zionism as it first appeared on the scene was a challenge and a danger, worse than assimilation or secularization, and in fact did represent one form of radical secularization. Zionism refused to leave Jewish identity and the Jewish community behind. It claimed them to itself, offering a radically new definition of what Jewishness meant. It actively rejected religion as representing passivity and ignorance. Zionism was a vote of no confidence in God and his Messiah, and an insult to 2000 years of tradition.

Most Orthodox reactions to Zionism were identical to the general Orthodox reaction to modernity and secularization. Orthodox leaders did not accept the Zionist definition of the Jews as a nation in search of a homeland, but remained faithful to the ancient definition of Jews as a religious community waiting for the Messiah. All over the world, including Palestine, pitched battles were launched by the Orthodox against Zionism beginning as early as the 1880s and the 1890s. The old Orthodox community in Jerusalem, for example, denounced Zionist newcomers to the Ottoman authorities and expressed horror at the revival of Hebrew as a secular language.

The success of Zionism among the Jewish intelligentsia and in negotiating with world powers made a deep impression on Orthodox leaders. There was a point when Zionism seemed to be invincible, gaining more support and collecting more success, which constituted a shock to the Orthodox who were losing members to assimilation.

Orthodoxy: Anti-Zionist, Non-Zionist, and Zionist

One characteristic of Orthodox Jewish life is the various grades and shadings of Orthodoxy, leading to competition and sectarianism. Thus one cannot speak of 'Orthodoxy' without specifying particular groups. A general measure of Orthodoxy would be the extent to which a group uses the Hebrew language versus Yiddish in everyday life. All ultra-Orthodox groups always use Yiddish; Zionist Orthodox use Hebrew.

Some non-Zionist Orthodox leaders see the coming Zionism and the founding of the state of Israel as an opportunity for Jews to improve their situation, but not as the beginning of redemption. The anti-religious Zionist groups will avoid any contact with the state because they see it not only as illegitimate, but as an act of blasphemy. For them the state is still a place of exile, until the coming of the Messiah.

Some of the ultra-Orthodox groups, though non-Zionist, are ready to cooperate with the state of Israel when it suits their purposes. Thus, they will accept financial support for their schools from the state as well as other forms of assistance. Unlike the Zionists however they will never see the state as having religious significance or being the 'beginning of redemption.'

There was a handful of Orthodox rabbis in the 19th century who were calling for a Jewish national revival, such as Rabbi Zvi Hirsch Kallischer of Posen, in Prussia. In 1862 he issued a call for the 'redemption of Israel', following the example of the Italians, the Poles, and the Hungarians. Such ideas, and such rabbis, were the rare exceptions rather than the rule.

In May 1912, 200 Orthodox leaders from Germany and Eastern Europe met in Kattowitz (Katowice) to start Orthodoxy's first organized response to Zionism, *Agudat Israel*, which exists today as a political party in Israel and as a political lobbying group elsewhere. Agudat Israel is an anti-Zionist Orthodox movement, the best-known political reaction of Orthodoxy to Zionism.

The ideologue of this movement was Nathan Birnbaum, a brilliant intellectual who collaborated with Herzl in the early days of political Zionism and then became disillusioned. He became convinced that the secular definition of the Jews as a nation was inadequate, and secularization would lead to the disappearance of the Jewish people. Orthodoxy had to take a firm stand against Zionism, in the form of a political organization. Agudat Israel was Diaspora-oriented. Its center in the years between the two world wars was in Poland, where about one-third of the Jews in that country were its supporters and where it had elected representatives in the Polish parliament in the 1930s.

Historically, Agudat Israel has been opposed to the idea of a Jewish state, but it was deeply affected by the Holocaust, and its opposition was softened. A major effect of the Holocaust was the loss of most of its constituency in Eastern Europe, resulting in Agudat Israel becoming more of a minority, more pro-Zionist, and more prepared to accept the reality of Zionist success.

In Israel after 1948, the party has been pragmatically involved in state institutions and accepts the state for all practical purposes. It supports governing coalitions and is rewarded with ample budgets for its Orthodox schooling system. The state of Israel is accepted *de facto*, but it is judged to be without the religious significance assigned to it by religious Zionists.

The Ultra-Orthodox Anti-Zionist

There is a small community in Jerusalem that continues the life of the Diaspora and preserves the historical tradition in the most authentic way, constituting a sort of living museum. *Neturei Karta* (Gardians of

the City—in Aramic) was created in response to the growing accommodation to Zionism on the part of Agudat Israel since 1948.

Members of the community do not use government identity
cards, do not use Israeli money or postage stamps, and do not accept
any services from the state. Neturei Karta represents today the classical ultra-Orthodox reaction to Zionism, viewing the latter as an
abomination, a heresy, and a blasphemy against historical Judaism.
The Zionist heresy is that of defining Jews as a nation. Jews cannot be
a normal nation because they have been chosen by God to be a Holy
People. The condition of exile will end when God wants it to end. Jews
were sent into exile because of their sins, not because of any worldly
weakness. Building up worldly strength is not real redemption.

The state of Israel was conceived and born in sin because Zionism is not just a rebellion against history but against divine judgment.
Such a rebellion will surely be punished and cannot be recognized in
any way. Jewish nationalism was an imitation of gentile ways, and
Jews should not rebel against gentile rule but wait for divine redemption. The Zionist state is a passing shadow, and the problems of Zionism in recent years represents divine punishment.

Religious Zionism

The beginnings of religious Zionism can be found in Eastern Europe
around the turn of the century. Several Orthodox rabbis accepted
Zionism pragmatically, as a movement that improves life for some
Jews but is devoid of religious significance. At that point it was clear
that Zionism and modernism were on the ascendant, and Orthodoxy
needed to move in the direction of accommodation. The Zionist religious camp was created in response to the successes and the vitality of
secular Zionism, and has grown or failed to do so in response to its
changing fortunes.

It was Rabbi A. I. H. Kook (1865–1935), who himself moved to
Palestine and served as chief rabbi there, who developed the concept
of Zionism as part of the divine plan for redemption. This notion made
possible a new alliance between Orthodoxy and Zionism, involving
only a minority of the Orthodox to be sure, but a significant group
nevertheless. This group was gaining from the vitality of Zionism, while
Orthodoxy seemed in real decline.

Kook was ready to sacralize the secular actions of Zionism, giving
the new settlements in Palestine a religious meaning. If Zionism was
the beginning of true redemption, even secular settlers were engaged
in positive action. The hope was that eventually they would see the

light, combine Zionism with Judaism, and return to religion. This view of Zionism having religious significance led to an active involvement in all aspects of Zionist activities in Palestine. After 1948, it meant that the National Religious Party has been a partner in most Israeli governing coalitions.

THE PRESENT: WHAT IS HAPPENING IN ISRAEL?

In Israel, differences among different groups can be illustrated in their attitudes towards Israeli Independence Day. The most anti-Zionist, Neturei Karta, fly black flags. For them, it is a day of mourning. They spend it reciting psalms and following other mourning customs. Members of Agudat Israel, which is considerably less extreme and slightly less anti-Zionist, treat the Day as a regular working day. They simply ignore it. Their school system, which operates independently of the state but enjoys government financing, stays open. Religious Zionists celebrate Independence Day with other citizens, but some of them, the most patriotic, carry out special religious services with thanksgiving prayers, thus expressing the belief that the state has religious meaning. These recent traditions of reactions to the secular state reflect early historical reactions to Zionism.

The settler on the West Bank, his head covered with the knitted skullcap and an Uzi slung over his shoulder, has become an emblem of Israel in the late 1980s. Much media attention has been directed toward incidents in which bus stop shelters have been burned or defaced after they were used to display advertisements showing scantily clad women. Less conventional, but perhaps more significant, reports and pictures appear to reveal Mr. Shimon Peres, the Labor Party leader, to be undergoing a process of Orthodoxization. First, Mr. Peres goes to the Wailing Wall after being sworn as prime minister in 1984, then he is observed taking Talmud lessons from a chief rabbi. That these displays of piety were subject to ridicule and derision is also part of the story.

Incidents such as the burning of bus stop shelters seem in this light to be the least significant, and this is confirmed when we learn that some feminists in Israel joined with the ultra-Orthodox in condemning the advertisements and sometimes in defacing them. This is reminiscent of similar cases in other places, such as the United States. Both parties to this surprising (and not so surprising) alliance, the ultra-Orthodox and the feminists, represent marginal groups, which essentially stand outside the Israeli political arena on most vital issues. The whole bus-shelter affair is totally unrelated to other, more important, issues of religion and ideology.

The now emblematic religious settler on the West Bank is a true reflection of events there, but he does not represent the majority of Israelis, or even the majority of Orthodox Jews in Israel. It is important to recall that there is still a clear negative correlation between Orthodoxy and Zionism among Jews. Those who are more Orthodox are less (or anti-) Zionist. The West Bank settlers rank high on the Zionism scale, but low on the Orthodoxy scale. Thus, for example, a woman has served as a secretary general of *Gush Emunim*, the settler organization. This would be inconceivable among the more Orthodox. The nationalist Orthodoxy of Gush Emunim is new and messianic, unlike that of most Orthodox Jews in the world.

One of the terms most commonly used in connection with the religion and political issue in Israel (and in other places) is 'fundamentalism'. When this term is used, in the case of Judaism in Israel, to denote Orthodoxy and nationalism, it is plainly wrong. Fundamentalism is a technical concept, denoting a specific Protestant movement, started in early twentieth century in reaction to religious modernism in the United States. The movement acquired its name from the 11 fundaments it adhered to, including such tenets of Christian faith as the Virgin Birth and the literal truth of the Bible. Using this term for other times and other places is misleading and counterproductive because it might hinder current perceptions of different realities.

One of the reasons for the attractiveness of this concept is that it leads immediately to associations with fundamentalism in other places, and often those using it would like to imply that fundamentalism and fundamentalists all over the world are the same, be they Americans, Iranians, or Israelis. While there might be an underlying common psychological component in various forms of fundamentalism, it seems that this term, growing out of a specific historical context, does not have much meaning beyond its native soil. Most Orthodox Jews are not nationalists and not Zionists. Religious Zionists in Israel, the so-called fundamentalists or fanatics, have little in common with Conservative Baptists in the United States or with Iranian Shiites who promote an Islamic republic.

Moreover, no religious Jew can be emblematic of the majority of Israelis beause that majority, despite all developments and appearances, is still nonobservant, if not consciously Zionist. Only around 20 percent of Israelis are observant, and they constitute a separate subculture characterized by its own life-style and separated from the majority of Israelis by the same structures that have separated Jews from their non-Jewish neighbors in the past—rules about diet, dress, and calendar. This minority subculture is clearly not becoming a majority. If there is a resurgence of religion in Israel, it can be found in several areas. The first is that of personal 'conversion', in which young and not-so-young Israelis, members of the nonobservant majority, make the personal decision to become Orthodox. Such cases in Israel have numbered in the thousands since 1973, and they constitute a considerable social movement.

Saying No to the Enlightment

This is a historical victory for Orthodoxy over Zionism as some of the sons and grandsons of those who rejected Orthodoxy and embraced Zionism are moving in the opposite direction. Moreover, it is a rejection of secular culture. It is "the Enlightenment in reverse" (Marmorstein 1969, 107), going against the historical secularization of the Jews, of which Zionism has been an integral part. The grandson of Isaac Gruenbaum, a famous antireligious Zionist leader in Poland before 1940 and in Israel after 1947, is a celebrated Talmudist today, having rejected his secular family, and he is only one among many such cases. The newly Orthodox express their rejection of Israeli identity by using traditional Jewish names for their children and by speaking Hebrew in the Diaspora pronunciation, or even Yiddish.

Of course, psychological factors are important in the search that leads Israelis to become Orthodox Jews. The religious camp points to the emptiness of secular life in Israel, and is quite correct in its diagnosis. These individuals search for community and for a moral order, looking away from the selfish, empty materialism of most secular Israelis.

Two observations need to be made in this context. First, the movement from secularism to religion, however significant, has not changed the minority status of the Orthodox in Israel. Second, most of the returnees to Judaism, according to the (negative) correlation presented above between Orthodoxy and Zionism, turn non-Zionist or even anti-Zionist as a result of their change of heart. They seem to be saying "we have tried all modern answers, including Zionism, and they didn't work."

Political Discourse

The second realm in which we can observe a significant change is that of political discourse. What we can observe, and this has been going on since 1967, is the growing use of religious symbols by nonreligious leaders and, even more so, the growing confidence of religious politicians in making pronouncements about matters both religious and secular. It is important to recall that most members of recent Israeli cabinets have remained totally secular in their behavior and political discourse, and this includes some of the more visible Israeli leaders, such as Yizhak Shamir, Shimon Peres, Ezer Weizman, Yizhak Rabin, Ariel Sharon, and Moshe Arens. It is also important to recall that among Israeli nationalists, secularism is still common.

The secular nationalists should not be discounted or ignored. There are atheist Zionists who are as militant about their atheism as about their Zionism, and this phenomenon exists quite openly and quite emphatically in Israel. Meir Uziel, a popular right-wing columnist (and a grandson of a chief rabbi), writes about attempts by his religious allies in nationalism to make him a believer. "And none of them succeeded. Why? Because there is no god. The Holocaust is the scientific proof for that. The Holocaust is also the theological proof of that. The Holocaust is God's way of punishing man for believing in him. That is His way, Blessed be He, to show us that there is no God" (Uziel 1985, 35). It is hard to imagine such blasphemy published in the United States, but in Israel it has not aroused much response.

Well-known nationalist leaders such as Yuval Neeman or General Rafael Eitan have never been known to attend synagogue in their lives. Nevertheless, all Israeli politicians recognize the new vitality of the Orthodox minority and, like politicians elsewhere, will use it to suit their own goals.

The problem of Zionism since 1967, and the severe crisis of Zionism since 1973, have created a relative, and only relative, 're-Judaization' of political discourse in Israel. After 1967, religion was needed to justify holding the whole of Eretz Yisrael, and after 1973, it was needed to provide hope for the future. On the one hand, religion is a source of energy for Zionism. On the other hand, the return to religion remains a symptom of the decline of Zionism. Religion is seen as the only answer to the crisis of justification that Zionism has been undergoing. It might indeed be. Only two generations ago Judaism seemed doomed and Zionism was full of vitality. Now the tide has turned, and religion offers hope and justification while Zionism appears to be in decline.

The Failure of Secularism

An important part of the Zionist revolution was the attempt at cultural secularization. Not only personal secularization, the experience of most Zionists (or their parents), but a cultural one, secularizing

Jewish life and language. The problem was that Jewish culture had been totally religious for hundreds of years. The movement for cultural transformation from religion to secularity was deliberate and energetic. Secularization has meant not only the negative process of rejecting religious traditions, but also the positive process of creating a secular identity and a secular worldview. Actually, much of humanity is still busy constructing a secular culture to replace religious traditions that are part of human history everywhere. Has the cause of secularization succeeded completely anywhere?

Because secular Jewishness is defined negatively, through an absence of something, while the historical Jewish identity was defined positively, the whole enterprise of Jewish secular culture suffers from a basic weakness. No one could doubt the authenticity of the Orthodox tradition. No one can doubt the Jewishness of the Orthodox who have the legitimacy of historical continuity. The secularists cannot claim that Orthodoxy is false to Jewish tradition; they can only claim that their own version is just as legitimate.

If there is a struggle and competition between secular and religious groups in Israel, the secular groups are at a disadvantage. They consistently claim that they represent an authentic brand of Jewishness or Judaism. They claim that Judaism was always 'pluralistic'. On the other side are the Orthodox, and they have the advantage of not having to justify their Jewishness. No one will doubt their Judaism or their Jewishness. They are historically authentic and don't have to prove their claim to this authenticity. When the secular majority claims the mantle of Jewish continuity, it is on shaky ground. The religious minority can claim it without any challenges. If one wants to claim an authentic Jewish identity, clearly the Orthodox have the upper hand.

One version of secularism is based on admitting that Jewish culture has been totally religious, but it represents the humanist-universalist values of justice, peace, equality, and charity. Jewish traditions are thus reinterpreted in a universalistic way, but the basic structure, such as the calendar of Jewish holidays, remains in place. The need for rites of passage is met by the traditional religious ones.

The attempt to create a viable secular Jewish identity and mythology has been only a partial success. After 100 years of secular Zionism, the basic questions about secular culture in Israel remain. What is a Jewish identity, and if it is Jewish, how can it be secular? The callow tradition of a secular identity cannot compete with the richness of the Judaic heritage. There are almost no secular rites of passage, with the exception of secular weddings or funerals. The majority of Israelis wanting to keep their claim to Jewish identity, support keeping the

Jewish nature of the state, even though this term is interpreted in many different ways. A majority support some role for Judaism in the state, and tying public behavior to Jewish tradition (Liebman and Don-Yehiya 1983).

The defeat of secularism and the relative desecularization of Israeli life is tied to other ideological changes. Secularism is usually ' tied to universalistic values, but these values are weak in the Israeli context. At the same time, it is crucial to realize that the Israeli elite is still thoroughly secular. This includes government leaders, the military, and the academic world.

THE NEW ORTHODOX CONFIDENCE

The crisis of Zionism has been accompanied by the rise of Judaism in its historical form including a resurgence of what has been despised as the culture of the ghetto. The failure of the Zionist secular revolution has led to growing Orthodox vitality, with Orthodox groups feeling confident enough to challenge the secular majority on a variety of issues.

The new confidence and energy of religious groups, both Zionist and non-Zionist, is the third realm in which changes are evident. Orthodox groups in Israel are showing vitality and confidence, which are striking against the background of the demoralized nonobservant majority. They take more initiatives than in the past and are ready to demonstrate and take public stands on issues, both "religious" and general.

Non-Zionist Orthodox groups are more confident as they witness the crisis of Zionism and the demoralization in the nonobservant majority. The failure of Zionism is the source of renewed energy and hope. The failure of the Zionist secular revolution has led to growing Orthodox militancy, with Orthodox groups feeling confident enough to challenge the secular majority on other than purely religious issues.

The Orthodox in Israel and in the Diaspora have been showing their new confidence in renewed political efforts and in recruiting new members among secular Israelis. The crisis of Zionism has led the non-Zionist Orthodox to a sense of heightened confidence and has resulted in greater demands vis-a-vis Zionist and secular parties as well as from the religious Zionists.

Ideological developments in recent years can best be explained as reactions to the crisis of Zionism and attempts to overcome it. The return to the religious source is an attempt at renewal in the face of crisis and disintegration. Because other ideological justifications for

Zionism cannot do the job, religion as a source of legitimation has become more popular. Zionism has been in the throes of a growing crisis of legitimacy, and religion has became an extremely important source of aid in this crisis. In the alliance between Zionism and religion, the benefits and needs used to be mutual, but now, clearly, Zionism is the more needy of the two.

The *Gush Emunim* movement offers rejuvenation to Zionism, and rejuvenation to the moderately Orthodox. This double-headed renewal represents a double-headed crisis. Zionism is in trouble, and religious Zionists have not escaped unscathed. Gush Emunim is the heir to the Orthodox Zionist tradition now in sharp decline. The reason for the decline is the crisis of Zionism, leading to the resurgence of non-Zionist Orthodoxy. The choices for religious Zionists are to move towards the more Orthodox and leave Zionism behind, or to try and keep Zionist faith through an injection of messianic Judaism.

While the non-Zionist Orthodox gain their confidence from the failure of Zionism, the religious Zionists demonstrate their faith in the future of Zionism through reliance on messianic hopes, which seem more substantial than what is available to secular Zionists. Only Gush Emunim and similar groups have solid answers in the form of religious justifications. Its members can offer revitalization for Zionism through religious faith because all other methods of justifying Zionism have proven inadequate. It is sufficient to believe in God and in Old Testament divine promises, and the justification for the praxis of political Zionism follows with flawless logic. The influence of those who could present religious justifications consistently and naturally has grown with time.

Today there is a retreat of religious Zionists in the face of the non-Zionist Orthodox, and a process of Orthodoxization among religious nationalists as they become less Zionist and more Orthodox. The moderately Orthodox nationalists have been moving to towards stronger Orthodoxy, which in turn means a growing distance from Zionism.

THE CURRENT SITUATION: A COAT OF MANY COLORS

Traditional Judaism, at least in the European context, was challenged, as we noted earlier, by the breakdown of the ghetto walls, the siren call of modernity, and the nationalist response in emergent Zionism. Traditional Judaism everywhere in retreat, but still a potent force in the struggle against the inroads of the world of the "others," seemingly suffered a death blow with the destruction of East European Jewry in the

Holocaust. Concomitantly and largely as an outgrowth of these
shocking events, the Zionist-secular vision achieved at least part of its
aims with the establishment of an independant Jewish state in Palestine. Clearly the balance had shifted away from religious traditionalism and towards secular nationalism. Had the script been followed in
its logical entirety, the Jewish people would have relinked themselves
to temporal history with religion assigned its limited place in the context of modernity as upholder of the sacred order, repository of collective memory, and dispenser of limited ritual and ceremonial tasks. But,
as has been noted, traditional religion has emerged as a key player in
the drama of a reemergent Jewish political entity and, rather than act
as a mere backdrop the religious enterprise, has assumed considerable importance.

Almost all of the chapters comprising the present volume under-
score this development in one way or another. But the emergent picture is not an uncomplicated one. While the religious factor looms
large, no less important are questions concerning ethnicity *within* the
Jewish community and the place of Arabs within the larger context.
One major thrust of the essays of Sobel and of Ayalon, Ben-Rafael, and
Sharot is the continuing valence of ethnicity and an almost inchoate
and certainly unformulated wish that religion fulfill a binding, healing
role. Ayalon et al. observe that most secular Israelis see the religious
secular division as more sharp and divisive than ethnic and class
divided, this tends to hold on the cognitive level. At the affective and
evaluative level, we are told that "ethnicity and class prove to be more
important ... than religious or secular positions." Similarly in the case
study analyzed by Sobel, one finds the religious "threat" providing a
framework and context for what quickly becomes apparent as a class
and ethnic split undergirding the communal structure. In fact, as
demonstrated in this essay, the potentially divisive role of religion is
tempered by the growing concern with an outside threatening force
(Arabs) wherein intracommunal splits—whether ethnic, class, or religious—appear eminently bridgeable in the face of a common enemy.

Not unrelated to a sense of external threat represented by Arabs,
is the spectre of a seemingly largely secular, at least behaviorally secular, population in thrall to upholders of an antimodern traditionalist
position that runs counter to the way most Israelis behave and to their
presumed secular-nationalist ethic. Secularization seems preemi-
nently the path being followed by most Israelis, and yet, as Beit-
Hallahmi observes, thousands are involved in the return movement,
and though only a small minority are actively affected, public opinion
is largerly supportive.

What has happened here? What is the meaning of this seemingly perverse embrace of a life-style so out of sync with that of the majority of Israelis? Why does the movement have a relatively high rate of retention—an accomplishment not shared by the various non-Judaic sects and cults that have lately enjoyed some growth in Israel?

Clearly the traditional religious context provides a dimension of legitimation and anchored continuity that these groups could not supply. The seeking of communal and individual legitimation through association—passive or active—with a core element of Jewish praxis and past is high up on the societal agenda. Some of the evidence brought to the fore by Kedem clearly demonstrates just how extensive is this curious traditionalism in a population of apparent secularists, where some 70 percent of a student sample expressed religious emotion tied to national events and where large numbers were in favor of religious legislation against the raising of hogs, for store closing on the Sabbath, for exclusively religious marriage, for religious education in secular schools, and so on. Separation, notes Kedem, as understood in an American context, is far from the reality of Israel, as is the way in which Israelis relate to non-Orthodox representation of Judaism. While one might contest Beit-Hallahmi's assertion that Israelis have not responded to "Reform and Conservative messages... because they do not feel the need for another type of Judaism," there is little question but that alternative forms of Jewish religious practice and identity have been slow in appearing. As Weber observed, tradition might be viewed as the authority of the eternal yesterday, and Israelis collective yesterday remains an important strut in their affirmation of today.

Nowhere is this affirmation of traditional modes more apparent than in the growth and expansion of religious education and, more specifically, the yeshivot. Bar-Lev speaks of the pressures towards the 'Haredization' of religious education where after a "try" at making some accommodation with modernity the present trend is backward, to a world of isolation, segregation, and particularism. The traditional yeshivot, while allowing the introduction of hints of modernization on the administrative level, rather supinely neglect dealing with any of the attendant problems of modernization involving Israeli society, such as the role of religion in the secular context, ethnicity, inequality, and other matters of no less central importance. The traditional yeshivot appear to be fighting the battles that marked the secular-Zionist world two or three generations earlier, such as Hebrew versus Yiddish as the language of instruction, the world at large or the shtetl, outreach to the masses or to an elite minority.

It is in the hesder yeshivot with their symbolically charged combination of sword and text that a glimmer of change, of modernization, is filtering through into a world still anchored in the nineteenth century. Clearly, the road to modernization within Israeli Judaism holds more promise of movement coming from this more indigenous, highly traditional context than from movements viewed as essentially foreign and indeed sectarian, such as the Reform and Conservative streams that have succeeded in capturing the majority of American Jewry. Indeed, as Tabory asserts, Reform and Conservative in striving for legitimacy are denied the possibility of presenting themselves as something new, as a true alternative. The hesder yeshivot recognized their "newness" but attempted (and succeeded to a point) in demonstrating how the new (army service) was in fact a device making the old (Torah study) feasible in a new context. Not only on the pragmatic level could justification be found, but on a more abstract religious level where the new was transformed into a commandment having meaning in and of itself with respect to participating in the divine plan for bringing people, book, and land into alignment.

The Reform movement undermined the traditional normative system. The change represented in the new yeshiva trend upholds the normative system, albeit with changed methods, but with the core value system left intact and assertively enhanced.

Orthodoxy in Israel is prepared to accept if not embrace the irreligious, or even the quirky, but is not so inclined with respect to organized ideologically fueled alternatives that are viewed as sectarian threats to the normative order. And in this the Orthodox rabbinical leadership seems to enjoy wide support from not only the observant and traditional but among the otherwise religiously indifferent as well.

Tabory demonstrates how Israeli Judaism and the major non-Orthodox streams of Diaspora Judaism occupy increasingly divergent universes. Israeli Judaism is inextricably linked with politics and the political process, while Diaspora Judaism—certainly in the United States—defines itself in terms of community and communion but quite apart from the political process.

But this is not the only fulcrum of divergence between the Diaspora and Israel. A number of the essays in this volume point to the existence of a growing chasm of experience and outlook that seems to point not only to difficulties of a politico-religious nature but of an experiental and expressive one as well. Tabory is no doubt correct in assuming the nontransferability of social, political, and religious movements from one environment to another. How much more should this be the case where histories—personal and collective—are so different. A key but unremarked upon aspect of Israeli society is that it is overwhelmingly only one or at most two generations removed from Orthodoxy. This is true of European and even more so for the Sepharadi majority of Israel's population. Most Israelis did not come out of a Zionist, antireligious, or religiously neutral background, but in fact might be said to have drifted into secularism and/or non-Orthodoxy without perforce rejecting in any categoric fashion their orthodox roots.

The Jerusalem funeral that is highlighted by a use of mystical metaphor can itself be seen as a metaphor of the relations between Orthodox religiosity and the secular or largely nonobservant majority of Israelis. Though the individual mourner and the collectivity might both evince overriding need for comfort and closure, it is ritual tradition that might not clearly supply these, which is ultimately determinative of behavior.

This again poses a key question. How is acquiescence secured from nonobservant people to ofttimes unfathomable and perhaps even socially and individually dysfunctional behaviors with little or no protest or opposition? As Abramovitch notes, "In Jerusalem, the special cult of purity and kabbalistic concerns over the sacred nature of procreation led to a series of ritual innovations in which the demands of social support were momentarily set aside in favor of the special needs of aiding the spirit of the deceased make the dangerous transisition to the world to come." This clearly is difficult to comprehend or explain to the Orthodox noninvolved or peripherally involved, and acceptance on their part can only be explained by a certain passivity or malleability that might characterize the bereaved generally. But in addition, it would seem to reflect (albeit with some anger and impatience as often as not) the willingness of the nonobservant to have the observant define the ritual parameters of their lives either for lack of an alternative, passivity, and not caring or perhaps because of the sense of legitimacy that hangs like an aura above Orthodox practices in most phases of collective life. Alternatively, however, the emergence among some of a "funeral within a funeral" might presage a reaction to the ritual monopoly of orthodoxy, but *not* a revolt against it: a felt need unanswered in ritual to be expressed, yes; an overturning of sacred ritual, no! Abramovitch is taken with the 'mismeeting' dimension, the anger many of the nonobservant felt toward religious society for forcing them into a pattern they find absurd or nonmeaningful. One might as easily be impressed with the overwhelming compliance with and lack of protest about these practices and the failure to actively seek change which characterizes the 'mismeeting'.

Even with those leaving the religious fold in its most Orthodox manifestation—the Haredi sector—there is a tendency to feel delegitmized and somewhat inauthentic. If religious conversion can be likened to falling in love, as William James has observed, leaving a religious context might be akin to falling out of love. Shaffir highlights similarities and differences involved in both; in drawing nigh and stepping away from deep religious observance. In many respects the process is similar: a break arrived at through a slow process rather than a sudden revelation. It would appear that Jews still largely convert and apostatize in a rather traditional fashion—step by step, rather than through radical and instantaneous upheaval. It is not accidental that we tend to have much more data about *hozrim betshuvah* than about *hozrim beshe'elah* or those who reject extreme Orthodoxy. It confirms in still another way what we have asserted throughout—the organic and deep legitimating function of religious Orthodoxy in a society demonstrating pervasive need for this kind of affirmation. Shaffir's research is one of the first efforts at breaking through this web of sanctified obfuscation in an effort to reach beyond armoured piety, showing cracks in a wall that the highly Orthodox, the merely traditional, and even some secularists feel a need for.

Unsurprisingly, and as foreshadowed in the work of Shaffir, the sacred canopy extends beyond matters of societal legitimation and reaches down to the behavioral and value contexts. Weller provides us with a sweeping survey showing how religiosity intersects with central patterns of individual behavior, such as family planning, attitudes towards sex, women's roles, attitudes towards minorities (Arabs), and ethics among other subjects. The research done in these areas thus far suggests that the less observant tend to be more "liberal," and the more observant tend towards the illiberal end of the scale. Clearly, as is shown in research done with doctors, social workers, and other professions, being religious has an effect in behavioral terms. It is not a mere cloak thrown over an otherwise "regular fellow." One should of course not be surprised by these findings, but in an age of cynicism, one can nevertheless still find oneself surprised that forces other than those that highlight the Acquarian apotheosis have substance.

One finding noted in Weller's essay does in fact surprise but, on deeper reflection, demonstrates an important point about the way in which religion does and does not function in Israel. We here refer to a study wherein religious pupils scored higher on a test of cognitive morality and achieved higher results on a test of moral reasoning but cheated on exams significantly more than secular peers. One could posit a whole host of possible reasons for this strange finding, ranging from an inbuilt powerful survival instinct having religious justification that overtakes lesser values such as temporal honesty, to a kind of dissonance that highlights the abstract over the practical, the cognative over the active. But Judaism is a religion of action, of doing, of being, not of abstract principle or theorizing. We think it rather demonstrates the thoroughgoing weakness of the pastoral function within the rabbinate and the almost virginal absence of a broad ethical dimension in preaching or teaching centered within the religious structure. In this a rather traditional line is being followed but with a vengeance. One is therefore not shocked at how little input there is coming from the religious leadership with respect to any of the chillingly threatening issues with which Israeli society is confronted other than those with a ritual or halachic ramification. The rabbinate does not speak—at least so that one could hear—about racism, minority rights, the debased position of women, business ethics, overall honesty in interpersonal relations, or myriad other subjects of related weight. The focus and thrust of rabbinic authority and of the religious enterprise is in the realm of Torah study for its own sake and ritual correctness as the behavioral norm. All else is commentary.

The only enlargements on the role assumed by religious authority in the nineteenth century shtetl is to be found in its muscular politicization and in its providing a type of framework for justification, continuity, and unity. While this is substantially the case for the Ashkenazi minority, it assumes somewhat different dimensions among the Sepharadi, largely Middle Eastern and North African majority of Israel's population. Here too, the search for continuity for reaffirmation, of a collective past results in the thrusting forward of the religious factor that appears as the cultural anchor most rescuable or recallable from out of the wreckage of the immigration trauma. If the European immigrants can be said to have been buffeted by the effects of upheaval and resettlement in a new and, in large measure, unfamiliar environment, even more so was this the case for most of the Asian-African migration. At least in the case of the Europeans, the basic societal institutions were products of a common background and were, as such, recognizable and, most importantly, approachable. For the immigrants from North Africa, and to a lesser extent from Asia, all of this plus the very notion of political Zionism itself was somewhat foreign, which tended to result in the shocks of immigration being that much heavier. Bilu has interestingly demonstrated how these shocks can at least somewhat be absorbed and cushioned through the reimplantation of an indigenous religious framework into the new, strange, largely unwelcoming context. Saints and the hagiolatric tradition that enjoyed an important place in the vernacular religion of Moroccan Jewry were transported to the most unlikely sites in the new country, which made these places attractive and the believers presence in them reasonable. For Israelis at large Biblical religion can be viewed as a deed of ownership for the land of Israel and perhaps as an affirmation for being "here" rather than "elsewhere." For the thousands of Moroccan immigrants whose immigration trauma was perhaps more devastating than for other groups, the relocation of familiar saints to obscure outposts often seen as dumping grounds for low status North Africans not only legitimated "here" over "elsewhere" but additionally suggests continuity and, more importantly, higher purpose for their specific "here" that was otherwise without a saving sense of attraction.

The collection of studies presented in this text provides a ground-level view of the complexities outlined in this *Introduction*. Taken together, they make up a panorama of religion as lived by individuals and communities in contemporary Israel. It is our hope that the book will both help to provide a realistic assessment of the religious situation in this society as well as lead to and stimulate more research efforts on these and related issues.

REFERENCES

Liebman, C. S., and E. Don-Yehiya. 1983. *Civil religion in Israel*. Berkeley: University of California.

Marmorstein, E. 1969. *Heaven at bay*. London: Oxford University Press.

Uziel, M. 1985. Talking to the preachers. *Maariv*, 7 March.

Part I

The Communal Dimension

1

Conflict and Communitas:

The Interplay of Religion, Ethnicity, and Community in a Galilee Village

ZVI SOBEL

INTRODUCTION

Peter Berger once observed that the sociological world seemed to be divided into those who are intimately related to computers and those who study the theories of dead Germans. In a parallel fashion, studies of contemporary Israel apear to be divided between those who view the society as a case study in nation building and others seemingly overcome by its sui generis nature. While truth is doubtlessly to be found somewhere along a continuum in both instances, one cannot but be struck by the centrality of paradox, of trend and countertend, of conflicting reality and definition, that spring at the observer of Israeli society from every point of the compass. Although it might be a truism, the blatancy and pervasiveness of paradox is unavoidable, creating serious difficulties for analysis and understanding.

Israelis are an old people in a new nation state with a shared sacred and, to some extent, temporal history. At the same time, separate experience and history divide its various groups like a chasm. The social political structure is heavily interlaced with and overlaid by a religious 'over structure', but the majority of the population defines itself and acts largely in secular fashion. The country is urbanized, but mythically tied to a vision based on the land and on entitlement by and

*The research upon which this chapter is based was partially supported by a grant from the Wenner-Bren Foundation.

through those who cultivate it. Israeli society emphasizes science and technology and strives to reach the cutting edge of both, but withal is backward and among the developing nations in more ways than the mythmakers can be comfortable with. Israeli society is educated and largely literate, but it harbors significant segments of illiteracy—both functional and total—and population pockets bearing closer ties to folk organization than to modernity. It is self-consciously Jewish, almost obsessively so, and yet in so undefined and frayed a fashion as to elude any substantial, rooted, and widely shared conception as to what constitutes a Jew. It is committed to peace and the sancity of the individual life, and yet resorts to war perhaps more readily than objective observers can profitably justify. Israel is an Asian nation, embedded in a vast Oriental culture pool, but emulates Europe, choosing it as a societal and personal model, and along with far-off America, it is conscious of the meaning—existentially and historically—of minority status, yet with a brooding conviction that separate and unequal is an unavoidable destiny and result of societal heterogeneity. It is a society whose stated motto is autonomy and self-realization, although it is almost totally dependent on the financial largess and political commitment of a foreign power. And finally, while sharing an underlying conviction that the state represents the culmination of an ancient historical dialectic wherein people and land must come together in a logical and sought after synthesis, Israel is discovering that not only have the vast majority of the world's Jews rejected this proffered opportunity for wholeness and historical closure, but that growing numbers of those already within the state are opting out.

Presented with such a canvas of paradox, one can easily understand recourse to the computer and the attempt to achieve order and clarity in small corners, to uncover facts and to quantify the apprehendable, such as it is. Conversely, one might take refuge under the wings of the 'Germans' or their system-building successors, looking for the universal, the nonparochial, the all-embracing, in every small exemplar of human and societal endeavor. One could argue—from shaky conviction rather than outright despair—that understanding comes in diverse ways and through strange combinations, and that an intensive and extensive view of the small patch can illuminate a much larger area, let the tools be what they may—computers, 'Germans', or a judicious mix of the two.

The small patch, some key features of which we will attempt to understand in an effort to cast some light on the overwhelming complexity and paradoxality of contemporary Israel, is Yavneel. This is one of the oldest Jewish settlements in the country, settled at the turn of the century, that in a circumscribed but defensible fashion reflects much that characterizes Israel as a whole. Circumscribed because while Israel is highly urbanized, Yavneel is rural; while the typical Jewish Israeli is at most the second generation born in the country, Yavneel is into its third and fourth generation of native born. While the vast majority of the population is concentrated on the coastal plain, Yavneel is in a valley basin in Lower Galilee far from the 'action' of the center. Notwithstanding these important differences, Yavneel is reflective of the Israeli reality in a startling array of ways. Like Israel as a whole, its two thousand citizens include a majority of Sephardi Jews, most of whom came in the great immigration wave of the 1950s. It has an establishment core of settler-farmers whose forebears arrived at the end of the nineteenth century from Russia and Romania, which included religious traditionalists and so-called radicals or freethinkers. It has a small group of people whose grandparents converted to Judaism in Russia, two Hebrew-Christian families, and a Yemenite community that settled in 1912. Its middle-class core is Ashkenazi with a sparse addition of upwardly mobile families from among the new immigrant Easterners, or Sephardis, while its substratum of poor industrial and agricultural workers is drawn overwhelmingly from Sephardi background. Its religious range includes Hassidic families, traditionally Orthodox, partially traditional, and secular groupings. Like most of the country, Yavneel was formally aligned with the Labor party and has moved steadily right since 1977, with a majority opting for the Likud in the last national elections. While once farm oriented to the virtual exclusion of other occupations, it is steadily moving away from agriculture with less than 20 percent of the households farming at present. There is, however, a factor characteristic of Yavneel and about a dozen similar communities that highlights an important difference between it and the larger society: Yavneel has a rooted yeomanry with ties to the land and a relatedness to place not readily found outside these few settlements. This core group of old settler families sees matters through a prism unfamiliar and, in many respects, not understandable to the majority of their fellow citizens not only in the community itself, or in Israel, but in the Jewish world at large. It is a core group that sees itself, if not divinely appointed, at least cosmically guided to provide the spearhead for a return to roots and values heretofore understated, ignored, or obscured in the Jewish praxis. (The Yavneel farmer looks and sounds very much like an American midwestern wheat planter, or a Swedish homesteader. The younger farmers even affect aviator sunglasses and baseball caps with the logos of agricultural machinery producers emblazoned on the visor.) The existence and placement of this yeomanry is an important factor apparently unique on the Israeli scene, of which more later.

Setting this feature aside, we see in Yavneel something of a microcosm of Israeli society after forty years of evolving statehood. In Yavneel the paradoxes, conflicts, absurdities, and something of the mystery of renewed Jewish sovereignty in Zion emerge to exaggerated and thus, for the analyst, highly useful prominence.

A small corner perhaps, but as Eudora Welty observes, "one place comprehended can make us understand other places better, Sense of place gives equilibrium; extended, it is a sense of direction." As noted, Yavneel is not Israel and Israel is not Yavneel. Distinguishing and unique features abound and delineate both the larger and smaller canvasses. But having stated the caveat, one is struck by the usefulness of the smaller entity as a sounding device for analyzing whether in opposition or fit, some prominent and dominating features of the larger context. In the very smells and sights of the town, in its human geography and its history one is constantly made aware of what I have called the paradoxes and confusions of Israeli society, and in no small measure the conflicts that undergrid and define its reality.

I am here especially concerned with two of these—ethnicity and the religious factor—that seem to enjoy prominence in the society at large as well as in Yavneel. Israel is confronted by four overarching and dominating societal challenges that can be summed up dicoto-mously as peace-war, Arab-Jew, Sephardi-Ashkenazi, and religious-secular. All four can be studied profitably in the microcosm of Yavneel, but the latter two almost literally spring forth from the very visage of the village in a blatant, relentless, and compelling fashion. A short stroll through the community exposes one to an almost promiscuous heterogeneity of form and practice. The smells are the smells of a farming community, turned earth, manure, fertilizer, fruit trees in blossom; the sounds that dominate are mooing and sheep bells; the machinery heard is the tractor pulling farm machinery, the truck carrying crops to market or packing house, or the lumbering combine. Against this backdrop one can also hear the singsong chant of residents studying Talmud, or see walking alongside the heavy farm machinery a black-clad young Hassid, bearded and earlocked. The accents include the lilting gutteral tones from North Africa, the broad flat sounds of the American immigrant, the Yiddish-accented Hebrew of the core group, and the sabra synthesis, which ultimately swallows and levels all.

But lest one be lulled into Edenic euphoria by this picture of Zion-ist fulfillment, it must be noted that these paradoxical cohabitations encompass a complex system of delicate symbiosis shot through with potential and actual conflict and disarray. What appears to be an idyllic exercise in religious and ethnic pluralism tends, on closer observation, to be fraught with unresolved tensions—new and Old— and with potential and existent conflict threatening stability and order.

Victor Turner notes of conflict that "it seems to bring fundamental aspects of society, normally overlaid by the customs and habits of daily intercourse into frightening prominence, with people taking sides,... according to deeply entrenched moral imperatives and constraints often against their own personal preferences" (Turner 1974, 35). Conflict profoundly enlarges and defines what might disturb under the surface, and what Turner calls "social dramas" emerge to highlight and expose underlying process (Turner 1974). He derfines *social dramas* more precisely as "units of disharmonic process arising in conflict situations" (Turner 1974, 37-38), with stages identified as breach, crisis, redressive action, and reintegration or irreparable schism. The concept of social drama seems apt and useful, placing in perspective an emergent and ongoing pattern of conflict in Yavneel and casting light on three of the four dichotomous central challenges pervasive in Israeli society at large.

A RELIGIOUS CRISIS IN YAVNEEL

The religion of Yavneel reflects and imitates the religion of Israeli society in miniature: the same observation can profitably and correctly, if cautiously, be made concerning almost any smaller unit of a larger societal entity. Thus the religion of Middletown no doubt reflects to a large degree the religious oeuvre of American society, and that of Nancy the religion of France, and so on. What is notable in the present case is the extent of the fit with a highly variegated religious 'over structure', given the smallness of the community exemplar. Unlike the case of Middletown and, I presume, Nancy—representative but not inclusive—Yavneel is close to being inclusive not only in the religious streams and emphases represented, but in its pattern of reactions to prominent concerns developed around and with respect to the religion issue in Israel. For example, the somewhat talismanic format through which the broader society and its institutions relate to religion has come to be known as the "status quo agreement" established by Ben Gurion together with representatives of the Orthodox community in 1947. The major thrust of the agreement was to assert a minimal baseline that made participation of the observant in the core structure of public life feasible, while recognizing the fact that the majority is essentially unobservant. It recognized and institutionalized the need for inclusiveness and refused to ghettoize the observant Jews. It also took into account what Bellah called a "religious ground bass" (Bellah 1980, 92) that characterizes the society at large, wherein Jewish religion functions in what Weber terms a *bedeutungszusamenhang*.

Yavneelim have for some three generations followed an unwritten and unheralded status quo agreement akin to the written document that guides and underlies the religious-nonreligious accommodation in the larger society. Its essential point was and is that blatant violation of broad, generally accepted religious norms such as minimal public Sabbath observance, fasting on Yom Kippur, eating matzoth on Passover, ritual circumcision, Jewish marriage and burial, and abstention in public from pork, would not be countenanced. Basic holy texts (the Hebrew Bible and a bit of the Rashi commentary) as well as basic prayers (the morning prayer and the doxology) would be taught in schools. But beyond this very basic, stripped down "Jewishness," no one was to make anybody feel bad about what he did or did not do—out of public view. Most Yavneelim, like Israelis generally, believe that a bit of religion cannot be harmful especially if the individual citizen—within reason and consensus—can pick and choose. Additionally and importantly, religion in it broadest sense is a way of piously affimring continuity with a past that otherwise threatens to slip away, leaving an ideational void. It also quietly legitimates existence in a hostile and essentially rejecting political environment. It is perhaps *the* major and singular legitimating device in the face of the historical and continuing claims and counterclaims to a land contested with relentless ferocity.

Thus for almost all Yavneelim, the religious leadership of the late Rabbi L who was the communal rabbi in the late 1950s and 1960s, was perfect. The Rabbi reminded all, in look and bearing, of the departed forebears—pious, self-effacing, highly learned in religious subjects and, in addition, having more than a mere patina of secular knowldege and wisdom. He was gentle, quiet, and unassuming, and important above all, he generally (and most liberally) acceeded to the New Testament dictum of rendering unto Caesar what was Caesar's, leaving a bare minimum for God. He bore a religious message and without question sought to advance its cause, but did not contend, did not cajole, and never attempted to force his viewpoint on others. He was quite prepared to accept the community's ideational and behavioral norms as they were, and to compromise his own in the face of potential conflict. He was, as one might surmise, much beloved by all.

The customs and habits of daily intercourse that overlay the fundamental aspects of society were rudely and rather seriously jolted by two still murkily related events. Rabbi L died and was replaced by Rabbi F some thirteen years ago; and a Hassidic leader, Rabbi S, appeared in the village two years ago, with part of his flock. Thirteen years of Rabbi F's tenure as communal rabbi prepared the soil for a conflict. The harvest was to be reaped with the arrival of the Admor, the Hassidic rabbi and leader, bringing to the fore an almost classic example of a social drama as a unit of "disharmonic process" demonstrating the various stages defined by Turner.

The breach, the overt breach or 'deliberate nonfulfillment of some crucial norms regulating...intercourse of the parties" (Turner, 1974, 37) is witnessed in two complementary though not completely symmetrical occurrences. The newly arrived Hassidic group attempted to further an extreme non-Zionist, nonfarming (indeed non-laboring) structure in the midst of a textbook exemplar of the nineteenth century Zionist vision, defying basic communal values of the veteran community and generating a widespread communal response. This in turn challenged the principle that any Jew can and indeed should be encouraged to settle anywhere in the Land of Israel.

Rabbi F, unlike his predecessor Rabbi L, is contentious, combative, and unwaveringly committed to the *haredi*, or extreme camp of religious ultra-orthodoxy. Where Rabbi L always sought the religiously acceptable lightening of religious imperative, the fit with widely accepted communal norms, Rabbi F interpreted his role to be that of the avenging sword, the protector of right doctrine, and a purifier of the temple precincts. Rabbi F, who came to the community at the remarkably young age of 20 (he is said to be one of the youngest men ordained in Israel) presumably with little experience of the world, immediately set forth to act as the proverbial new broom. He demanded stricter public observance of the Sabbath, the closing of the community center on Sabbath and holy days, and more religious instruction in the public school. He exhorted sinners and interpreted personal tragedies as a sign of God's disfavor and anger. He first fought the construction of a community swimming pool, and then insisted on an opaque wall down its very center and into the changing rooms, in order to separate the sexes. But aside from specific exhortations or acts, three elements acted as particular catalysts of growing communal disfavor: (1) his inclination to dabble in local politics; (2) a reputed lack of fervor for the widely accepted norms of Zionist fulfillment; and (3) what many interpret as an abrasive personality. Rabbi F, early in his career in Yavneel, presumably decided that his major constituency was to be found not among the core group of old settlers and their descendants who like himself were Ashkenazi, but among the newcomers who were overwhelmingly Sephardi, traditional and highly respectful of the rabbinical role, and constituted a growing majority of the town residents. He extended aid and favors wherever possible among this group and sought successfully to place their representatives on the religious council and in various other local bodies. He has attempted to influence the selection of candidates to the town council and to play a role in coalition wheeling and dealing for the selection of mayor. If this 'politicization' of his role were to have moved in a direction distant from the highly sensitive ethnic arena, reactions of core group members might have been more restrained and tolerant. But inasmuch as he chose as his context not only politics, but ethnic politics with the added fillip of extreme Orthodoxy, the reaction could easily have been foretold. Having exposed himself to widespread disfavor, however, does not necessarily entail the active opposition and almost violent antipathy expressed towards him by so large a proportion of the town's residents, including many from his target group of Sephardim. For this points 2 and 3 above came together to assure his status as the most disliked public figure in the village. His reluctance until this year to display the national flag at his home on Independence Day, and above all the fact that he has never served in the army are sufficient to brand him anti-state, anti-Zionist, and thus unacceptable as a public figure to large numbers of residents.

His protests notwithstanding, he is viewed, though native born, as essentially foreign and hostile to some of the most sacred communal and national norms. Thus for a number of years a growing rift has been developing, largely below the surface, between the official representative of religion in the community and large numbers of residents. Though officially embodying one basic desideratum of community in Israel as the formal representative of the Jewish religious entity that is seen as a given of statehood, he is seen as standing in opposition to the state itself. If Israel is defined as the Jewish state, Rabbi F is seen as the bearer of a message attempting to bifurcate and separate state from Jewish. By attempting to shift religion from the 'ground bass' of communal life to a determinant or at least dominant coloration of normative daily behavior, he set himself—and to some degree the religious context he was seen to represent—in opposition to other crucial norms of the community. But while this challenge to the crucial norms lingered near the surface, not erupting in any serious manner for a full decade, the arrival of the Admor and his Hassidic followers provided the spark or catalyst that led to the emergence of the breach and the resulting crisis.

Rabbi S, or the Admor, is a claimant to leadership of the Bratslav Hassidim, the only Hassidic group that has never had an official successor to leadership following the death of its founder, Rabbi Nahman, in the early years of the nineteenth century. There is reason to believe that Rabbi S views himself as a successor to Nahman and has thereby earned disdain and caused consternation among other subgroups adhering to the same sect, known for its asceticism and rigid rule. They are perhaps the only Hassidic group that is teetotaling, accepts reincarnation, and practices a form of ritual mystical separation known as *'Hitbodedut'* wherein the followers undertake regular nocturnal visits into the forest and desert in order to commune with the diety as well as to "clear" spiritual passages making this communion possible. In most other respects they are clearly defined as one of many Hassidic groups that have emerged in the course of the late eighteenth and nineteenth centuries in Eastern and Central Europe. But being followers of a long dead Tzaddik, or spiritual head, most offshoots have not developed the role of a present Tzaddik or spiritual mentor—and Rabbi S as a possible claimant to such a role seems to be undermining this position. For many years Rabbi S has made his home and base in New York, though he grew up in Jerusalem. His Israeli following of perhaps 150 or so males has come to him largely through his extensive pamphleteering—dozens of booklets of 15-50 pages called *Contressim*—giving spiritual advice and guidance on a simple level and marked by repeated assurances of God's love and, perhaps immodestly, the love of Rabbi S as well. He and his booklets are reportedly popular among Israel's prison population, where he has enjoyed some small success in returning prisoners to religion. One such returnee, a man referred to as Rabbi A, came to Yavneel a few years ago, and a short time later Rabbi S himself announced to a startled town council that he intended to settle in the community. He requested public land for the establishment of *hatzer*, or Hassidic court, and at this point brought to the surface the dormant conflicts resulting in breach. Protests were mounted by groups of town dwellers, and the request for public land was rejected. Rabbi S, digging in his heels, privately purchased property in town and proceeded to build a villa for himself, which included a synagogue-study hall and a ritual bath.

If Rabbi F, the communal rabbi, was seen to be in violation of crucial norms, then Rabbi S, the Admor, and thirteen families of his followers, who soon moved into town, were viewed as having changed the unacceptable into the unbearable. Passages were uncovered in the writings of Rabbi S where he is said to have recommended not serving in the army. This, together with the fact that in this laboring community few of the Admor's followers held gainful employment, resulted in formal protests, some acts of small sabotage, and the emergence of a group led by a young town-born veterinarian to prevent what was fast

coming to be viewed as a foreign invasion with succession as its ultimate aim.

Among the core group—though not very extensively among the
'newcomer' Sephardim—the appearance of Rabbi S and his followers,
on top of, and some contend as a result of, the active efforts of Rabbi F,
represented a serious breach of Zionist values and deeply held communal norms. Moreover, their own efforts also represented a breach
in the fact that they were seen to oppose the Admor's coming, thereby
violating a key Zionist norm that one may not prevent a fellow Jew
from settling in the land or any part thereof. If the Rabbi held an image
of Zionist fulfillment as he claimed (he wants, after all, to immigrate to
Israel), it was an image in most ways contrary to the communal norms,
and this was widely understood. It constituted a competing view,
based on imminent messianic hopes bearing all the hallmarks of a
counterreformation, and calling into question the very legitimacy, not
to mention the life-style and history, encoded in the prevailing normative structure.

The breach, outwardly based on the religious issue and the felt
sense of threat to the ideational-normative structure, widened and
fanned out, to encompass another smoldering question—the ethnic
matter, or the relationships between the core group of Ashkenazi old
settlers and the majority group of Sephardi 'newcomers'. As Turner
notes, "the phase of crisis exposes the pattern of current factional in-
trigues hitherto covert..." (Turner 1974, 38). The religiously based
breach exposed the pattern of hitherto covert antipathy of an essentially ethnic nature. A conflict emerged that, as Turner observes
"seems to bring fundamental aspects of society normally overlaid by
the customs and habits of daily intercourse into frightening prominence" (Turner 1974, 35). He adds, "people have to take sides in terms
of deeply entrenched moral imperatives and constraints, often
against their own personal preferences. Choice is overborne by duty"
(Turner 1974, 35).

The breach and the churning of conflict, or more correctly, the
exposure of conflict gives way to crisis that is one of those "turning
points or moments of danger and suspense when a true state of affairs
is revealed, when it is least easy to don masks or pretend that there is
nothing rotten in the village" (Turner 1974, 39). It is, says Turner, liminal. "It ... dares the representatives of order to grapple with it. It cannot be ignored or wished away (Turner 1974, 39).

Until the arrival of the Admor, Rabbi S, and the breach and resultant crisis, the villagers could and indeed did ignore and with a high
degree of aplomb wish away the frustrations and antagonisms of the
'newcomers'. Many claimed to be unaware of the very existence of

these frustrations. Others attributed it to sour grapes, or to the normal jealousy and antagonism directed at the 'haves' by the 'have nots', or more comfortably, to a difficult but passing stage in the absorption process. The core group ignored or at least downplayed the fact that they were the only real holders of property, had the most direct and potent access to central and local sources of power and decision making, and zealously guarded the portals of both against the intrusion of others. However, this lack of consciousness was accompanied by a lowering sense of guilt, if not generated than constantly piqued by Rabbi F, the communal rabbi, not concerning the core group's treatment of the 'newcomers', but of their presumed violation of the basic ancestral code of public religious norms thought to have been set in place by their fathers and grandfathers. The legitimate context of communal public expression was asserted to be religious Orthodoxy, as expressed by both the institutional setup and the individual behavior of the forebears' generation. The coming of the Admor was seen as a conscious, planned attack upon what was differentially viewed as the legitimate religious undergirding of the community; an attack from within (Rabbi F) buttressed, supported, and reinforced by blatantly outside forces (the Admor and his followers) using as agents members of a disprivileged group (the 'newcomers'). A fact known by all, but rarely voiced by core group members, was that the 'newcomers' were in fact approximately two-thirds of the town's residents, and "our town" was becoming or had become "their town." It was no longer possible to pretend, to don masks. It was a situation that did indeed have the hallmark of liminality: lines were drawn, sides were taken, postures assumed. If the breach occurred against the matrix of religion, the crisis escalated, becoming "coextensive with ... [a] dominant cleavage" (Turner 1974, 38)—the ethnic chasm that afflicts Israeli society at large.

A committee was fomed to fight the entry of the Admor and his followers into Yavneel. It was demonstratively formed exclusively of core group residents, with the singular exception of the mayor who is of Iraqi origin, but not, as the majority of newcomers, either working class or North African. The committee met frequently, drafted positions, circulated a petition, and granted interviews to the press. Certain members appeared on a TV documentary made about the event —but it did or could do little else. Could they actively prevent Jews from coming to live in a Jewish town in Eretz Israel? Could they foment a pogrom against the religious with themselves in the unassimilable role of the Cossaks? Although matters did get out of hand on a few occasions—air let out of car tires, slogans painted on walls, a push here, a shove there—it quickly became evident that little of an active nature could be done against the Hassidim and that the committee must bide its time until signs of religious coercion were evident, at which point, one was assured, "blood will flow." A good deal of the fear and hostility felt toward the outsiders was deflected to Rabbi F, the community rabbi, who was blamed for having engineered the Hassidic arrival in order to destroy the core group's way of life and bring about a religiously dominated regime of a different ethnic composition than the prevailing one. The widely accepted definition of the situation among the core group was that the Sepharadim were more supportive of both rabbis because they saw in this an opportunity to aggravate if not punish the old establishment, which was so discomfited by the evolving new situation. Their presumed support was also explained as the result of a higher degree of unquestioning religiosity, as well as from a certain simplicity larded by greed. "They were," it was widely asserted, "bought."

Thus a drama, triggered by what was presumed to be a religious cause, quickly assumed a more complex mien wherein other tensions were given vent and expression. A consciousness of "us" and "them," previously below but close to the surface, emerged, and the previously dominant cleavage became a religious dispute that clearly threatened communal stability by challenging and undermining the normative struture that had hitherto contained it.

Both the religious and the ethnic contexts represent basic factors of extreme importance in understanding the societal underpinnings and legitimation structure of Israeli society; this is amply demonstrated on the smaller canvas herein discussed. One might ask why, if the majority of Yavneelim and Israelis are not particularly observant, does the issue of religion—what kind and how much—concern them to the extent it does? One might further ask, given the societal commitment to the ideal of *mizug galuyot* (one people), how one explains efforts to maintain ethnic borders and emphasize differences, or at least account for the inability to lower ethnic consciousness.

One sees a reaching out to religion on the part of the nonobservant or partially observant to legitimate what is variously experienced as of, at best, questionable legitimacy—the state itself. What after all justifies a return to Zion and the displacement of the indigenous population, if not the holy entitlement of biblical promise and prophetic fulfillment? What better deed to ownership than holy writ and a contract of ancient provenance and cosmic force such as that concluded between our ancestors and our God? For such enhancement and confirmation of what is subliminally viewed as possibly questionable and even morally tainted, there is a price to be paid and a widespread willingness to pay it. The price is to tolerate a large measure of religious involvement in certain aspects of public and private life. On the public plane, this price includes extensive funding of religious institutions, religious legislation that irritates a fairly large number of the nonobservant, and political power out of proportion to the percentage of the population represented by the Orthodox. On the private level, it includes key matters of personal status, the monopolization of ritual life cycle events by the Orthodox establishment, and the abased position of women, which places some 50 percent of the population in a subservient status. On the whole this arrangement snakes along with little in the way of probing and feinting for advantage on the part of the minority—the observant and their political rabbinical leadership. Thus it works reasonably well because that most valuable of social commodities—legitimation—is provided from under the sacred canopy. When, as happens from time to time, there is a probing for advantage, for extended power and increased influence of the religious sector, a counterreaction on the part of the majority nonobservant population can be foretold. Yavneel's reaction to the religious challenge set forth by Rabbi F, and the release of tension made possible by the coming of the stranger, the Admor and his committed and threatening followers, is an example of this dynamic process.

Religion, for most Yavneelim as for most Israelis, is seen as providing a sacred and symbolic framework for carrying on the business at hand. Its niche, while wide on the symbolic level and fairly extensive in terms of life cycle events and matters of legal personal status, is withal defined and delimited. Trouble arises when this framework is challenged and breached.

THE CRISIS AND ITS RESOLUTION

A modus vivendi of another kind characterizes relationships between Jewish ethnic groups in Israeli society and in Yavneel as well. As Ben-Rafael observed, following Parkin, in looking at Israel one sees a model wherein

> ... a dominant class maintains itself by controlling entry to valued positions through reliance upon criteria of achievement, while the 'hidden' assumption is that only a predictable few can meet these. Thus *mizug galuyot* (one people) and other tokens of the national consensus simply blur the reality of class antagonisms to the advantage of the better off. They hinder the growth of a political class-consciousness among ethnics who belong massively to the working class and on the other hand undermine

their readiness to engage in ethnic politics. (Ben-Rafael 1982, 228).

Ben Rafael is troubled by the fit between Parkin's conflict theory approach and the Israeli reality, which he sees as being ready to endow membership on newcomers, and the general societal generosity that is demonstrated towards the 'ethnics'. But the fit exists, I think, because of a heavy dose of ambivalence in which the whole encounter and the very idea of mizug takes place. Just as a religious framework of legitimate and legitimating provenance is sought and kept at arm's length at one and the same time, so with mizug. The core group both wanted, on its own terms, the integration of the newcomers, and rejected it; wanted equality of opportunity, and needed the context of exploitation; elevated the idea of meritocracy, and fell back on theories of innate inferiority. The reasons for this ambivalence are varied, but there exists scant doubt that interests combined with deep-seated cultural conservation played a distinct role.

In both the response to the religious challenge and to the changing positioning between the ethnics and the core group, we witness a rather classic instance of the forces of conservative structure maintenance attempting to prevent the breach and crumbling of a normative context, and its replacement. The tie-in between the two variables can be found in the perceived coalition between the threatening religious invaders and the ethnics who are seen as receptive to religious blandishments, both in order to strike a blow against the core group who oppose increasing public religious observance and because of their presumed closer adherence to traditional religious modes and standards. Their alliance with the religious invaders in fact increasingly provides a platform for the expression of manifold and essentially nonreligious differences between the groups, which can no longer so readily or easily be expressed in purely ethnic terms. A Moroccan or Tunisian immigrant, and certainly the sons and daughters of these immigrants, can no longer dress, play, or vote along these ethnic lines—but he *can* reach some sort of comfortable and assimilable way of praying so that neither his ethnic identity and loyalties nor his broader national Israeli identity will be compromised. In fact, embracing the Ashkenazi religious model (the Hassidim) can be seen as less a desertion of inner being than a moving towards a national synthesis where input is not unidirectional. After all, both the Hassidim and the ethnics see themselves as deprived groups, but the Hassidim bear a strong claim to relationship with the dominant core group, albeit in conflict with them as are the ethnics. Curiously though understandably, an alliance between the Hassidim and ethnics provides something in the way of a thrust inwards towards a national legitimating channel, made by the former for the latter, without demanding a process of deracination. This tendency is reinforced in Yavneel by the use of highly self-conscious syncretism wherein the Hassidim incorporate Sephardi modes of prayer into their own basically Ashkenazic forms, thereby providing a sense of full and equal participation for both streams.

With the breach and resultant crisis, based as it was on the two-pronged constellation of the religious and ethnic factors, one was able, as Turner phrases it, to see "... how deep structure may be revealed through surface anti-structure or counterstructure" (Turner 1974, 34). Clearly, matters that had bubbled below or close to surface level for many years emerged to full prominence, revealing in the process a truer picture of social reality than had hitherto been visible or *allowed to become so*. But at the risk of perhaps excessive organicism, I would aver that the social corpus seeks quiet and fears disorder more than it seeks truth and understanding. Fears generated by the exposure of deep conflict and fissures raised the specter of arbitrariness and communal disarray. There was a sense that if the community was to return to some level of stasis, redressive action in Turner's terms was required. Here, Turner tells us, both pragmatic techniques and symbolic action reach their fullest expression. A new situation can emerge. A sort of liminality marks this phase, which can result either in reintegration (cure) or the positing of irreparable schism.

In Yavneel a symbolic common ground was sought after it was recognized that things were getting out of hand, that bitterness was rampant, splits were enhanced, and that the sense of place and alignment were threatened. This symbolic common ground was revealed in two related, though quite distinct, phenomena: the events of Memorial-Independence Day 1988 and the reaction to the Day of Peace protest in the Arab sector that same year.

Israel has evolved a linkage often commented upon in celebrating Independence Day contiguous with Memorial Day for the fallen in its many wars. In what has variously been thought of as an exercise in communal split personality or an untenable combination of disparate emotional expressions, deep reflection and sadness is followed immediately by the expectation and reality of often raucous joy and celebration. In Yavneel, the split along ethnic and religious lines is reflected in the manner in which both of these linked events are observed. Memorial Day tends to be the exclusive or near exclusive purview of the core group with only the most visibly minimal participation of the *edot* (Sepharadim) and the religious ultra-Orthodox. Some 32 Yavneelim have fallen in Israel's wars. Of these, only one was from among the edot, and he died in the service due to illness rather than combat. If two values can be said to have been accorded central place in the normative structure of the community, they are 'work' in the building up of the country and as a fulfillment of the *felt dicta* to change the Jew's relationship to his environment, and 'defence' or the willingness to fight, and to die, in maintaining 'Eretz Israel' in confrontation with its enemies. On the gravestones of Yavneel's founding generation one sees inscribed over and over again: "He was a good and devoted worker," and the community had a special building erected as a shrine to its war dead. It appears to be a temple with a nave opposite the entrance, and in this area are the pictures, in uniform, of each of the 32 fallen. Though a temple, its flavor, interestingly in view of the Russian origins of most of the founders, is that of an Orthodox church rather than a synagogue. The structure is totally bare apart from the pictures, which seem to be nothing less than ikons, even to the memorial lamps lit beside each of them. The structure has no chairs (again as in the Christian Orthodox tradition) and visitors file past or stand in near darkness before the nave in silent contemplation.

Once a year, on Memorial Day, the building is opened and the community is invited at 4 P.M. to gather on the front lawn for the ceremony, followed by a communal visit to both cemeteries. The ceremony follows a ritualized format and consists of individuals paying their respects before the pictures of the fallen, two schoolchildren standing at attention, and relieved by two others every 15 minutes, in front of a bank of national flags set up on the left. The ceremony is opened by a resident who is always drawn from among the veteran settlers or the sons of veteran settlers, who begins by asking the town choir to sing one or two renditions. The songs are properly somber and the choir is inordinately bad, but no one seems to mind or indeed to notice. This is followed by reading poetry associated with the founding of the nation or the sacrifices of war, and usually a wounded war veteran makes some kind of speech about ultimate dedication. *Kaddish*, the memorial prayer for the dead, is said by an old settler whose son is among the fallen, an additional song or two is sung by the choir, and the crowd moves to the cemeteries.

In Yavneel there are two cemeteries, both quite beautiful. The older cemetery nestles high above the town and overlooks not only the village itself but the Sea of Galilee, the Golan Heights and the pink-hued mountains of Moab in Jordan. It is densely covered in trees and shrubs, and on the hottest of days there is a cool breeze. The newer cemetery is in the Bet Gan section. It too is covered with flowers and shrubs and is situated in a basin within a magnificent copse of pine and palm trees.

In 1987, one of the main expressions of the crisis phase occurred on Memorial Day. The town Rabbi, Rabbi F, has always refused to take part in the ceremony at the memorial building, asserting that he could not in view of the mixed choir that constitutes a prominent feature of the event. Resentment over his imputed lack of patriotism, to wit, his lack of an army service record, and his refusal to display the national flag at his home on Independence Day, has grown and festered from year to year. With the tension brought to the surface by the arrival of the Admor and his seemingly outspoken anti-Zionist positions, hostilities long-harbored against the local rabbi broke forth. A group of townspeople led by a veteran settler who, while non-Orthodox, heads the local *Hevra Kaddisha*, or burial society, announced that in view of the rabbi's boycott of *their* ceremony and because he had not served in the army, they were calling in an army rabbi to officiate at the cemetery. Ceremonies there were in the past, and are now, traditionally religious and involve reading passages from Psalms, chanting the memorial prayer "God of Mercy," and reciting the mourners prayer, Kaddish. The local Rabbi has carried out these rituals over the years. Rabbi F refused to accept this slight and said he intended to fulfill his legally appointed function, and in fact was waiting at the cemetery for the ceremony at the memorial building to be completed. He was waiting with some of his supporters, mostly from among the *edot*, as a protective measure in case of trouble. But the Yavneelim turned the tables on him and switched the order of cemetery visits, thus effecting a *fait accompli* by having the army rabbi fill the role of local rabbi. A fistfight nearly broke out at the grave of one of the fallen soldiers when a local Orthodox stalwart from the core group insisted that the local rabbi be called and allowed to fulfill his duty.

Anger and readiness to do battle were palpable as the parents, family, and friends of the fallen soldiers insisted that it was their wish and their right to have an army rabbi fill the role. At the second cemetery, as noted above, Rabbi F was already waiting. A quick compromise was reached and Rabbi F and the army chaplain each did parts of the service thus avoiding imminent violence.

The Independence Day celebrations, which begin in the evening at the conclusion of Memorial Day following in this the religious practice, continued to reflect the religio-ethnic split of the earlier commenoration. The community celebrated with performances by outside entertainers, the youth band of the village, the communal choir, and dances by grade school pupils. In addition the town council head or mayor made some pertinent remarks. Here too, in 1987, participation was overwhelmingly of the core group, Ashkenazi, and non-Orthodox. In asking some members of the edot group why they were so little in evidence, I was given to understand that it was a sort of spontaneous boycott brought on by the sense that *their* culture was not represented and the Ashkenazi culture was not only dominant but exclusive. A sense of *their* Independence Day celebration rather than *ours* has festered among the edot over the years, gaining expression in the quasi-boycott only at this juncture. On the following day, too, expression was given to this heightened sense of communal split and indeed segregation: certain undertakings were of the *edot*, others were Ashkenazi, and nothing of an ultra-Orthodox nature was evident. For example, the annual adult basketball game was played by and for an audience of almost exclusively core group members in the lower town. In the upper town, a key event was a soccer game that was almost exclusively edot, both as to audience and players. Both groups were aware of the segregated nature of the celebrations. The core group tended to explain matters in cultural terms, for example, basketball is a middle class, western game, while the edot tended to see soccer as the poor man's game, as against games of the rich. Though similar in observation, the underlying conceptions were quite different. The former envisioned the edot gradually moving towards the dominant mode with time and westernization. The latter viewed the differences as hardened by cultural and class inclinations and choices, and by an unstated but palpable symbolic distancing practiced by the core group even in what should have been a communal ritual of unification and unity. The day concluded with what has become a widespread Independence Day practice—cookouts, family picnics, and the gathering of friends at one or another's residence. In this one could again witness widespread segregation.

Thus, Memorial-Independence Day 1987 clearly reflected the breach and developing crisis phases in the community around the bipolar phenomena of the growing religious rift and the ethnic tensions festering for over 35 years. Feelings of "us" and "them," growing resentment, increasing expressions of "anti" sentiments, were all present in heightened and dangerously explosive form. Masks that had been worn for over three decades fell, revealing that indeed "something was rotten in the village."

If a split with accompanying disintegrative and possibly violent aspects was to be avoided, some form of healing, of bridging, of what Turner refers to as 'redressive action' was clearly required. Recognizing this, though never in an overt or verbalized fashion, common ground was sought on a symbolic level. The committee formed to prevent the coming of the Admor and his Hassidim faltered, and met less and less frequently. When it did meet, hostility to the Admor was increasingly displaced onto the communal rabbi. Efforts to have him removed, involving accusations of financial malpractice, were made to the Ministry of Religion and the police. It was increasingly recognized that in the absence of concrete efforts by the Admor to prevent the non-Orthodox from living their lives as before, steps to prevent him settling were untenable on both legal and moral-ideological grounds. Meanwhile, economic problems more and more consumed the interest of the farming core group members. Increasingly they asserted that the financial reverses afflicting their group were in fact accomplishing what volition never could—a leveling that, they claimed, brought the core group and the edot closer on objective economic grounds. Both, it was said, are now in the same economic boat. While the core group was harmed by government policy, the edot, it was asserted, were deprived by lesser energy and talents, but the end result was seen to be the same—impoverishment. (This definition of the situation was, of course, not shared equally by the two groups.)

But the catalytic agent for redressive action was provided by an occurence outside the community and in a format assuming classic dimensions—the recognition of a common enemy, more threatening, more dangerous, and less assimilable than the challenges facing the smaller entity. What was called the Day of Peace was organized by the Association of Arab villages in Israel. It resulted in some acts of violence against the state and its representatives including, in a few instances, the stoning of vehicles, the raising of the Palestinian flag, and verbal expressions of identity with the wider Palestinian cause. Rage was the predominating emotion among all segments of Yavneel's population in response to what was seen as this revelation of Israeli Arabs' true colors. They, it was widely said, were part and parcel of the *Intifada*, which their cousins in the West Bank and Gaza had launched against us, and their aim was the same—the destruction of Israel. At the very least, it was noted, we, the religious, the edot, the old core settlers are all Jews, all Israelis; and the enemy, the real enemy, was to be found elsewhere.

A closing of ranks with resultant signs, if not of healing, then certainly of truce, was evident. Memorial Day 1988 passed quietly, again with little participation of the edot, but with both the communal rabbi and the army chaplain splitting ritual responsibility on an agreed basis. The celebrations of Independence Day were still heavily imprinted by Ashkenazi culture, but large numbers of *edot* as well as core groupers participated. The rabbi and some of the ultra-Orthodox displayed the national flag from their homes. Though it was a more somber occasion than in the past, given the riots in the West Bank and Gaza and renewed suspicion of the intentions of Israeli Arabs, there seemed an unstated pervasive definition of the situation shared by all groups. It suggested a setting aside of what could only be described as family trouble in order to deal with the real threat. It was, in fact, backing away from the results of breach, and an almost inchoate striving for communal healing.

Redress too, says Turner, has its liminal features. It is being betwixt and between, and when redress fails, there may be a return to crisis. In a small community, he notes "regression to crisis tends to become a matter of endemic, pervasive, smouldering factionalism, without sharp overt confrontations between consistently distinct parties" (Turner 1974, 4). This, in fact, seems to sum up well the current status of Yavneel's social drama. Clearly a process of reintegration has not occurred, and if anything, Turner's alternative to a happy ending in phase four, that is, the legitimation of irreparable schism, appears a more likely result.

But clearly the actions of the various segments involved indicate a strong pull away from the abyss of communal dissolution and toward some form of bridging, of reaching out and healing. More correctly, what seems to be evident here are two opposing tendencies vying for ascendancy and dominance: one which pounces on separatist dissolutive elements that naturally abound in a heterogeneous social context, raising these to prominence and centrality, and another that seeks a coming together of disparate forces and the bind of community. This is true for both the society at large and for the village where, when all is said and done, it is 'communitas', which lies beyond structure, which exercises the ultimate pull. "Group binding memory" is sought rather than the bold imperatives of structure, which involve the dryness of duties and roles as well as the impieties implied in the pursuit of group as well as personal interests.

In striving for 'communitas', efforts are made to downplay ethnic tensions and emphasize ameliorative tendencies on the part of both groupings—the core veteran group and the edot. These tendencies are not symmetrical: the former cite its efficiency much more readily than the latter. However, there seems to be a certain subliminal awareness that if these ameliorative tendencies are not representative of the reality, then the idea of communal coexistence not only on the village level but in the state itself is nonviable. Similarly the factor of religion operates on myriad and complex levels involving as it does a context for memory, a framework of identity, going beyond constrictions of local or even family frameworks, and is, as well, a political, social, and even economic force within the community writ large and small. The Admor both can and cannot be an enemy to others in the community. His vision is not that of the majority, whether of core group or *edot*. His life-style, behavior, reactions to, and definition of reality are utterly distinct—even idiosyncratic when measured against community models; but for all that he is kin, flesh of our flesh, and thus unthinkable as an enemy. There are decided limits to what kinds of opposition can be mounted against his coming. Fears with respect to future action on his part or those of his followers are not sufficient cause for his active exclusion or for other than verbal grumbling about his otherness and nonassimilability. Above all the desire for a religious umbrella of legitimation is a seeking of communitas on the most profound and perhaps the safest level. Social structure and all that it implies and brings in its wake in the sense of a cold calculus of rights will not or cannot satisfy this primary need. With Turner, one might postulate that "the coherence of a completed social drama is itself a function of communitas" (Turner 1974, 50).

REFERENCES

Bellah, R. 1980. The five religions of modern Italy. In *Varieties of Civil Religion*, ed, Bellah and P. Hammong. San Francisco: Harper & Row.

Ben Rafael, E. 1982. *The emergence of ethnicity: Cultural groups and social conflict in Israel*. Westport, Conn.: Greenwood Press.

Turner, V. 1974. *Dreams, fields and metaphors: Symbolic action in human society*. Ithaca, N.Y.: Cornell University Press.

Personal Motivation and Social Meaning in the Revival of Hagiolatric Traditions among Moroccan Jews in Israel

YORAM BILU

INTRODUCTION: SAINT VENERATION AMONG THE JEWS IN MOROCCO

Beliefs and practices related to the folk veneration of saints (*hagiolatry*) played a major role in the lives of many Jews in Morocco. Because Moroccan Jews have venerated their saints in a distinctively Maghrebi 'North African' style (Stillman 1982, 499), it is reasonable to assume that the proliferation of hagiolatric practices among them was influenced by North African Muslim *maraboutism* (veneration of holy men thought to have supernatural powers) that, in scope and profoundity, has no equivalent in any other Muslim society (Eickelman 1976; Geertz 1968; Gellner 1969). At the same time, however, it was also reinforced by the deep-seated conception of the *saddiq* (sainted, pious man) in the classical Jewish tradition. In various Jewish groups outside North Africa, Sephardic as well as Ashkenazic, pious rabbis and charismatic sages were accorded saintly attributes, and their tombs became centers of popular pilgrimage. Hence the phenomenon under discussion, although intimately related to indigenous Moroccan traditions, is also grounded in Jewish folk religion.

The predominance and centrality of the saints in the lives of the Jews in Morocco has been amply documented in recent studies (Ben Ami 1984). Ben Ami identified no less than 650 saints whose sanctuaries were scattered all over Morocco, but this number is far from conclusive. It appears that virtually every Jewish community had its patron saint. These saints were charismatic individuals, distinguished by their erudition and piety. They were believed to possess a special spiritual force, the manifestations of which are similar to the Moroccan Muslim *baraka* (see Rabinow 1975, 19–30; Westermarck 1926, 35–126). This spiritual force, which does not fade away after the holy man's death, might be utilized for the benefit of his adherents.

In terms of popularity and importance, the saints can be placed on a continuum ranging from local peripheral saddiqim known only in particular congregations through regional holy men to popular saints venerated by large groups of Jews in various parts of the country. In the densely populated pantheon of saddiqim these popular saints whose reputation transcended regional boundaries constituted a small select group. Most famous among them are figures like Rabbi Ya'acov Abu-Hatsera, Rabbi Amram ben Diwan, and Rabbi ou-Moshe.

In terms of "authenticity," some of the saints were well-known historical figures, at times founders or descendants of veritable dynasties of saddiqim (such as the Abu-Hatsera and Pinto families), while others seemed to be legendary figures; most of the popular saints belong to the latter group. The historical vacuum that envelops many saddiqim is congruent with the fact that most of them were not known during their lifetime but were recognized as sainted figures after a posthumous apparition in dreams.

The life stories of the nonhistorical saddiqim are stereotypical and highly symbolic. They were depicted as messengers from the Holy Land who were sent to the Jewish communities in the Moroccan Diaspora to collect funds for the inhabitants of Jerusalem. Sometimes, their mission was presented as a forced exile, imposed by an older rabbi whose authority they had challenged. Most of these messengers from the holy land met their death on the road, before accomplishing their mission, and were buried in remote desolate, places. Following their death, a spate of miraculous episodes would disclose the unknown, hidden tomb, and its inhabitant's saintly status would be established. The life story of the legendary saddiq, based only on popular imagination, without the constraints of historical events, encapsulates and reflects major themes in the collective Jewish experience in Morocco: a continuing Jewish existence, in exile, geographical mobility, and a wish to return to the Holy Land that does not materialize. The Israeli origin of many saddiqim seems conducive to current attempts, reported in this study, to transfer saints from Morocco to Israel symbolically. For it is only natural that these cultural identities will ultimately return to the place where they originally belonged, the more so after their adherents have done so.

Generally speaking, the presence of the saint was a basic given in the culturally constituted reality of Moroccan Jews. The *saddiq* constituted a central idiom through which a wide range of experiences were articulated (Crapanzano 1977, 11). The main event in the veneration of each saint was the collective pilgrimage to his tomb on the anniversary of his death and the *hillulah* (celebration) there. In the case of the more renowned saints, many thousands of pilgrims from various regions would gather around the tomb for several days, during which they feasted on slaughtered cattle, drank *mahia* (arak), danced and chanted, prayed, and lit candles. Deep spirituality and flesh and blood concerns combined in ecstatic devotion, in a relaxed and at times frivolous picnic-like atmosphere, that made the hillulah a variegated event that all the participants irrespective of age, sex, and social status could and did enjoy. Sociologically, those hillulot (pl.) constituted cultural patterns that highlighted and reinforced Jewish solidarity and fraternity as manifested in the spirit of *communitas* (Salnow 1981; Turner 1973) that prevailed in many aspects of the celebration. On the other hand, the hillulah was also a setting for conspicuous consumption and display of material wealth most explicitly demonstrated in the ritualistic auction of candles and glasses of mahia dedicated to the saint.

In addition to collective pilgrimages, sanctuaries drew a continuous flow of pilgrims who turned to the saint individually in times of distress, with a vast array of human afflictions. These included physical ailments and psychological disturbances of all sorts, economic difficulties, and a wide range of romantic, intrafamilial, and interpersonal problems. In fact, no human misery was considered irrelevant to or insoluble by the saddiq in his primary role as intermediary between God and mortals.

Collective and individual pilgrimages to the saints' tombs do not exhaust the complex of hagiolatric beliefs and practices. The presence of the saint was also strongly felt in daily routine as people would utter his name and dream about him whenever facing a problem. At homes, candles were lit, festive meals were organized, and male newborns were named after him. In many cases the enduring and pervasive nature of the relationship with the saint has amounted to a symbiotic association spanning the entire life of the devotee.

FOLK VENERATION OF SAINTS: THE ISRAELI SCENE

The massive migration of Moroccan Jews to Israel during the 1950s and 1960s confronted the newcomers with a major challenge of maintaining cultural traditions rejected by the Israeli mainstream. Saint veneration as a whole, being ultimately related to Jewish folk religion, was less liable to invoke stigmatic images than, say, traditional beliefs in *jnun* (demons) and *shur* (sorcery); but in the new country it was closely linked to physical loci now remote and inaccessible. The annual pilgrimages to the saints' sanctuaries had been the high points of hagiolatric traditions in Morocco. At these sacred sites the deep sentiments towards the saints could be rejuvenated and reaffirmed. Emigrating to Israel meant, among other things, a painful dissociation from the blissful milieus of the saddiqim; exacerbating the trauma of aliyah (immigration to Israel) even before the predicaments of the first harsh years in the new country were overcome. Clearly, the messianic fervor generated by the establishment of Israel compensated for this loss, but not for long. Facing enormous difficulties after immigration, the support of the saddiqim was a cultural resource that people could not forego easily. The cultural shock felt by the newcomers, often amplified by cultural suppression on the part of the absorbing agencies, contributed to the general diminution and decentralization of the hillulot. But the idiom of the saint was too central to disappear entirely, so the hillulot were celebrated in small numbers on a domestic level, at homes and in neighborhood synagogues. At the same time, however, these attenuated, family-based hillulot served the function of preserving the tradition during a transitional period after aliyah (Ben Ami 1981, 303).

Contrary to a naive melting pot conception, the relative progress in the socioeconomic conditions of North African Jews in Israel has enhanced their consciousness of their distinctive ethnic identity. In proudly asserting their culture heritage, the folk veneration of saints played a major role as an idiom to be recultivated and reemployed. But the fact that the sites associated with the saints had been left far behind has called for flexible accommodations. Actualizing these accommodations proves the tenacity with which hagiolatric traditions were maintained and indicates their significance in the contemporary Israel scene.

Three major alternatives have been employed as substitutes for the original sites associated with hagiolatry in Morocco.

"Annexing" Old time native Pilgrimage sites

As mentioned before, folk veneration of saints in Judaism was not restricted to Morocco. In the Land of Israel, tombs attributed to charismatic figures, mainly from the Biblical and Talmudic eras, have drawn pilgrims from the Middle Ages, if not earlier. Most renowned are the sanctuaries of Rabbi Shimon Bar Yohai in Meron and Rabbi

Meir Ba'al Haness in Tiberias. Observations made in these sites during recent hillulot (Bilu and Abramovitch 1985) show that most of the pilgrims are of Morrocan origin, and their participation is growing steadily over the years. As a result, these hillulot have undergone a process of "Moroccanization," reflected in their style and form in dress, food, and music.

Creating New Contemporary Saints

Because the emergence of saints has always been a dynamic process, it was only natural to assume that contemporary rabbis and sages would be posthumously alloted saintly attributes, and their tombs would become centers of mass pilgrimages. The most impressive example for this process is that of *Baba Sali*, Rabbi Israel Abu-Hatsera, who was considered a holy man even in his life time. Since his death in 1984, his tomb in the southern development town of Netivot has become a center of huge gatherings, second in popularity only to Rabbi Shimon's sanctuary. Another interesting case is that of Rabbi Hayyim Houri, a Tunisian rabbi whose tomb is in the municipal cemetery in Beersheba. Although highly respected in his lifetime, the first anniversaries of his death attracted few participants, mostly family members. Since the 1970s, however, the image of the late rabbi was transformed into a sainted figure, a divine healer, and his hillulah now attracts thousands. As in Meron and Tiberias, the overwhelming majority of the celebrants here and in Netivot are Moroccans, and the number of the pilgrims is growing over time. The fact that both places are located in the southern part of the country is significant, given the relative paucity of ancient sacred sites there.

Renewing Hagiolatric Traditions

This option can take two major forms: "transferring" a saint from Morocco to Israel, and discovering a sacred site associated with a local tradition. In both forms one deals with a spontaneous initiative of an individual who is inspired by a dream series in which a saint appeared and urged the dreamer to erect a site for him at his home.

The main concern of this chapter is with the latter mode, certainly the most innovatie and demanding in terms of personal involvement. This substitute is also more intimately tuned to the needs of veteran adherents of saints' cults in Morocco, as it serves a restorative no less than compensatory function, summoning the venerated cultural characters of the past.

PLAN OF THE STUDY

During the years 1981–1984 I conducted in-depth interviews and observations in various locales in Israel where traditions of saint veneration had been renewed. Most of the data were collected in two sites in Northern Israel:

1. The House of Rabbi David ou-Moshe in Safed
2. "The Gates of Paradise" in Beit She'an

The sanctuary of Rabbi David ou-Moshe, one of the most popular saints in Morocco, is near the village of Agouim in the High Atlas region. His hillulah on the first day of Heshvan, the second month in the Jewish calendar, drew thousands of visitors from various parts of the country. In 1973, a forestry worker names Avraham dedicated a small room in his modest apartment in Safed to Rabbi David ou-Moshe following a dream series in which the saddiq informed him that he had left Morocco and indicated his wish to reside forever with him. Avraham promulgated his first dreams as "announcements to the public" and circulated them among Moroccan synagogues all over the country. The impact was extraordinary. Within a few years the new site was transformed into an important pilgrimage center that, for most of the saint's adherents, constitutes a legitimate substitute for the original burial site in Morocco. During the day of the hillulah, the trickle of supplicants that frequent the place throughout the year becomes an impressive throng of some 20,000 celebrants. Among the new sacred sites erected through individual initiative, Rabbi David ou-Moshe's House in Safed is no doubt the most successful, having acquired the status of cardinal station on the "sacred map" of saints' sanctuaries in northern Israel.

According to a legendary tradition mentioned in the Talmud, the entrance to the Garden of Eden in its terrestrial form is found in the town of Beit She'an in the Jordan Valley. in 1979, a man named Yaish, a leader of a cleaning team in the local municipality, announced that he discovered this entrance in the backyard of his house. The discovery was precipitated by visitational dreams in which Elijah the Prophet appeared to Yaish, disclosed the place to him, and guided him in and out. In the beginning of the month of Elul, the twelfth month in the Jewish calendar, a hillulah for Elijah is conducted at the site, near the small synagogue erected over the presumed entrance. The site has not acquired total legitimation as yet and is virtually unknown outside Beit She'an. Most of the visitors are from Yaish's neighborhood. In terms of popularity, then, the Beit She'an site cannot compete with the House of Rabbi David ou-Moshe. The fact that it was erected only a year and a half before the beginning of the study enabled us to document the initial phase of its development—a stage that in the Safed shrine, founded six years earlier, we could only reconstruct.

While most of the fieldwork was conducted in Safed and Beit She'an, our main objective was to identify common themes in the revival of hagiolatric traditions that transcend the singularities of a particular site and the idiosyncracies of its founder. To that end, brief investigations were made at other sacred sites related to saint veneration in Ofakim, Kiriat Gat, Netivot, and Hatsor. All these settings are development towns founded in the 1950s in which the majority of the inhabitants are from Morocco. Safed is no exception because the small nucleus of the old town is surrounded by new neighborhoods that in design and population do not differ from most development towns.

The study of the new sites in Safed and Beit She'an involved three levels of analysis. First, the *personal motivations of the initiators* to establish these sites and to develop them were thoroughly researched. This was done through lengthy and detailed interviews with them, through which their life histories were meticulously documented. Second, the impact of the new sites on the *community* and the extent to which they function as cultural resources were examined through interviews with individuals involved—on different levels of intensity— with the site and its patron saint. An attempt was made to map the whole gamut of life problems with which supplicants turned to the saint, in order to locate points of stress in the lives of North African Jews in Israel. Third, the development of each *site* in terms of physical setting and social activities was documented through regular visits. This documentation included both the hillulot and the daily functioning of the shrines.

A phenomenon as complicated and multifaceted as the veneration of saints can be approached and analyzed from various perspectives. In this presentation, I chose to concentrate on the life histories of the founders of the sites in Safed and Beit She'an and to describe it in detail. Following this, the significance of the new sites in the context of present-day Israeli society is examined and explicated. The "personalistic" bias of the study is justified by the fact that the personal initiative of the founders echoed the wishes and sentiments of many others in their group. What had been precipitated by a few dreams has swiftly culminated in mass pilgrimages in which many thousands of people participate. In reviving cultural traditions that others were eager to adopt and follow, the initiators gave expression to something that transcends individual psychodynamics. In fact, their initiative was modeled on the collective Moroccan experience in Israel. The

complicated, at time painful process of "homecoming," with its conflicting themes of continuity and change, of segregation and intergra-
tion, has found a symbolic expression in the renewed forms of saint
veneration, as I later attempt to show.

THE INDIVIDUAL HISTORY OF A SACRED SITE FOUNDER

Avraham and Yaish, the founders of the sites in Safed and Beit She'an,
were in their early fifties at the time of their first revelations. The fact
that they emerged from the rank and file is reflected in their modest
living conditions and the low-status occupations they continue to hold
following the revelation. Their simple appearance and modest, unpre-
tentious demeanor appear congruent with their professional status.
Designations such as "charismatic leader" or "popular prophet" seem
entirely out of place in the case of Avraham and Yaish. They do not
exhibit excessive ardor and fervor conducive to inspiring others, and
their discourse is not very coherent. Yet behind their modesty, gentle-
ness, and even awkwardness, one senses tremendous dedication and
resourcefulness. The continue to respond to their calling uncondition-
ally and tenaciously, and this total commitment endows them with a
convincing aura of authenticity. What are the sources of this persever-
ence and indefatigable energy?

Avraham and Yaish are both natives of Southern Morocco. The
former grew up in Imi-n-tanout, a fairly large village 90 km southwest
of Marrakesh, while Yaish was born in the smaller village of Oulad
Mansour, near the town of Demnat. In both places Jewish life could be
maintained fully and piously despite the distance of their communities from the rabbinical centers. The fathers of Avraham and Yaish
were simple and humble men who earned their living through manual
work. Avraham's father was a cobbler who spent most of his weekdays
in the surrounding villages seeking customers for his products. Yaish's
father was a seasonal laborer, a jack-of-all-trades, who worked mainly
in agriculture. Until this day both fathers are active and industrious,
but their vitality and assiduity cannot hide their lack of spirituality
and erudition. It is hard to conceive of them as the inspirational
models for their sons' enterprises. In fact, both are quite dissociated
from the latter's initiatives, the origins of which should therefore be
looked for elsewhere. At the same time, however, the parents of both
founders inculcated in them from early childhood a profound sense of
faith and trust in the lodal saddiqim. Yaish's earliest memories involved the hillula of Rabbi David Dra Halevi, a popular saint buried
near Demnat. To this day he retains vivid recollections of the happy

and joyful days spent by the family near Rabbi David' sanctuary. Avraham's infantile memories are also embedded with visits to the three saddiqim of Imi-n-tanout buried ona nearby mountain.

These vivid recollections, however, do not separate Avraham and Yaish from a host of Moroccan Jews in whom, too, the image of the saddiq as a basic constituent in the construction of social reality was imprinted during their formative years (mostly by their mothers as Brown 1976, 106, has shown). Yet in the case of our protagonists, other more personally involving experiences, related to family figures, played a critical role in molding the motivational bases from which their future enterprises have emerged. Matrilineally they had among their ancestors venerated rabbis and sages who were deemed saddiqim in their communities. In both cases, the last representative of this thread of piety and sagacity in the family was the maternal grandfather, with whom Avraham and Yaish had close contact in childhood. As a result, both are convinced that they have been invested with ample *zekhut avot* (rights by virtue of ancestry: this term may be seen as the Jewish equivalent of the Muslim *baraka*). More than by this conviction, however, it seems that their inspiration and commitment were shaped by awareness of the conspicuous gap between their grandfathers' aura of sanctity and spirituality and their fathers' lack of it. Because blessing and virtue in their families were enveloped exclusively in the maternal, less cardinal line of ancestry, their share in it, far from guaranteed, had to be validated and reaffirmed. Through the symbiotic liaison with their "own" saddiqim (which reflects, as I later attempt to show, a symbolic reunion with the grandfathers), their claim to the family zekhut could be made forcefully and convincingly.

Yaish's grandfather, Rabbi Issakhar Amar, was considered so pious and devout that he could stop a flowing river with his prayer. His great-grandfather, a renowned healer, had absolute control over the *jnun:* "with one word from his mouth he could summon them, chained, at his feet." Avraham's charismatic ancestor too left an indelible mark on his development and, presumably, on his later project. He reports that as a child he spent more time with his grandfather, Rabbi Shlomo Timsut, who was a *shohet* and *mohel* (ritual slaughterer and circumciser), than with his own parents. In the house of Rabbi Shlomo he had ample opporunity to observe the multifarious expressions of respect and admiration bestowed on the old patriarch, and the latter's reciprocal hospitality and generosity. Whenever he slaughtered a cow, Rabbi Shlomo would allot a portion for the needy. Every Sabbath evening a large number of Jews from the local community assembled in Rabbi Shlomo's house to receive his blessing. His importance for Avraham was manifested in the latter's desperate attempts to retrieve some souvenirs from his house, particularly one of his handwritten books and a giant tea urn from which the grandfather served his visitors. These attempts proved abortive as Rabbi Shlomo's son and heir (Avraham's maternal uncle) refused to give these objects away, falsely claiming that they were abandoned in Morocco. (This episode might well reflect the tension between various factions in the Timsut family as to the worthy heir of Rabbi Shlomo.) In any case, the symbolic import of these two objects appears evident: the sacred book embodies the spiritual blessing, transferred through Rabbi Shlomo's erudition and moral ascendance, while the tea urn symbolizes the material blessing given in the prosperity and generosity characteristic of his house. It can be argued that with these two distinctive yet comlementary aspects of his ideal past Avraham strives to reintegrate in the House of Rabbi David ou-Moshe.

Avraham's attempts to take possession of some tangible objects of his late grandfather's might have been invigorated by the profound sense of loss and privation that the particular circumstances of the rabbi's death created in him. Although Rabbi Shlomo lived most of his life in Imi-n-tanout, he died in the coastal town of Es-Saouria (Mogador), where he received medical treatment during his last months. The Jews of Es-Saouira, well aware of the deceased's virtues, refused to send him back to his native village and hastened to bury him in their cemetery. For 13-year-old Avraham, who as devotedly attached to his grandfather, the sudden disappearance constituted a traumatic experience of separation exacerbated by the absence of a burial site, where the relationship with the deceased could be maintained. In establishing the site for Rabbi David ou-Moshe, Avraham might have unconsciously compensated for the vacuum created by his grandfather's disappearance. The initial situation in which a family saint had been "appropriated" by others to be buried far away was reversed by bringing a saddiq from afar into the house. It should be noted that Rabbi David ou-Moshe's abode in Safed is considered by many of his adherents as his reconstructed tomb.

One of Rabbi Shlomo's predecessors, also called Rabbi Shlomo, was the most renowned saddiq in the Timsut family. His miraculous feats were depicted in the annotated corpus of Jewish Moroccan saints (Ben Ami 1984, 563–565). This rabbi had been treacherously assassinated by Arabs who entombed his mutilated body in a house wall. Through a miraculous dream revelation, the late rabbi informed his wife where he had been put and exposed the identity of the murderers. His tomb in Marrakesh swiftly became a pilgrimage site, a scene of innumerable miracles. This narrative, part of the family myth, might have tacitly influenced Avraham's initiative, also propelled by a dream revelation and involved a transfer of a saddiq from one place to another. A more compelling association with Avraham's enterprise is evident in a legend attributed to another sainted ancestor, Rabbi Ya'acov Timsut. One month after his funeral in Marrakesh a letter arrived from Jerusalem announcing the marvellous appearance of a gravestone with the name of Rabbi Ya'acov in the cemetery on the Mount of Olives. Hence, a model for transferring a saint from Morocco to Israel had been in existence in the family tradition long before the project in Safed, which should therefore be deemed restorative no less than innovative.

Both Avraham and Yaish review their Moroccan past with nostalgic affection. Life in Imi-n-tanout was qualitative in three distinctive domains: First, the social relations within the Jewish community as well as with the Arab neighbors were peaceful and harmonious. Second, the land was prosperous, and the natural resources abundant and uncontaminated. Third, the life-style of the Jewish community was characterized by spirituality, piety, and strict observance of the Law. If this retrospective view is positively biased, it stems from the painful contrast with the difficulties of life in the new country. Particularly Yaish, who was only 11 years old when he moved to Israel, tends to idealize his recollections from Morocco, probably because as a child he was spared the adversities of adult life there. Hence "the predicaments of homecoming" (Deshen and Shokeid, 1974) had a very strong effect on him. A quotation suffices to convey the atmosphere of prosperous life and spirit of gemeinschaft that prevailed in Oulad Mansour: "Everything was plentiful there. We had beans, pears, grain; we used to fill up with all sorts of fruits, and dry them. From the river we brought large quantities of fish. People used to work there only six months a year. During the winter, when it snowed, we stayed home, chatting, eating and drinking. People were strong and healthy and happy too. The water was pure, the air fresh and clear. Nothing got spoiled there. All the inhabitants of Oulad Mansour, Jews and Arabs were like brothers."

Upon hearing this nostalgic reminiscence one might ask whether Yaish, in discovering the "gate of paradise" in his backyard, is not re-creating the lost paradise of his childhood. This supposition is rendered more plausible when the spiritual dimension is introduced. Both men emphasized the central role of religious studies in the *sla* (synagogue), but it was Yaish again, the younger of the two, who was irrevocably removed from the path of learning upon immigrating to Israel. In Oulad Mansour, under the strict discipline of the rabbi, he studied the Torah from the morning prayer to the late afternoon, showing determination and assiduity. But this willpower evaporated rapidly after aliyah, in the adverse conditions of the *ma'abarah* (transit camp) days, in a municipal school dominated by negligence and apathy. In Yaish's words: "Here it was free and easy, without authority. I became less and less conscientious. There, we did what we were supposed to do. In any case the Rabbi would not let us deviate from the course of study. Here, the teachers do not care. That's why the children can do whatever they wish." At age 11 Yaish left his school in order to become, two years later, a seasonal laborer in the neighboring kibbutzim. To this day he laments his truancy that distanced him from strict observance and spirituality. In establishing the sacred site, however, he was able to repair partially his childhood negligence. Inspired and intimidated by his proximity to the sacred—which he himself had created—Yaish feels obliged to dedicate his free time to reciting Psalms, hymns, and prayers. Within the complex he intends to build in his yard, he has reserved a central place for a Talmud Torah (religious school) for children roaming aimlessly in the streets of Beit She'an, who will study there under the guidance of a local rabbi. Yaish is well aware that in so doing he will heal his own wounds, the consequences of his traumatic transfer from Morocco to Israel.

Avraham and Yaish both came to Israel in 1954 and were sent immediately with their families to the towns of Safed and Beit She'an respectively, where they live to this day. In both cases, the families were not separated and, consequently, their members could preserve a sense of togetherness typical of their life in Morocco. Today, more than 30 years after their aliyah, Avraham and most of his seven siblings, of whom he is the oldest, still live with their families within walking distance of their father's apartment. Indeed, as the family's married children also tend to find residence in the neighborhood, and with the fourth generation being born in the 1980s, an impressive cross-generational stability has been established. As later shown, this stability has contributed to the creation of the sacred site and was reinforced by it in turn. Of Yaish's four siblings, only one has left Beit She'an. All the others, including Yaish, live in the same neighborhood as their father.

Avraham was 24 years old when he moved to Israel. He was already married to Masouda, a neighbor's daughter in Imi-n-tanout, and father to a six-month-old daughter. He had to give up his former occupation, shoemaking, inherited from his father, and the two men, together with many of their fellow newcomers, found their living as afforestation workers. Unlike most of them, however, Avraham has stayed in this job, one of the lowest in prestige and income. As I later show, however, the actual work conditions on the job, in which he managed to acquire some specialization over the years, were conducive to Avraham's growing involvement with Rabbi David ou-Moshe's House.

Life in Safed was not easy in the 1950s. The apartment was tiny and, during the first year, devoid of basic comforts such as running water and electricity. Avraham's salary was not sufficient to sustain a rapidly growing family, and Masuda had to work as a maid in the evenings, until the House of Rabbi David ou-Moshe was founded. Notwithstanding these difficulties, Avraham was more than satisfied to live in Safed, a town inbued with a special mystic atmosphere and surrounded by numerous sacred places, mostly tombs of Talmudic sages and sixteenth century kabbalists. Some of the tombs are on the slopes of the Biriyah Mountains, where Avraham has spent most of his working time, and it is possible that the inspiration to establish a sacred site was acquired in part there. The multitude and density of sacred tombs in the region proved advantageous some years later, after the establishment of the new center, as it has been easily integrated into the popular itineraries of saints' visits in the Galilee. Hence, during the mass hillulot of Rabbi Shimon Bar Yohai, Rabbi Meir, and Honi Hame'agel in Hatsor, many pilgrims also visit the House of Rabbi David ou-Moshe.

Avraham's growing attachment to the local saddiqim was expressed in the names he gave his first two sons (he has ten children, six of whom are boys). His first son was called Shimon, after the venerated Rabbi Shimon Bar Yohai, while the second bears the name of Rabbi Meir (Ba'al Haness). The burial sites of these two sages, located at Meron and Tiberias respectively, are by far the largest pilgrimage centers in northern Israel. Both of them are visible from Safed. Avraham's third son, his fourth child, was given the name of his beloved grandfather, Shlomo. The juxtaposition of the latter to the two local saints is not accidental as the following episode shows.

In 1955, one year after aliyah, Avraham's economic situation was so poor that occasionally he could not buy special foods for the Sabbath. On one of these occasions he stumbled upon a large sum of money, with the help of which he could celebrate the Sabbath fittingly. The following night, this propitious event was explicated to him through a dream in which Rabbi Shlomo presented him to Rabbi Shimon. The latter gave him a loaf of bread and promised to take care of all his needs. The message of the dream is quite explicit: while in Morocco, Rabbi Shlomo had been the patron of his grandson, in Israel he transferred him to the custody of Rabbi Shimon, a most potent saint who resides near Safed. Thus the transition from Morocco to Israel was completed through symbolic reorganization of allegiances to saints. Eighteen years later, when Avraham established a liaison with Rabbi David ou-Moshe, Rabbi Shimon was present in some of his dreams, just as Rabbi Shlomo before him. Only Avraham's fourth son and eighth child was named after his own father, Isaac.

Like Avraham and his father, Yaish's father made his living in Beit She'an as an afforestation worker. Despite the difficulties of the ma'abara, he has never complained about life in Israel and inculcated in his children a solid attachment to and pride in their new home. More clearly than in Avraham's case, the father remained the center of the family. Yaish's strong attachment to his father was manifested when he turned down various financially attractive offers to live and work outside Beit She'an. Some of the offers concerned reconstruction work on archaeological sites, a domain in which he acquired some expertise after reluctantly accepting such work. It might be suggested that Yaish's involvement with work, the essence of which is uncovering and restoring a glorious past, predisposed him to discover the gates of paradise in his own yard. In fact, Yaish reluctantly particiapted in the reconstruction of the Massada National Monument; but after a short and unhappy period there, he came back to Beit She'an and spent 17 years as an industrial worker in a textile firm. There he met his wife-to-be, Hannah, also a native of southern Morocco. A short time before the revelation, Yaish joined the staff of the local municipality and became supervisor of a cleaning team. This move was significant as it is hard to imagine how he could have developed his site had he stayed in his former physically demanding job. In his new occupation, Yaish starts working before sunrise, but finishes before noon. Avraham's conditions are easy, and he can dedicate a large part of his day to the site he founded.

In Israel, Avraham could preserve his religious faith intact and even became the *gabbai* (treasurer) of the neighborhood synagogue —administrative work that was excellent preparation for his project. Yaish, on the other hand, was not strictly observant of religious laws in his youth. His progressive disengagement from religion could be attributed in part to childhood negligence, typical of his age group; but more than that, it was the result of a distrubing personal problem. Yaish, an introvert who felt at ease only at home, was liable to become anxious in various social settings, including the synagogue. Whenever he was called to read from the Torah, he became so upset that he stopped coming to prayers altogether. This avoidant behavior, however, did not bring him relief as any involvement with religious matters, such as praying and reciting Psalms, even at home, became unbearably agitating. Without delving into the psychological origins of his problem, it is clear that by erecting the site in his yard, Yaish has cured himself entirely. Since then, his life has been marked by an aura of spirituality, as he is surrounded by a host of saddiqim the inhabitants of Paradise, who would not let him skip a prayer or omit a precept. The centripetal orientation of Yaish's reconstituted life has redeemed him from his social malaise. As with other founders of sacred sites, including Avraham, most of his daily activities are centered around his place. Instead of socializing outside his house, he can host supplicants and pilgrims there. The synagogue that functions at the site on weekends has exempted him entirely from the burden of participating in the communal prayers in the neighborhood synagogue.

The general life situation of Avraham and Yaish prior to the revelations was quite similar. They continued to live in the same towns to which they had been brought in 1954 with their families, which they managed to keep intact. They survived the harsh post-immigration years, and with the general development of their towns, they experienced a modest but systematic improvement in their economic status. Approaching midlife, the growth of their families has been attenuated. By 1970, Avraham had eight children, four boys and four girls. Although the intrafamily relationships were generally harmonious, Avraham was occasionally bothered by casual expressions of nonobservance on the part of his adolescent sons. This growing secularization became particularly evident during the prerevelation period. The appearance of the saint effectively kept it at bay. Today all of Avraham's older children, except one, dutifully adhere to the religious code. In introducing Rabbi David ou-Moshe, Avraham was able to draw his children nearer to his own life-style without exerting direct pressure. One simply cannot be religiously negligent when residing in the same apartment with a saddiq.

In 1972, one year before Rabbi David ou-Moshe's first revelation, Avraham's dearest brother and neighbor died in a car accident. Avraham's religious faith had never before been so seriously shaken. Basically optimistic and complacent, he became despondent and could not find consolation. To his ninth child, born a few months later, he gave the name of his late brother. Here again it was the saddiq who put an end to Avraham's prolonged distress. In one of his first apparitions, he took Avraham to a magnificent garden and picked one of the most beautiful roses that grew there, explaining that in the same way God selects the best people to reside with Him. Under his explicit demands, Avraham stopped his mourning and complaints. The significance of the saint as an indispensable resource at times of personal crisis was thus well established. Indeed, car accidents are among the major plights against which the saddiq's intervention is called for in present day Israel. Avraham's brother, without the protective shield of a patron saint, died in a minor accident in which the car was not damaged nor any of the other passengers injured. (The absurd circumstances of his bereavement evidently exacerbated Avraham's depression.) By contrast, several of Avraham's relatives would be involved in car accidents, depicted by them as hazardous, nearly fatal events, after the revelation. None of the were seriously hurt, and this fact was attributed, of course, to the miraculous protection of Rabbi David ou-Moshe. The juxtaposition of their accounts to the brother's story dramatizes the wide gap between prerevelation vulnerability and postrevelation immunity and sense of security.

The death of his brother undoubtedly created in Avraham a state of emotional turmoil that constituted a fertile matrix for the appearance of the saddiq. The event that immediately precipitated his first visitation, however, was Avraham's firm intention to move to a bigger, more comfortable place in another neighborhood. The change was prevented at the last moment by the saint's announcements that he desired the old apartment as his permanent abode. As a result Avraham and his family were tied to their original place of residence by inextricable bonds. Interestingly, a firm decision to move to a less peripheral town or neighborhoos that was eventually annulled by the saddiq has underlain the erection of other sacred sites, including Yaish's. This recurrent precipitating factor might well reflect an ambivalence that initiators, along with many residents of development towns, have felt towards their communities. On the one hand, they are areas marked by lack of employment and educational opportunities, and by a rather poor public image. Many of these people find themselves linked to their localities through networks of friends and family. In many instances the conflict is solved by the saddiq, who sanctifies the old place of residence and compels inhabitants to stay there. This point will be elaborated later.

In contrast with the common pattern of dedicating a place for a saint following an ongoing liaison with him, Avraham claimed not to have known Rabbi David ou-Moshe before the revelation. This ignorance has contributed to his credibility and reinforced his claim for authenticity. Later on, however, he was able to retrieve a long-forgotten childhood memory that might have contributed to his particular choice. As children, Avraham and one of his brothers helped an old woman to collect money in the market of Imi-n-tanout for the hillulah of Rabbi David ou-Moshe. Incidentially, the brother who accompanied Avraham was the one whose death precipitated the apparition of Rabbi David ou-Moshe in Israel. The fact that Avraham altogether forgot that episode might have found expression in the saddiq's allegations during their first oneiric meeting: "Why have those who left Morocco forsaken me and deserted me? Where are all the thousands—my followers and believers?" A few months after the first revelation, Avraham's tenth child was born. As might be expected, he was given one of the saddiq's names: Moshe. Moshe was the last child of Avraham and Masouda. The apparition of the saint marked the termination of the fertile phase of family expansion, followed by a shift towards more spiritual concerns, more appropriate for midlife. It is significant that the room dedicated to the saint had previously housed the couple's bed.

When Yaish had his first revelatory dream, Rabbi David ou-Moshe's House was functioning for seven years with ever growing success. Clearly Avraham's successful initiative gave Yaish an inspiration as well as a model for action. Like many other Moroccan-born Israelis he was strongly moved by the "announcements to the public," circulated all over the country, in which Avraham's recent oneiric encounters with Rabbi David ou-Moshe were portrayed in detail. A few years later when Yaish promulgated his own dreams, he borrowed Avraham's introductory passage almost word for word. Beyond this general influence, however, Yaish became personally involved with the new center in Safed in a matter of utmost importance. After twelve years of marriage during which three girls were born, Yaish desperately desired a male descendant. In his distress, he frequented the tombs of many sainted figures, but it was only after a visit to the House of Rabbi David ou-Moshe that his wish was granted. As a token of gratitude, he called his newborn son, David, after the saddiq. This was Yaish's fourth and last child. As in the case of Avraham, his role as procreator was terminated with the apparition of the saint. This change was clearly congruent with the enlargement and 'spiritualization' of his preoccupations. Instead of dedicating himself to mundane concerns of family expansion and economic improvement, Yaish, inspired by the holy place he had longed for, invests all his energy in developing it and in accommodating the constant flow of visitors and supplicants.

The theme of leaving one's old place of residence that frequently preceded the revelatory episodes in other cases, was particularly pronounced in Yaish's initiative. Following a bitter family conflict, Yaish reluctantly came to the conclusion that he should leave Beit She'an. He decided to move to a town near Tel Aviv, where his wife had relatives. Two weeks before the intended departure, he dreamed for the first time that there was a holy place in his backyard. Obeying the orders of an old man, later identified as Elijah the Prophet, he saw and uncovered in his dream the entrance to a beautiful garden in which old rabbis were walking. It was only two days before moving that the identity of the garden was revealed to him in another dream. Following this stunning discovery, Yaish cancelled his plan to leave and took the first measures towards building the site.

As previously noted, the association between the Garden of Eden and Beit She'an was not born in Yaish's mind: a Talmudic tradition links these two loci (Babylonian Talmud, Eiruvim, 19a). However, the fact that it was he who revived and "materialized" that tradition attests to his strong personal ambition and sense of calling. Retrospectively, this calling in rudimentary form was present long before. Yaish recalled how in his youth he used to tease his brothers with the idea that in the World to Come he would be the gatekeeper of Paradise. When he assumed this role, his brothers would be entirely at his mercy to gain entrance. In employing a local tradition or "public myth" to discover the entrance to Paradise in his backyard, Yaish also managed to actualize a childhood fantasy or "private myth."

THE NEW SITES AND THE MOROCCAN EXPERIENCE IN ISRAEL

At first glance, the emergence of the new centers of saint veneration in Israel represents a mere return to the past. The traditional idiom of the saddiq, tenaciously maintained mainly by Moroccan Jews, has been employed to articulate sentiments and experiences constituted in the new country. This strong insistence on traditional symbols might give rise to the assumption that the phenomenon under study constitutes a segregatory mechanism obstructing smooth assimilation of Moroccan Jews in Israeli society. Later I attempt to show that this point of view is too simplistic to exhaust the multiple meanings of saint veneration. On a manifest level, however, one cannot deny that the new hillulot strengthen rather than dissipate ethnic boundaries. Most of the pilgrims and celebrants are from North Africa, mainly of Moroccan origin. The dominant language in these centers is Moroccan Arabic, and the Maghrebi past gains salience as reflected in the dress, food, and music typical of the hillulot. Ethnographically speaking, the patterns of the new pilgrimages follow the traditional Moroccan *ziara*, or Moslem pilgrimage to a holy man's grave.

On the other hand, one cannot ignore the fact that the emergence of the new centers was correlated with a relative improvement in the socioeconomic status of many Moroccan Jews in Israel, as well as with the hitherto unprecedented rise of some to power positions in the sociopolitical structure. Paradoxically, it seems that a sense of roots in and belonging to the new country should have been acquired before the renewed manifestations of saint veneration could appear. As mentioned before, the 1950s and 1960s, in which the newcomers were less "Israelized" than today, were mute years regarding the public collective expressions of hagiolatry. Their reemergence reflects a process through which traditional symbols are brought to the fore and reaffirmed as an integral part of the dynamics of homecoming. Pilgrimage centers in Israel, old as well as new, constitute arenas for mass gatherings that strengthen the collective consciousness of the Moroccan Jewish group—the largest Jewish group in Israel today— and contribute to the reconsolidation of their distinctive ethnic identity. In the cases described, this process has been reinforced by the vigorous efforts of the initiators to draw to their sites as many adherents as possible. This centripetal emphasis was manifested in numerous visitational dreams in which the saints unequivocally proscribed private hillulot as well as other saint-related activities outside the new site.

Until now, the renewed encounter with the saints was depicted as a multifaceted phenomenon that reflects a growing confidence in integration into the contemporary Israeli scene, as well as a sense of ethnic distinctiveness and an emphasis on cultural boundaries. These conclusions, however, should not be overgeneralized. The new sacred sites do not draw *all* Moroccan Jews in Israel. Among devotees of the saint, women, old people, and inhabitants of development towns and moshavim—the more traditional segments of the Moroccan community in Israel—are clearly the majority. Still, we deal here with mass celebrations that encompass many thousands of people, not with an esoteric and marginal phenomenon characteristic of a small minority.

An important Israeli aspect of the phenomenon under study concerns the significance of the saddiq for the town in which his abode has been erected. The appearance of a venerated saint in a development town, heretofore deemed peripheral and unattractive, might indicate a significant change in the image of the place, in the eyes of many residents. The saddiq imbues the town with an aura of sanctity and thus makes it more of a center. The town is cathected by the divine grace of the holy man and gains in positive valence. The appearance of the saints and the growing popularity of their sites cannot be separated, therefore, from the vicissitudes shared by many Moroccan Jews in their new country. Together with Avraham and Yaish, many inhabitants of Safed, Beit She'an, and other development towns have walked the long and weary road from the difficult ma'abarah years of the 1950s to the more prosperous 1970s and 1980s. Along this arduous trajectory, genuine feelings of homecoming and an authentic sense of belonging have been slowly and painfully acquired by many Moroccan Jews, though not by all! Thus, the appearance of the saints symbolizes and facilitates the process by which residents of development towns, once passive victims of an arbitrary policy of placement on the part of Israeli authorities, become rooted in the communities and develop loyalties. From this perspective, it is not surprising that people like Avraham and Yaish were among the prime movers behind this process. As mentioned before, neither of them has ever left the town he settled in after aliyah. Integration in their new locales was facilitated by the fact that their families remained together and could provide unconditional support in times of crisis. In both cases, the profound sense of integration in the place of residence has been reinforced by the stability and intergenerational continuity character-istic of these families within their respective communities. Four generations of both families reside today in Safed and Beit She'an. The precipitating factor underlying the revelation in both cases was the decision to move elsewhere, which seems particularly significant in this context. In describing their profound attachment to their sites located, it should be recalled, within their houses, Avraham and Yaish utilize phrases such as "(we are) inseparably tied to this land," "life prisoners of the saddiq." Both of them contend that the tradition they renewed will be perpetuated through their descendents.

The attachment to the house is fortified, of course, by the sense of well-being and personal security that the sacred site radiates. Both founders claim that the presence of the saddiq is strongly felt through abundant manifestations of his grace at times of need. Illnesses cured, economic difficulties solved, and in general, every problem settled are immediately ascribed to the saint's intercession. The centripetal orien-tation of the family towards the saddiq has been lucidly demonstrated in times of crisis, as in the following episode. In 1981, rumors of an imminent earthquake erupted in Safed. Many residents panicked and some of them temporarily left the town, which has suffered destruc-tive quakes in the past. By contrast, Avraham's children, including the two who lived outside Safed at the time, gathered in the tiny apart-ment, passing the night when the earthquake was supposed to occur in the saddiq's room. They were convinced that under the protection of Rabbi David ou-Moshe they were invulnerable. The same opinion was reiterated in accounts of many inhabitants of Safed and Beit She'an, who consider the presence of the saddiq as an important asset of their town. Some people, particularly those living near the sacred sites, frequent them whenever they face a problem, thus transforming the place into a genuine community center.

The Israeli aspects of the new sites have been most pronounced in times of war and military conflict. As Ben Ami (1977) showed, the miracles of the saint multiplied during the recent wars. It is interest-ing to note that the first *hillula* for Rabbi David ou-Moshe in his new site coincided with the cease-fire that terminated the Yom Kippur War of 1973. The most massive wave of miracles attributed to the saint was associated with the dire consequences of that war (locating soldiers missing in action; healing severely wounded soldiers). It was only natural, therefore, that in the "announcement to the public" the protection of soldiers took priority over all other concerns for which the saint's intercession was required. When a group of high school children from Safed were attacked and taken hostage by a Palestinian Liberation Organization (PLO) unit, some of the survivors testified that they had been saved by Rabbi David ou-Moshe in person: these pupils were living in the neighborhood of the site and witnessed its development. This correspondence between military crises and protective hagiolatry was lucidly demonstrated in the case of the tomb of Honi Hame'agel near the development town of Hatsor. Although the location of Honi's tomb near Hatsor is based on an old tradition, the place became an important pilgrimage center only following the wars of 1967 and 1973. In both cases Hatsor, an easy target for the attacking Syrians, was not damaged at all. The grateful inhabitants selected the Israeli Day of Independence as the most appropriate time for the *hillula* of Honi. It is interesting to note that this "patriotic" aspect of saint veneration, although consonant with the contemporary Israel scene, represents, in fact, a continuity with Morocco where the most common theme of saint intervention was a miraculous redemption from hostile and menacing Arabs.

To conclude, by discovering and establishing sacred sites associated with the saints, the more traditional segments in the Jewish Moroccan community express their integration into Israeli society. The circle is closed: the wounds inflicted by the painful separation from the saint are being healed at least partially, as these cultural identities that constitute the vital symbols of the group have been implanted in the new environment. This process, although far from involving all Moroccan Jews in Israel, recurs too regularly to be considered sporadic and episodic. It might be predicted that new sacred sites will continue to emerge in various concentrations of Moroccan Jews in Israel, serving the double function of consolidating the distinctive ethnic identity of the inhabitants and strengthening their local loyalties. This pattern already displays a strong sense of territoriality. Even though some of the new pilgrimages have transcended local boundaries, most of the population directly concerned with the sacred sites is essentially local. In Safed, Beit She'an, and other towns, the traditional model of a community centered around its "own" saddiq is being recreated. This tendency might be deemed functional insofar as it reinforces links to one's home town. The message it carries is as follows:

"Rabbi David ou-Moshe's assistance should be sought for not in the Moroccan Atlas but rather in Safed"; or "Beit She'an is not a desolate place to be abanonded, as it contains a center of utmost holiness." But this pattern is largely traditional, based on beliefs and practices from the past. The moral conveyed is clear: even the more traditional groups in the Jewish Moroccan community resourcefully find their own ways to overcome the "predicaments of homecoming." For those believing in a melting pot integration, this process might seem disappointing; it says, in effect, that only by preserving their Moroccan heritage as an important constituent of their identity can Moroccan immigrants and their descendants feel at home in Israel.

REFERENCES

Ben Ami, Il 1977. Studying war folklore—The saint motif. *Sefer Dov Sadan.* Jerusalem: Hakibbutz Hameuchad Publishing House (Hebrew).

Ben Ami, I. 1981., The folk-veneration of saints among Moroccan Jews. In *Studies in Judaism and Islam*, ed. S. Morag, I. Ben Ami, and N. A. Stillman. Jerusalem: Magnes Press.

Ben Ami, I. 1984. Saint Veneration among the Jews in Morocco. *Folklore Research Center Studies*, vol. 8, Jerusalem: Magnes Press (Hebrew).

Bilu, Y., and H. Abramovitch. 1985. In search of the *saddiq:* Visitational dreams among Moroccan Jews in Israel. *Psychiatry* 48:83-92.

Brown, P. 1976. *People of sale: Tradition and change in a Moroccan city, 1830–1890.* Manchester: University of Manchester Press.

Crapanzano, V. 1977. Introduction to *Case studies in spirit possession*, ed. V. Crapanzano and V. Garrison. New York: Wiley.

Deshen, S., and M. Shokeid. 1974. *The predicament of homecoming.* Ithaca, N.Y.: Cornell University Press.

Eickelman, D. F. 1976. *Moroccan Islam.* Austin: University of Texas Press.

Geertz, C. 1968. *Islam observed.* New Haven: Yale University Press.

Gellner, E. 1969. *Saints of the Atlas.* Chicago: University of Chicago Press.

Rabinow, P. 1975. *Symbolic domination.* Chicago: University of Chicago Press.

Salnow, M. J. 1981. Communities reconsidered: The sociology of Andean pilgrimage. *Man* 16:163-82.

Stillman, N. A. 1982. Saddiq and Marabout in Morocco. In *The Sephardi and Oriental Jewish heritage studies,* ed. I. Ben Ami. Jerusalem: Magnes Press.

Turner, V. 1973. The center out there: Pilgrim's goal. *History of Religion* 12:191-230.

Westermarck, E. 1926. *Ritual and belief in Morocco.* London: Macmillan & Co.

3

The Jerusalem Funeral as a Microcosm of the 'Mismeeting' Between Religious and Secular Israelis

HENRY ABRAMOVITCH

FUNERAL: TEXT AND PERFORMANCE

In this chapter, I consider the Jewish funeral in Jerusalem from two distinct aspects. First, I present an anthropological/ethnographic description of the unique aspects of Jerusalem mortuary against the background of more general Jewish custom. In addition, symbolic aspects of the ritual are discussed in an attempt to reveal social and psychological functions of funeral ritual as part of the mourning process.

In the second part, I discuss the Jerusalem funeral as it is performed in practice. Specifically I focus on the situation in which secular mourners (Israeli Jews from a nonreligious background) participate in burial ceremony as part of the religious monopoly of rites of passage, such as weddings and funerals. As a result, nonreligious, nonobservant, secular Israeli Jews, are forced to participate in an Orthodox religious ceremony. Such an Orthodox ceremony reflects basic values dissonant with those secular Jews. The funeral, instead of reinforcing basic shared values and group cohesiveness (Durkheim 1969; Huntington and Metcalf 1979), might promote dissension and disharmony. Indeed, the confrontation of values in the Jerusalem funeral service is a microcosm of the 'mismeeting' between the secular and Orthodox Jewish communities in Israel as a whole.

In the first section, the funeral is considered, in its ideal form, as a text for a central social-religious drama. In the later section, specific performances of the social drama are analysed against the backdrop of the secular-religious conflict. Matrial for both sections was collected as part of a participant-observer study of the major Jerusalem burial society, which handles over half of all funerals in the Israeli capital and by far the majority of funerals for secular Jews.[1] By presenting both sides of the religious-secular divide as faithfully as possible, I hope to clarify the position of each and show the basic points of their mismeeting.

THE RELIGIOUS-SECULAR CONTINUUM

The terms religious (*dati*) and secular (*hiloni*) require some clarification. In practice, these polarized social categories reflect part of the contemporary folk classification of the nature of Israeli society. As in many other cases of conflict, be they religious, political, interethnic, or economic, there is a pervasive tendency to dichotomize social categories into in-group/out group, with us/against us polarities. Such a split serves to reinforce rigid group boundaries and exclusive identity, feeding the cause of extremists on each side. The social reality is much more complex, resembling a continuum more than a dichotomy. There are ultra-Orthodox individuals who hardly come in contact at all with nonreligious individuals and institutions. Likewise, there are atheist Israelis who have no contact with religiously minded Jews of any group, celebrate no Jewish holidays, know little or nothing of Judaism and even overtly refuse the religious burial ceremony. Both extremes, however, in fact constitute tiny minorities. Most Israelis lie, then, on a continuum of more religiously minded or more secularly minded. Many members of the *Hevra Kadisha* (burial society) studied here do reserve army service, albeit often in the burial unit. At least one has an advanced secular degree, though most studied primarily in religious educational settings. Most co-called secular Jews celebrate at least some religious holidays in addition to the holidays of the Israeli civil religion. Many secular Jews have or had religious parents or grandparents who directly or indirectly affect their perceptions. A common occasion of mismeeting is the situation in which an observant parent is buried with full ritual, to the dismay of the nonreligious children. Many secular Jews sit *shiva*, observe the seven-day mourning period as well as the 30-day commemoration (*shloshim*). Most observant Jews, the so-called knitted skullcap (*kipa sruga*) Jews, participate fully in mainstream secular Israeli society, with its mix of civil religion and Judaism. These individuals, while clearly in the religious camp, often have attitudes, opinions, and even behaviors similar to their nonreligious fellow citizens.

There are always individuals who defy the simple continuum, for example, an ordained rabbi who works for the secular Citizen's Rights Party; or secular Israelis keeping no rituals who following a death begin religious observance or, in extreme cases, become 'born again' Jews (*hozerim betshuva*). Thus the dichotomy religious/secular, while reflecting a basic cleavage of Israeli society, hides at least as much as it reveals.

In terms of funeral behavior, individuals to the religious side of the continuum are more likely to understand and share the worldview of the burial society. As mourners, they are more likely to 'know their parts' and to participate in the religious drama as it unfolds, without prompting. Individuals toward the nonreligious side are much less likely to comprehend or accept the Orthodox worldview. They are more likely to be confused by the sequence of events and react angrily to imposition of specific customs that offend their sense of a funeral aesthetic. Secular Jews are therefore less likely to agree with the ritual script the burial society proposes. The struggle in extreme cases is often acute because funerals are occasions in which the basic group values of a community need to be reinforced. The polarized extremes have few if any values in common, and the funeral ceremony becomes the battleground over which a set of values will be reinforced, elaborated, and even celebrated. Death is a time when people need to feel they have an answer to the meaning of life, to feel there is a reason to continue living. The tragic mismeeting occurs when the values and answers of the burial society are irrelevant or antagonistic to their secular clients.

THE TASK OF FUNERALS

Funerals, like other rites of passage, perform a number of simultaneous tasks in the social and psychological life of a community. In this section, I discuss the interrelationships between three of these tasks. For convenience, I shall refer to these three tasks as initiating mourning, providing social support, and ushering the soul of the dead into the afterlife. Each task refers primarily to one of the three main actors in the funeral drama, respectively, the chief mourners, the rest of the community, and the body and soul of the deceased.

Although ritual initiation of grief might begin long before the ritual disposal of the body, it is with the funeral that the initiating of grief is most pronounced. The survivors are confronted with the reality of

the death and their loss. Their social status is typically altered or reduced. They are obliged to display signs of their grief, such as changes
in diet, habits, clothing, ritual pollution, and so on. These changes help
the mourners in contouring the grief process and ultimately allow the
mourners to make a successful resolution of the loss.

Funerals are also occasions that bring people together. The community gathers in support of the mourners and helps them in their ritual tasks. Like other ceremonies, these rites serve to provide a renewed
sense of togetherness and social solidarity, at the very moment when
the continuity and permanence of the social group is threatened by the
loss of one of its members. Providing social support takes many forms.
It might include comforting the mourners, even feeding them or just
sitting together in silence. The comforting presence helps the mourners
in overcoming the sense of aloneness that death almost inevitably
brings and aids them in the completion of tasks of mourning.

The main formal task of funerals, however, is not with the living
but with the dead. It is concerned with the parallel obligation of appropriate disposal of the corpse while ushering the soul of the dead into
the culturally conceived afterlife. This transition is often fraught with
dangers and is in part dependent upon the behavior of the mourners.
The successful navigation of this transition, however, reenacts a symbolic victory over the reality of death through reference to a sacred
order that transcends everyday experience, what Geertz has called a
"religious perspective." Although the funeral usually only starts ushering the soul into another realm, it does provide a collective sense that,
even in death, there is a potential for continuity and even the regeneration of life.

These three tasks in the funeral process usually go hand in hand,
and indeed are interdependent. The mourners are supported by the
entire community, who as a whole take solace from the ushering of the
soul of the dead into the afterlife and the symbolic victory over death
this provides. The fortunes of the mourners are in some complex manner linked to the successful transition of their relative who, failing,
might return as a wandering ghost, or agent of misfortune. The dead
man's soul is often in turn dependent upon performances of specific
rituals by his relatives and, occasionally, the community to complete
this passage to the other world.

In describing the funeral process in these terms, I have emphasized their functional aspect. Circumstances might occur in which the
tasks might clash in a dialectical process, in which the demands of one
are temporarily set aside in favor of the needs of the other. In this
study, I want to describe a somewhat anomalous case, in which I will
argue that the demands of providing social support to the mourners

are set aside, indeed negated, at a crucial moment in ushering the soul in his passage to the afterlife. Specifically, I shall discuss an aspect of the Jewish funeral in the holy city of Jerusalem.

Prior to the start of a father's funeral, all lineal descendants, literally "all those who have issued from his loins," children and grandchildren, are forbidden to follow the funeral procession. In former times, when the body lay in state at home, these children were left behind and did not attend the funeral at all.

More recently, following the letter of the injunction not to follow their deceased father, children are sometimes permitted to walk in front of the procession, ahead of their father's body and arrive at the graveside in advance of the rest of the funeral party. In either case, this injunction, known as *herem Yehoshua bin Nun* (Hebrew, "the ban of Joshua son of Nun"), serves to set off a man's children and grandchildren not only from their father's body but also from the rest of the community at the very time when these lineal mourners are presumably most in need of psychological and social support.

THE JERUSALEM FUNERAL AND THE JEWISH MOURNING CYCLE

Before proceeding to analyse this custom of ritual exclusion, it is necessary to place it within the context of the Jerusalem funeral practice and the Jewish mourning cycle. In the course of this discussion, I shall restrict myself to Orthodox Jewish custom, which follows the *Shulhan Arukh* and other standard codes of Jewish law. My study of the specifics of Jerusalem burial practice (*minhag Yerushalayim*) is based on a participant-observer study of one of the larger Jerusalem burial societies (Hevra Kadisha). The contours of Orthodox Jewish mortuary ritual are shared by most Jewish communities, although in the details of burial and mourning, there is considerable heterogeneity. In Jerusalem, for example, in the British Mandate period in the 1930s, there were at least 32 different burial societies, and each *Hevra Kadisha* jealously guarded the specific traditions of its own religious practice.[2]

In the fifties their number was reduced, and today, in the eighties, there are about 12 active burial societies. Most of these are geared to an ethnically homogeneous immigrant group, for example, Persian Jews, North African Jews, or specific religious sects such as Hassidic Jews. The burial society in which observations were carried out is the sole nonsectarian organization and is used by Jerusalemites of diverse ethnic background, religious and secular Jews alike. In practice, they are responsible for over half the funerals performed in Jerusalem.

Most Jewish communities oblige descendants, especially children, to escort their father to the grave. Indeed, the Hebrew word for funeral, *hal'vaya*, derives from the root, *laveh*, 'to accompany'. All Jews are required by religious law (*Halaka*) to follow the funeral cortege, at least a number of symbolic steps, even if they are passing strangers. This restriction on children in Jerusalem burial custom stands out all the more in contrast.

Orthodox Jewish funerals are simple, standard, and rapid affairs. Virtually the same service is performed for all. No great expense is necessary. In Israel, standard burial plots and burial garments are covered by social security, though one can buy a specific plot if one so wishes, and the erection of a tombstone can be a considerable expense. In addition, certain Jews specify their will to be buried in Jerusalem, and transportation from overseas plus obligatory purchase of a plot and tombstone can run as high as ten thousand dollars. However, most people are buried free of charge, although this was not always so.

Ideally, a dead person should be buried as quickly as possible, preferably before nightfall of the same day. In many communities, it is, however, acceptable to postpone the funeral to the following day, or until the heirs and chief mourners arrive. In Jerusalem, the importance of immediate burial is greatly stressed on account of the sanctity of the holy city. As a result, individuals are often buried within hours of their demise, even at night. Because burial is not permitted on Saturday, the Jewish Sabbath, funerals on Saturday night, after the Sabbath is over, are common.

The Jewish mourning cycle divides up mourning into four distinct and time-limited phases. From the moment a person learns of the death of an immediate relative (father, mother, brother, sister, child, or spouse) until burial, he is considered an onen. An *onen*, 'one whose dead lies before him', is absolved of the fulfillment of all positive commandments. He is not required to pray or even answer greetings. His entire attention is absorbed by the obligation to make arrangements for the burial. After the funeral, the mourner becomes an *avel* (mourner) and begins the prescribed initial seven-day period of mourning, *shiva* (Hebrew, 'seven'). During the first seven days, a mourner is forbidden to work, to wash, to have sexual intercourse, to study, to offer greetings, to wear freshly washed clothes, to cut his hair or beard, or participate in any festivities. Usually he sits on the floor or on a low stool. He is not permitted to prepare his own food, nor should he leave his house. It is customary for members of the community to visit and sit with the mourners during the shiva. The shiva period is typically ended by a visit to the grave of the deceased.

Some of the prohibitions of the shiva continue until the 30 day *shloshim* (Hebrew 'thirty'), for example, wearing new clothes or cutting hair or beard. The shloshim is usually celebrated by a visit to the grave and a large meal, called feast of the thirtieth day (*seudat shloshim*). Except in the case of parents, formal mourning is completed on the 30th day. Mourning for parents continues for 12 months. The anniversary of the death is likewise observed by a visit to the grave, recitation of prayers, and often a meal. The anniversary is observed in a like manner every year.

These four phases, or statuses, *onen, shiva, shloshim,* and in the case of parents, the remaining 11 months of the year make up the four divisions of the Jewish mourning cycle. For each of these divisions, there is culturally appropriate social support that relatives and friends are expected to offer. In addition, each phase is said to mark stages in the transition of the soul of the deceased in the other world with the result that the fate of the soul and the cycle of mourning parallel one another. Indeed, the transition of the soul is in part dependant upon the actions of the mourners, who pray, study, and give charity in honor and aid of the deceased. The cycle is completed when the soul reaches its place in Paradise and may act as a cultural resource and intercessory on the behalf of his relatives, especially his children.

INITATING MOURNING

Rather than present a chronological sequence of Jewish Jerusalem funerary ritual, an account will be given in terms of three tasks of the funeral discussed previously. Unless noted, customs apply to Jewish funerals generally.

Upon learning of the death of an immediate relative, one is obliged to 'rend one's garmets'. Although this obligation should be performed at the moment of learning of the death, standing, with the phrase, 'Blessed is the True Judge', in Jerusalem, and elsewhere, it is formally incorporated into the funeral ritual. Thus just prior to the beginning of the formal ritual prayers, the leader of the Hevra Kadisha cuts a garment, such as a shirt or scarf, with a razor, which the mourner further tears. The mourner is then instructed in the appropriate phrase. The tear is the first behavioral indication of loss and seems to symbolize the tearing of the psychosocial fabric of society. The tear is never meant to be fully repaired, evoking the sense that once an intimate relative dies, something in the inner world of the person is irrevocably torn, never fully mended.

It is also customary in Jerusalem to spill all standing water. The reasons for this are complicated, even contradictory: to avoid effects of ritual pollution, or lest blood somehow enter the water supply, or to avert the Angel of Death. In any case, spilled water in a Jerusalem courtyard was a sign that a death had occurred. With the advent of indoor plumbing, this custom is only infrequently observed.

Concerning the status of onen, Lamm (1969) has written: "Practically, then, the *onen* must make immediate and significant decisions based on the reality of death. Psychologically, however, he has not yet assimilated it or accepted it" (p. 21). This initial phase corresponds to the stage of shock and disbelief, with a subtle psychological identification between the onen and his dead relative in that both are cut off from the demands and requirements of social and religious life. It is significant that at the funeral, which ends the status of onen, the mourner's main task is to say the Kaddish prayer and reaffirm his belief in God.

It is a usual concern of family members to provide for a vigil over the corpse because a dead body ought not to be left alone. In many cases in which the funeral is delayed overnight, the body is refrigerated, and in many cases no vigil is conducted.

At the end of the ritual purification in Jerusalem, it is customary for the members of the burial society to invite the eldest son to place earth over the eyes of his parent. My informants told me that this is done because the eye is the organ of desire and envy, and needs, as it were, to be specially treated in order for it to accept its demise. The symbolism of 'earth to earth, dust to dust' was also cited in this connection. For the son who places the earth over the eyes, this last direct encounter with the body dramatically brings home the reality of death. Although most communities outside Israel use some sort of coffin, traditional Jewish practice, still followed in Israel, rejects absolutely the use of closed coffins, and the deceased is dressed in seven burial garments enclosed by a winding sheet. These shrouds are often prepared by the deceased while still living, and in such cases, it is a family member who makes them available to the burial society. Moreover, the body wrapped in plain white sheet, lying on a simple bier, is itself another poignant reminder of the fragility of human life.

In Jerusalem, the funeral begins with the leader breaking a bit of porcelain over the doorway saying the Hebrew phase from Psalm 124:7: 'The snare is broken and we have escaped'. My informants were not clear about the meaning of the phrase, and whether it referred to the soul of the deceased (in which case it concerns the ushering of the soul into the afterlife), or whether it concerned the break between the world of the living and the realm of the dead. In any case, like the rending of garments, the metaphor of something broken is clear.

In the funeral service, the chief mourner's main task is to recite the Kaddish. Although the Kaddish is often referred to as the prayer for the dead, it means literally 'sanctification' and its use is not limited to mortuary ritual, but is a regular element in daily prayer. It contains no personal reference to the dead person. Rather, it is a public declaration of faith and an affirmation of divine sovereignty now and in the time to come. The text of the prayer, however, is mostly in Aramaic, a language incomprehensible to Israeli Hebrew speakers, and so it has some of the mystic flavor of an incantation.

From a dramatic point of view, the recitation of the Kaddish by the eldest son or other male relative is the high point in the funeral service.[3] It is at this moment that great emotion is displayed both by the man reciting and by the assembled crowd. Often, the chief mourner has difficulty completing the prayer when he is overwhelmed by feeling. It is at this point that he must show publicly that he accepts the divine decree.

The structure of the prayer is a sort of ritual dialogue between the individual mourner, who recites the main text, and the assembled quorum, who respond 'Amen' or 'May His Name be Blessed' in the appropriate places. The Kaddish highlights the interdependence of mourners, the community, and the dead. In Jerusalem, the Kaddish is recited thrice, once before the funeral, again when the body is placed in the funeral van, and again in a more elaborated version at the graveside after burial.

SOCIAL SUPPORT

Social support for the family of the deceased is provided by the burial society (Hevra Kadisha) and by the community of relatives, friends, neighbours. The Hevra Kadisha, literally a sacred society or holy fellowship, takes upon itself the work of preparing the dead for burial. Originally, it was a voluntary organization of high status and prestige in the community, and only members of highest standing were invited to join in this highest form of loving kindness (*gemilut hesed shel emet*). With the bureaucratization of mortuary care, the increase in the number of daily funerals, the status of the individuals who work full-time in the Hevra Kadisha has seriously declined, especially in the eyes of secular Israelis. This clash of values in the Jerusalem funeral between secular Israelis and religious Israelis is exacerbated because burial is a monopoly of the Ministry of Religion, which does not allow, except in kibbutzim, any secular funerals. Moreover, the black garb of most of the workers of the burial society and the routinization of this sacred activity has contributed to their stigmatized work identity.

From a religious point of view, however, the Hevra Kadisha performs a vital function. When a death occurs in a town, by Orthodox law, all the inhabitants are forbidden to perform any work. If, however, there is an organized burial society to see to the needs of the deceased, then work and normal social life for those not immediately involved can continue. In addition, some authorities argue that once the Hevra Kadisha assumes responsibility for the care of the dead, then the mourners are released from the constraints of the *aninut*, i.e. the status of onen. The Hevra Kadisha brings the body from home or hospital, undertakes the ritual purification of the body, dresses the body in shrouds that they provide, except as stated above, and makes all the formal funeral arrangements. At the funeral, the leader performs *kri'a*, the rending of garments, breaks the shards, recites various prayers, assists the chief mourner in reciting Kaddish if necessary, while the rest of the members of the society make up a prayer quorum, if there are less than ten adult men. They also help carry the body and accompany it to the cemetery while reciting Psalms. At the grave, one of the members lays the body in the ground, assists in covering it with earth, while the leader performs further prayers. As in many communities, in Jerusalem the mourners are given a pamphlet that explains most of the mourning customs and memorial prayers. In addition, a rabbi associated with the burial society visits the family during the shiva period.

As we shall see below, most of the activities of the burial society are for the purpose of honoring the dead (*kvod hamet*), but many of their actions provide practical help for the mourners, who would otherside be obliged to carry out many of these duties themselves. Despite their loss in status and their stigma, the Hevra Kadisha act as ritual experts guiding the mourners through the funeral drama, coaching them in their roles, and reminding them of the religious commandments. It is the leader of the Hevra Kadisha who informs the children of the ban of Joshua son of Nun.

Members of the community provide a display of support at each step of the funeral. Their very presence reassures the mourners that they are not entirely alone. In cases where there are no mourners, the Hevra Kadisha performs the funeral.

During the formal prayers, community members surround the mourners, and say the responses in Kaddish. Often they will carry the deceased, first to the funeral van, and later from the van to the grave. At the grave, they follow the example of the leader of the Hevra Kadisha shoveling earth into the grave, taking care not to pass the spade directly from hand to hand. Later, they will also place a stone over the covered grave, a custom common to Jerusalem and a number of other communities.

The nonmourners assume their ritual roles as comforters in the recessional from the grave. At the end of the graveside service, they form two lines, through which the mourners pass. As the mourners walk by, those present recite the formal words of comfort: "May the Lord comfort you among the other mourners of Zion and Jerusalem." Concerning this custom, Lamm has written: "The purpose of the recessional is to redirect our sympathies and concerns from the deceased to the mourners. It marks the transition from *aninut* to *avelut*, the new state of mourning which now commences. The theme changes from honoring of the dead to comforting the survivors." (p 66-7). Comforting the survivors is continued through visits to the shiva, bringing food, which serves to nuture the mourners, and participating in a special prayer quorum at the house of mourning.

USHERING THE SOUL OF THE DEAD TO THE AFTERLIFE

It was Hertz (1960) who first pointed out the parallels "between the state of the corpse, the fate of the soul and the ritual condition of the mourners." As we have observed, everything up to the funeral is done to honor the dead, and thereafter, in support of the mourners. The fate of the soul, however, is bound up with the actions of the mourners but also with the decomposition of the body. Only at the end of the mourning cycle, when the body has decomposed to the bone, may the soul achieve its ultimate destination and be bound up in the 'bundle of life' (*tsor hahayim*). Death merely initiates the ultimate process of separation of body and soul to their respective fates. This attitude is aptly summed up by the motto, written in large Hebrew letters above the funeral chapel of the Hevra Kadisha in which I did my study, that read, "The body returns to the earth whence it came; while the soul returns to Him who gave it."

Jewish custom forbids touching a dying man unnecessarily lest this hasten the departure of the soul. Ideally a prayer quorum of ten adult males should be present to attend him, to hear his confession, and to help him with his final prayers. If he is reluctant to make his confession (*vidui*), he is reminded, "Many have confessed and not died; many have died and not confessed." In one Jerusalem hospital, it was the custom for one God-fearing man to say the confession publicly with all the patients answering "Amen." If a person cannot speak aloud, he is permitted to say it in his heart.

After death, candles are lit, windows opened up, and the body undressed. Covered by a top sheet, the body is later lowered to the floor so that the back is in contact with the floor. Thus begins the symbolic journey of the body toward the earth. Special care is taken so that the face is covered because one is forbidden to look into the eyes of the deceased. Usually mirrors and pictures are likewise covered.

The body should be watched at all times and Psalms recited during this vigil. Eating, drinking, blessings, or study are forbidden in the immediate presence of the corpse. These prohibitions are based on the notion that one must not 'mock the poor', as the dead are called in their impoverished ability to perform any religious commandments. It further seems to serve as a guard against the envy that the dead would thus feel towards the living.

The handling of the corpse is guided by three concepts of Jewish culture: the honor due to the dead (*kvod hamet*); the uncleanness of the dead, or ritual pollution of the corpse (*tum'at hamet*); and ritual purification of the dead (*taharat hamet*). The honor due to the dead, as discussed above, requires that the dead body be treated with appropriate respect. Common American mortuary practices, such as embalming, autopsy, wake, viewing the remains, and cremation are all forbidden because they are not in keeping with the notion of *kvod hamet*.

Rabbinic literature often compares the dead body with an invalid ritual object, such as a defective Torah scroll. Such a scroll is proscribed for ritual use, yet it must be handled with the care and respect of a valid one, in accordance with the holiness it once possessed. Likewise, a dead human body must be treated with respect. Like the dead body, any ritually defective material, bearing the Divine Name, must be buried or stored in a *geniza* (repository), and the Hevra Kadisha has set aside a plot of land in which such material is buried. Under certain circumstances, a Torah scroll will be given funeral honors.

Honor due to the dead requires that the corpse undergo ritual purification, and in Jerusalem, that it be buried according to the burial custom of the holy city. Alternative forms of disposal are unacceptable to Orthodox Jewish law. Even the ashes of one burned to death must be buried. Likewise, a corpse ought not to be left overnight because it is not keeping with the honor due to the dead, the sanctity of Jerusalem, or the danger that an unclean spirit might enter the dead body. At the close of the graveside service, the leader, in the name of the Hevra Kadisha and all those assembled, addresses the spirit of the dead person. He says that if any fault was unintentionally committed, it was performed "in his honor according to the custom of Jerusalem." He goes on to ask forgiveness from the dead person and absolves him of membership in any association he might have been a part. Stripped of his social roles, or any grudge toward the living, the soul is free to make his journey toward the world to come.

Jewish beliefs concerning purity and pollution are exceedingly complex and intricate. For the purposes of this article, it is important to note that human corpses are a major source and, in some senses, are considered the archetypal source (*avi avot hatumah*, literally 'the father of fathers of uncleanness'), that is, the primal category of pollution. Corpse pollution transmits uncleanness not only to anything that comes in direct contact with it but even through the shadow of a building in which the corpse lies. Moreover, any person or object polluted in these ways becomes a carrier of the ritual pollution, for example, a man might become ritually unclean if he touched a vessel that has lain in the shadow of a house in which someone has died. The earth is the only object that does not receive nor transmit corpse pollution, and once the corpse is buried it is no longer subject to the laws of uncleanness.

Prior to burial the corpse must undergo ritual purification (taharat hamet). The purification process is divided into two parts: the physical cleansing of the body and the actual ritual of purification. It is a fixed rule that men wash men and women, women, in keeping with the 'honor due to the dead'. My informants did mention one unusual case, in which no woman was available in the Hevra Kadisha to perform the cleansing and purification. In this extreme case, a man was blindfolded and participated in the ritual cleansing. It is important that the members of the Hevra Kadisha themselves undergo daily ritual immersion to remove the source of corpse uncleanness and restore themselves to a state of purity and hence be in a ritually pure state during the act of purification of the dead body.

Before beginning the purification procedure, the senior member of the company leads a prayer for mercy and forgiveness on behalf of the deceased. The physical cleansing of the body commences following right/left, sacred/profane dichotomies first noted by Hertz (1960). The head, neck, and right side of the body are washed to the accompaniment of special prayers for each body part. The left side is treated without any benediction. The body is then turned over and once again the right side is washed, with prayer, the left silently. Finally, the body is placed on its left side and the anal cavity is cleansed by enemas until the water comes out clean without any smell. The anus is then sealed with a wad of cloth. This 'internal purification' (*tahara pnimit*) is peculiar to the burial custom of Jerusalem, but it is not performed in the case of infectious diseases, or upon doctor's orders, or in the presence of blood, such as after an operation. If at any time the presence of blood is detected, the internal purification procedure is stopped. Indeed, any individual 'whose blood is upon him' such as in violent death receives no purification, external or internal, Such individuals are often buried in their bloodied garments because blood is equated with life (compare Genesis 9:5).

In many communities, care is taken to trim fingernalis. In Jerusalem, however, all the dirt under fingernails and tonenails is removed, so that no direct barrier can be said to come between the body and the waters of purification.

After the physical cleansing is complete, the body is immersed in a ritual bath (*mikveh*), if available. If no mikveh is available, or when it is used only for the highest status individuals, the corpse is raised to an upright position and about 20 liters (the so-called 9 kavim) are poured over it. The corpse is then declared pure by the threefold repetition of the Hebrew word *tahor* (pure). At this point, the corpse is in an inner state of purity, while continuing to radiate corpse pollution.

The shrouds are made of plain white material, flax or cotton, and should be hand sewn. In many communities, a man's *kittle*, a long white garment used for his wedding, for the Day of Atonement, and for Passover festivities, is used. There are seven standard burial garments. In the order they are put on, they are: a square head covering, a loin-cloth, pants without openings for the feet, a tunic (or kittle), a long thin triangular eye cover, a hood, and the winding sheet. During the dressing, the eldest son is invited in to place earth over the eyes. Three external knots are tied to keep the arms and legs together during transit to the grave and are only untied when the body is placed in the grave, so that the person leaves the world as he entered, 'without ties'.

A large prayer shawl is placed over the body in the case of males, while a *parochet* or Torah curtain is used for females, once again highlighting the equivalence of Torah and human body. The body is then placed on a bier and carried across the hall from the purification chamber to a small chapel where candles are lit and the family may gather for a prayer vigil and a last intimate farewell.

The ban is announced to the children, just prior to the funeral proper. It is known as the "ban of Joshua son of Nun" (*kherem Yehoshua bin nun*), but none of my informants could give an explanation for the term or even whether this Joshua is the same man described in the Bible. It is possible that the name was given to give the relatively recent practice an aura of antiquity. Scholars (Tuchinski 1948; Scholem 1965) assert that the ban is probably no more than 250 years old. All those who have issued from his loins are informed that according to the 'custon of Jerusalem' (*minhag Yerushalayim*), they are prohibited from following their father to the grave. The ban applies only to children of males (to fathers, not to mothers) but does apply to both sons and daughters, grandsons and grandaughters. Formerly, when the body was taken from the home of the deceased, the children would recite the traditional prayers at the doorstep of the house. They would remain behind, while the funeral procession continued by stages to the cemetery.

Although, the language of the injunction forbids actually following, it is permissible to walk in front of the father and arrive at the grave ahead of the rest of the funeral party. Many observant Jerusalemites elect to follow this practice, fulfilling the letter, if not the spirit of the injunction. In contrast, secular Jews, unfamiliar with this practice, often react with anger and confusion. Many refuse to comply. I have heard reports in which the children were forcibly prevented from following in the procession, but I have never witnessed such an altercation. On the contrary, the members of the burial society where I did the bulk of my observations stated that it is not their job to enforce the ban, which in any case, was for the honor of the deceased father. As one man put it succinctly, "We are not policemen."

It must be emphasized that this ban on children is not only peculiar to Jerusalem, within Judaism, but apparently anomalous within the anthropological literature on mortuary ritual (Rosenblatt et. al. 1976; Aries 1977; Huntington and Metcalf 1979; Humphreys and King 1981; Bloch and Parry 1982; Palgi and Abramovitch 1984).

Moreover, the custom seems to violate one of the cardinal functions of such rites of passage. Durkheim taught that one of the major functions of funerals is to bring together the survivors in an increased sense of social solidarity. "The foundation of mourning," he wrote "is the impression of a loss which the group feels when it loses one of its members. But this very impression results in a bringing them into closer relations with one another in associating all in the same emotional state and therefore in disengaging the sensation of comfort which compensates for the original loss." He concludes, "Since they weep together they hold to one another and teh group is not weakened in spite of the blow which has fallen upon it." (Durkheim 1969, 401).

The ban of Joshua son of Nun sets off the children physically not only from their fathers but also from all other nonlineal relatives and the rest of the community, just at the very time when they are most in need of a reassuring sense of solidarity and emotional support.

THE FLAW IN MALE SEXUALITY

In religious (halakic) terms, burial marks the ritual transition from the deeply liminal status of "those whose dead lie before them" (onen), who are absolved of all positive religious commandments, to the social status of *avel* or mourner, who sitting low on the ground have a restricted but clearly defined social standing. For the children who do not follow their dead father, the passage from *onen* to *avel* is blurred. They do not actually witness the burial itself and therefore do not know precisely when the change of mourning status is effected.

How are we then to understand this ritual separation? One hint comes from the liturgy of the funeral itself. It begins with an extract from the *Ethics of the Fathers* (3:1):

> Akavia Ben Mehalael used to say:
> Look upon three things and you shall not enter into sin: Whence have you come?
> Where you are destined to go?
> and before Whom you must stand in final judgment?

The answer to the initial ontological question, "Whence have you come?" is given in an undertone, *sotto voce* so that none of the assembled can actually hear what is being said. The whispered answer is "from a vile drop," that is, one's father's semen; and the text is not spoken aloud out of respect for the children of the dead man.

The great student of Jewish mysticism, Gershom Scholem has discussed the background to this peculiar doctrine:

> To the Kabbalists, the union between man and woman, within its holy limits, was a venerable mystery, as one may judge from the fact that the most classical and widespread widely circulated Kabbalistic definition of mystical meditation is to be found in a treatise about sexual union in marriage. Abuse of man's generative powers was held to be a destructive act, through which not the holy, but the 'other side', obtains progeny. An extreme cult of purity led to the view that every act of impurity whether conscious or inconscious, engenders demons. (Scholem 1965, 155).

Spilling one's seed even in a nocturnal emission constituted a terrible flaw in the nature of masculine sexuality. Such wasteful ejaculation was considered worse than murder, creating irreparable damage to the 'upper spheres', and, moreover an act not amenable to repentance (Zohar 62a 219b; Green 1981, 56; Benayahu 1983).

The flaw in masculine sexuality derives from the fact that a man's first sexual experience is with a wet dream or nocturnal ejaculation. This dream experience was conceptualized by the Kabbalists as a sexual encounter with female demons, usually Lilith, Adam's first wife. Cohabitation with such demonic female spirits engenders the 'semen demons' who are relegated to the spirit world like their 'mothers' seek to claim paternity from their erring father. It is noteworthy that Lilith was allegedly rejected by Adam because she wished to engage in 'forbidden' sexual practices, namely, to assume the superior position in sexual intercourse. Since then Lilith, symbolizing the banished destructive feminine aspects, is conceived of as a threat to infants, newlyweds, and other liminal individuals because she is often in search of semen with which to construct bodies for her wandering spirit children.

Ejaculated semen engendered a sort of disembodied demon, ever seeking to incarnate. These 'spirits of harm that come from man' unless prevented, would appear at their father's funeral. Their appearance was not only out of keeping with the honor due to the dead, but worse, these 'semen demons' might dispute or demand their share of the father's inheritance or harm the more legitimate heirs. To prevent this, a series of antidemonic rites were devised to guard against these illegitimate demon-children.

One of these devices was a strange 'dance of death' still performed occasionally in Jerusalem for men of high standing.

> Before the body was lowered into the grave, ten men danced round it in a circle, reciting a Psalm which in Jewish tradition has generally been regarded as a defense against demons (Ps. 91), or another prayer. Then a stone was laid on the bier and the following verse (Gen. 25:6) recited: 'But unto the sons of the concubines, which Abraham had, Abraham gave gifts, and sent them away.' This strange dance of death was repeated seven times. The rite, which in modern times has been unintelligible to most of the participants, has to do with kabbalistic conceptions about sexual life and the sanctity of the human seed. (Scholem 1965, 154)

Many diverse cultures express the mysterious connection between sexuality and death in mortuary ritual (Bachofen 1967; Bloch and Parry 1982). In many cases, the victory over death or transformation into rebirth "is symbolically achieved by a victory over female sexuality and the world of women who are made to bear the ultimate responsibility for the negative aspects of death" (Bloch and Parry 1982, 22). The dangers of the female might be implicit in Jerusalem rite because formerly, in many cases, women did not accompany the corpse to the grave or even attend the funeral at all. What is unusual in the custom of Jerusalem is that focus on masculine sexuality as 'dangerous and unproductive', when separated from the sanctified fertilizing act of procreation. It is precisely this disembodied masculinity that endangers the funeral process.

The sixteenth century Kabbalist, Abraham Sabba, according to Scholem, was the first to formulate the funeral link between father and his spirit children. He poignantly describes the final meeting:

> For all those spirits that have built their bodies from a drop of his seed regard him as their father. And so, especially on the day of his burial, he must suffer punishment; for while he is being carried to the grave, they swarm around him like bees, crying: "You are our father," and they complain and lament behind the bier, because they have lost their home and are now being tormented along with other demons which hover (bodiless) in the air. (quoted in Scholem 1965, 155).

In order to prevent such a tormenting and pathetic scene, various antidemonic tactics were contrived. The most potent was a sort of sympathetic magic. The presence of a man's biological offspring seemingly allows the 'semen children' to attend the funeral as well. By banning one set of heirs, the absence of the other is assured.

This explanation is the one my informants gave me and continue to give bereaved children just prior to the funeral. As in other cultures (Bloch and Parry, 1982), there is a folk explanation that parallels the official esoteric account. This explanation I heard mostly from women. They claimed that all children are prohibited from following a father's bier because a man is never sure whether his children are truly his own biological offspring. The ban acts to prevent the public disgrace of a bastard being included in the funeral procession, even if the father is not aware that a child is from another's seed. What is interesting is that the folk explanation and the official explanation deal with the same issue, namely, the exclusion of illegitimate offspring. Whereas the official version focuses on illegitimate beings in the spirit realm, the folk version is concerned with illegitimate children in the flesh. Both versions agree that there is no need for a similar ban in the case of mothers, who are in all cases sure about the maternity of their progeny, in a way that no father can be confident about his paternity.

There is at least one matrilineal society, the Fante of West Africa, in which the children, who have no share in their father's inheritance, are set apart during the funeral procession. The children, who provide only the coffin and no other funeral expense, walk in front while the rest of the relatives follow (Chukwukere 1981). Unlike the Jerusalem case, Fante children are obliged to walk in front of the coffin and certainly to attend the funeral rite. Chukwukere convincingly argues that their position within the procession reflects their peculiar status within their father's family and more general male/female dichotomy in which a man's children belong not to his own but to his wife's lineage. Similarly, Goody (1952, 1976) has shown how peculiar customs night reflect changing conflicts concerning family and inheritance.

SEPARATION OF BODY AND SOUL

Kabbalistic views of death placed emphasis on the separation of the soul from the body. One tradition, for example, described how the soul leaves the body organ by organ and continues to wander from the grave to the home of the deceased in the initial period following death. Moreover, the separation of the body from the soul was said to parallel the original fusion at the moment of conception. My informants stated that the soul could hear everything said in the presence of the corpse at least until burial. Indeed, the graveside service is only complete when forgiveness is asked of the dead man, as well as absolving him from any lingering obligations. The soul in its wanderings from house to grave is said to be 'mourning' over its body, and the link is only finally severed with the decomposition of the flesh, whose duration is said to equal the period in which the soul undergoes punishment for his sins. In the rocky soil of Jerusalem, certain plots are favored for their alleged capability to hasten decomposition. In this way, as in many cultures, the fate of the body does to some extent parallel the fate of the soul in the afterlife.

Death, however, placed both body and soul in a vulnerable position. Some texts (Trachtenberg 1974) pictured the dying man as surrounded by evil spirits waiting to pounce. Demon spirits were thought to try to gain possession of the corpse in the period between death and burial. This danger is expressed in the phrase: "The body is like a house and the soul its inhabitant; when the tenant leaves the house there is no one to look after it" (quoted in Trachtenberg 1974, 47). Numerous aspects of Jewish mortuary ritual were designed to guard against such demon attacks. The vigil, the sealing of orifices, rapid burial before nightfall—a time given over to unclean spirits—were all designed to protect the body against such evil influences. In Jerusalem, right/left dichotomies during ritual washing/purification and the recitation of antidemonic chants, for example, Psalm 91, were added for additional protection against the dangers of the liminal phase. Only with burial did the danger of demons cease because it was well known that demons have no power under the earth (Tuchinski 1948; Benayahu 1983).

Funeral ritual everywhere enacts a symbolic victory over death. Often, achieving a collective sense of symbolic immortality (Lifton 1979) requires overcoming the biological material nature of man (Bloch 1982). In Jewish funerals, this physical aspect of man is usually represented by the 'stinking corpse', the archetypal source of ritual pollution. The material aspect of the person, in this case the physical body, must be cast aside in order to release the crucial nonphysical essence, which then begins its journey to Paradise in the afterlife. In Jerusalem, this physicality takes on an additional presence, in the form of the felt presence of a man's ejaculations that come to haunt him and his children in the cultural entity of spirit or demon offspring.

The Kabbalists focused on spilt semen as the epitome of the anti-reproductive act, which threatened the triumph over the physical nature of man and hence the funeral process itself. In this process, the image of these semen demons became an "image of ultimate horror" (Lifton 1989), that is, a collective image of extinction.

This image crystallized the fear that a man will leave behind him, not children and children's children, but only a vile drop. Thus spilling of the seed is considered an expression of the antilife forces, which work against the symbolic continuity of father and son. The danger represented by these symbols of disembodied masculinity threaten the very principle of biological continuity represented by lineal descendants, and indeed the very symbolic victory over death.

Funerals, we have argued, initiate mourning, provide social support, and usher the soul of the deceased into the world to come. In normal circumstances, these three functions go hand in hand, mutually reinforcing each other, as in the Jewish funeral outside Jerusalem. In Jerusalem, the special cult of purity and Kabbalistic concerns over the sacred nature of procreation led to a series of ritual innovations in which the demands of social support were momentarily set aside in favor of the special needs of aiding the spirit of the deceased make the dangerous transition to the world to come. Because of the flaw in masculine sexuality, which conceived of a man as inevitably the father of semen demons, the presence of any children would threaten the funeral process, especially the symbolic victory over death, sin, and the biological, material nature of man. The needs of the descendants for social support could thus be sacrificed in favor of the assuring magical protection for the soul of the deceased.

This anomalous case highlights how different cultures make selective use of diverse aspects of the funeral process to mediate and modulate various dilemmas on its own cultural agenda. Indeed in the

Jerusalem case, the usual rhythm of initiating mourning, followed by ushering the soul to the world to come, and then providing social support is maintained. It is precisely at the transition point between ushering the soul and providing social support that the two clash. Once the man is buried, however, as in all Jewish practices, the non-mourners come to make condolence visits to the house of mourning.

The custom emphasizes the latent role of sexuality and fertility in funerals even when it is not overt in the ritual. As Maurice Bloch (1982) has argued, societies with traditional authority based on a timeless ancestral realm have difficulty with temporal, unpredictable events like birth and death, which seem to violate the realm of eternity. Such societies, he claims, tend to bifurcate their relation to the body and soul of the deceased, identifying the corpse with dirty pollution, something to be thrown away, as the spirit ascends to the ancestral realm, associated with the eternal values. Block gives examples from the Merina society of Madagascar that practices a second funeral in which the bones are removed from the earth and placed in communal ancestral tombs.

His argument, however, seems to apply to the Jerusalem material as well, which is likewise a religious system based on a purported timeless ancestral realm of values. The corpse is considered archetypically polluting and, in that sense, needs to be thrown away to allow the soul to rise to Paradise. Unlike the Merina, in which the rotting corpse is identified exclusively with women and female values, Jerusalem Jewish custom adds to that dichotomy the male division between fruitful and barren sexuality, that is between sacred sexual procreation and intercourse with demons in the form of seminal ejaculations. Just as the spirit must be separated from the body, so too must the demons be kept away from their father.

In this section, we have examined an anomalous funeral custom of Jerusalem, *herem Yehoshua bin nun*, in which lineal descendants are prohibited from escorting their father to his grave. This practice effectively isolates these sets of mourners, just at the very time when it is expected they would most be in need of social support. The emic explanation concerns the Kabbalistic conception about the flaw in male sexuality. A father's seminal ejaculations engender disembodied half souls, or demons who would seek to claim paternity at the funeral unless all children were banned.

For the Kabbalists, the funeral initiates a process in which the body and soul of the father begin a process leading to ultimate separation, the body returning to the earth and the soul to its Creator. Just as body and soul need to be separated, so too a man's biological children need to be distinguished from his unwanted spirit offspring. Whereas the former are vital symbols of continuity, the latter are considered threatening and disruptive. In a symbolic sense, these two sets of creations should not meet at the time when the separation of the father's body and soul is begun.

From a functionalist point of view, the prohibition remains problematic. Nevertheless, one can discern in the structural contrast of sacred fertility to barren masturbatory sexuality and the difficulties inherent in the task of the funeral, namely, the symbolic victory of the spiritual over the material.

RELIGIOUS CEREMONY/SECULAR MOURNERS

Until now, I have presented the funeral dynamics from the perspective of the burial society and the religious establishment it represents. I have also tried to make sense in symbolic anthropological terms of some of the peculiar customs of the Jerusalem burial tradition.

The performance of the funeral, the actual versus the ideal, varies tremendously. I have seen beautifully evocative ceremonies "which not only do the work of burial, but also much of the work of mourning, creating a momentary sense of unity among the mourners, but also uniting all those gathered" (Abramovitch 1986). In particular, one is impressed with the person who enters the open grave to receive the corpse as it is passed down. He lays the corpse in the grave and undoes the last slip knots in the shroud, symbolically undoing the final ties between the dead and the living. Likewise, asking for forgiveness from the deceased is often a beautiful moment, indicating the reality of dialogue between living souls and dead ones. The American scholar Jacob Neusner describing such a funeral ritual has written: "Jerusalem's Hevra Kadisha is deserving of its name, 'the holy society'. Those beautiful Jews showed me more of what it means to be a Jew, of what Torah stands for, than all the books I ever read. They tended the corpse gently and reverently, yet did not pretend it was other than a corpse" (Neusner 1974).

Not all funerals are so successful. I have also witnessed embarrassing, disruptive, burials. The initial dilemma concerns the asymmetry between the bereaved and the Hevra Kadisha. As in other professions, the emergency of the former is the routine of the latter. Individuals who participate in funerals on a daily basis do not always display a sense of empathy and concern concomitant with the mourners' unique feeling of loss. Indeed, for the members of the Hevra Kadisha the emphasis is on finishing the ceremony as quickly as possible, often in order to set the stage for the next funeral. As a result, corpses are often buried before most of the bereaved are assembled. Even more disturbing, it is not unheard of for the driver of the funeral van to honk noisily just after the conclusion of the graveyard service to call the pallbearers to reassemble.

The handling of the corpse in practice does not always attain the ideal of reverence. I have seen corpses get wet in the rain, splattered with mud, banged as they are placed in the grave. But perhaps the most astonishing thing is the simple fact of the corpse wrapped in shrouds lying on a bier. For myself, coming from a North American background, it was the stark confrontation with the shrouded corpse that was the most striking and disturbing aspect of the funeral, far more disturbing than the collection of alms at the graveside, which many secular informants found exceedingly distasteful.

At the end of the graveside service, it is traditional to place a stone on the grave and to do so on the occasion of each visit to the tomb. The number of stones thus becomes an indication of postmortem popularity as well as a unobtrusive indicator to regular visitors to the grave that others have been there as well. The origin of the custom is obscure, but probably derives from the use of rock cairns instead of gravestones in former times. Stone, however, is an appropriate symbol of permanence, highlighting the separation of the decaying body from the eternal soul. In contrast, many secular mourners bring flowers to the grave. To the Orthodox, flowers are not only inappropriate as non-Jewish symbols but also on account of their impermanence. Flowers that wither cannot symbolize the cultural values of eternity, union with the Creator, or the passage to everlasting life. The clash between the Hevra Kadisha and its secular clients is a conflict of differing basic enduring cultural values to be reaffirmed as part of the ritual process.

Many nonreligious Jews in Jerusalem are passively compliant with the guidelines of the Hevra Kadisha. This is not surprising because many disoriented individuals are glad of the structure the ritual provides, even allowing a culturally sanctioned regression to acts and attitudes belonging to their own childhood. Others, however, are deeply disturbed, even enraged, although part of their anger might be displacement of the anger felt concerning their loss. Some of the secular reaction must be seen as part of the resentment at encroaching religious control of social life. Religious monopoly on burial is seen as a case in point. Second, the physical appearance of the members of the Hevra Kadisha makes them the target of epithets like "crows," or "vultures." In addition, professionalized mortuary care, formerly a voluntary activity, is considered by nonreligious as a stigmatized occupation, in contrast to the traditional Jewish view in which it is the highest form of charity (*gemilut hesed shel emet*).

Most of the rituals done in accordance with the custom of Jerusalem are incomprehensible and often offensive to secular Israelis. It is also my feeling that many secular individuals are upset by the lack of any artistic contouring to the funeral proceedings. The absence of a coffin, the ban on lineal descendents, the rapidity of burial, the collection of charity, the frequent lack of solemnity, or even the placing of burial implements on tombstones, go against their Westernized sensibilities. Secular mourners do not know their roles in the funeral drama. They need to be coached when to say Kaddish, where to stand, when to pass through the lines of consolers, as well as the details of observance of the *shiva* period in the seven days following burial. On the other hand, I have occasionally seen secular Jews perform a funeral within a funeral, when after passing through the lines of consolers, the traditional exit from the cemetery, the individuals return to the grave for further orations, devotions, or tears. It is at this secular funeral, resembling the kibbutz funeral in some ways, that secular mourners and their friends are able to express some of the positive basic values of their culture and special relationship with the deceased, unfettered by halakic restraints.

The basic clash between religious and secular cultures is one of worldview. Within the context of funerals, the Orthodox perspective is personalistic, mystical, other worldly, concerned with the unseen. Their task in the funeral is to aid in the transition of the soul from the body to the status of ancestor dwelling with the Eternal in Paradise, reunited with the Creator. The funeral is also the occasion for the demise of the social person, as well as the end of the status of *onen* for his or her ritual mourners and their transition to the status of *avel*. The entire ritual is founded on a profound belief in an afterlife under a Just Judge; that death can be retribution for sin; and as we have seen, that there is a hidden connection between death and male sexuality.

In contrast, most secular Israelis are uncomfortable with such eschatological notions of reward and punishment, afterlife and paradise, eternity and damnation. The soul of the deceased is not usually understood to continue a nonmaterial existence, except perhaps in the memories of those about them. The burial is thus a marker of the transition from life to "nonlife." Those who ordinarily engage in such ritual are implicitly stigmatized and tainted by their regular contact with the dead in a way quite different from halakic concerns with ritual impurity. Moreover the Jerusalem funeral does not include any spontaneous personal expression of one's emotional relation to the deceased beyond the standard tears and eulogies. Such a personal relationship is one of the basic life values in secular society, and the development of the funeral within the funeral is therefore one attempt to reaffirm this basic cultural value.

If funerals are social occasions for reasserting basic life values, which address questions of ultimate meaning in the face of ultimate loss, then Jerusalem burials are indeed a flash point in the ongoing tensions between Orthodox and secular Jews. Each group or ideology struggles to maintain its worldview as paramount. In the funeral, this struggle centers on the question, implicit in alternative worldviews: "Where are the dead?."

For the Orthodox, the answer is clear if mystic. The dead, separated from the body, return to the Creator where they may find response in Paradise. The main function of the funeral is to help the soul attain its proper position in the hereafter, a transition that is fll of dangers.

For secular Israelis, the dead do not function as cultural resources, mediating between man and God. Hence, there is no need for prayer, charity, and good works to ensure that the soul completes his spiritual journey. Secular Jews come to the funeral mostly, I believe, to say goodbye, to mark the parting from life. There is a general concern for the peace of the deceased, but it is not tied to any specific ritual tasks, as it must be for the Orthodox. Once the dead are buried, they might not be forgotten, but in a metaphorical sense, they are indeed, dead.

THE MISMEETING

Martin Buber made up the word *vergegnung*, mismeeting, to designate the failure of a real meeting between men. In his "Autobiographical Fragments" he discusses how he learned from a playmate, a girl several years older than himself, that his mother would never return. He writes:

> We both leaned on the railing. I cannot remember that I spoke of my mother to my older comrade. But I still hear how the big girl said to me, "No, she will never come back." I know that I remained silent, but also that I cherished no doubt of the truth of the spoken words. It remained fixed in me; from year to year it cleaved ever more to my heart, but after more than ten years I had begun to perceive it as something that concerned not only me, but all men. Later I once made up the word "Vergegnung"— "mismeeting" or "misencounter"—to designate the failure of a real meeting between men. When after another twenty years I

again saw my mother, who had come from a distance to visit me, my wife and my children, I could not gaze into her still astonishingly beautiful eyes without hearing from somewhere the word "Vergegnung" as a word spoken to me. I suspect that all I have learned about genuine meeting in the course of my life had its first origin in that hour on the balcony. (Buber 1971, 18)

Although Buber is discussing his parents' divorce, all experiences of loss and reunion are fraught with the danger of mismeetings. In the article, I use Buber's notion of "mismeeting" to discuss the failure of a real meeting in Jerusalem funerals, which in turn mirrors the broader social conflict between religious and secular Jews in Israel. The conflict becomes more acute when those in charge of running the funeral, members of the burial society (Hevra Kadisha) who are exclusively Orthodox if not ultra-Orthodox religious Jews, serve fully secular Jews, who do not share the worldview of the religious community but, on the contrary, are actively hostile to it. The service relationship common in American funeral homes, in which the mortician seeks to accommodate or ingratiate himself with the client mourners, does not exist. The Hevra Kadisha is a charitable, honorary voluntary association, formerly of very high social status. Its allegiance to the precepts and values of its religious community involve religious concepts of the "honor due the dead" (kvod hamet), ritual purification of the deceased (*taharat hamet*), and the sanctified local burial custom, known as 'the tradition of Jerusalem' (*minhag Yerushalayim*). Everything up to the actual burial is done to honour the dead, afterwards it is the mourners who might take precedence. From a dramaturgical point of view, the religious members of the burial society perform the funeral to assist in the final separation of body from soul, and so that the latter might begin the dangerous and difficult transition to the next world (*olam haba*, literally, the world to come). Most of the complicated and strange prayers and rituals are designed to further this mystical transition. The secular families of the deceased, who usually reject any notion of an afterlife, misperceive these rituals as an attempt by religious ritual experts/authorities to impose their will on secular outsiders. Far from seeing these actions as part of the honor due the dead, they see in many of the rites indignity and humiliation, which block their own spontaneous expression of grief and secular life values.

If many secular Israels reject the religious text of the Jerusalem funeral, they are hard pressed to replace it with a ceremony of their own. Secular Jews do not dwell on issues of death, transitoriness of human life, and the reification of transcendent values. In this way, they are at a great disadvantage in relation to the religious communities who have a tradition and ideology that addresses such issues in theory and praxis. In the one instance of the secular funeral, in kibbutzim, no established form of ceremony for funeral and burial has taken hold, in contrast to success in many aspects of communal ritual life. Indeed the very first kibbutz funerals were held in silence or inevitably fell back on variations of traditional Jewish custom. For a secular community, constellated only in polarity to the religious communities' attempts at domination, it is not clear what are the basic group values to be celebrated.

Unlike those who fall in the midrange of the secular-religious continuum, for those near its secular pole the funeral does not serve as a holding environment, containing the intense conflicting feeling to which death and loss inevitably give rise. As a result, angry feelings might be inappropriately vented on the Hevra Kadisha in a way that interferes with the naturally working through of the mourning process. Most secular Israelis do perform the *shiva*, at least in part, staying at home to receive condolence visits but not reciting *shiva*-appropriate prayers nor sitting on low seats. Often the bitterness of the mismeeting within the funeral remains, however, leaving a lasting sense of grievance and mistrust. Such a sentiment is poetically expressed in a contemporary Greek funeral lament, which seems to express sadly the potential for mismeeting:

> Songs are just words. Those who are bitter
>   sing them.
> They sing them to get rid of their bitterness,
>   but the bitterness doesn't go away.
>   (Danforth 1982, 146)

Within the contexts of such mismeeting and misperception (witness Franz Rosenzweig's bitter motto: It is worse to be misperceived than to be mistreated), there is a further struggle over the priority of the tasks of the funeral. While the members of the Hevra Kadisha formally do the work of initiating mourning, they are unable to provide much social support, especially because their main task is focused on ushering the soul into the afterlife. Secular Israelis, bereft of an afterlife, find much of the funeral ritual absurd. Many seek to avoid the ritual act of rending one's garment, the formal sign of mourning. Their feeling is "I refuse to place myself under your moral authority," or more simply, "You cannot tell me what to do." This struggle over moral authority and the transcendent group values is at the heart of the mismeeting between religious and secular Israelis.

REFERENCES

Abramovitch, H. 1987. Death. In *Contemporary Jewish religious thought*, ed. A. A. Cohen and P. Mendes-Flor. New York: Scribners Sons.

Abramovitch, H. 1986. The clash of values in the Jerusalem funeral: A participant-observer study of a *Hevra Kadisha*. *Proceedings of the Ninth World Congress of Jewish Studies*. Jerusalem: World Union of Jewish Studies.

Aries, P. 1977. *L'Homme devant la mort*. Paris: Editions du Seuil.

Bachofen, J. J. 1967. *Myth, religion and mother right, Trans. E. Mannheim*. London: Routledge and Kegan Paul.

Benayahu, M. 1983. *Concerning death processions, circumambulations and the ban on children following their father's bier*. *Sinai* 92:58-65 (Hebrew).

Bloch, M. 1982. Death, women and power. In *Death and the regeneration of life*, ed. M. Bloch and J. Parry. London: Cambridge University Press.

Bloch, M., and J. Parry. 1982. *Death and the regeneration of life*. London: Cambridge University Press.

Buber, M. *Meetings: Autobiographical Fragments*. La Salle, IL: Open Court, 1971.

Chukwukere, V. 1981. A coffin for the loved one. *Current Anthropology*.

Danforth, L. M. 1982. *The death rituals of rural Greece*. Princeton: Princeton University Press.

Durkheim, E. 1969. *The elementary forms of the religious life*. New York: Free Press.

Geertz, C. *The Interpretation of Culture*, p. 110. New York: Basic Books.

Geertz, C. 1957. Religion and social change: A Javanese example. *American Anthropologist*, Vol. 59. 32-54.

Green, A. 1981. *Tormented master; A life of Rabbi Nachman of Bratslav*. New York: Schocken.

Goody, J. 1962. *Death, property and the ancestors*. Stanford: Stanford University Press.

Goody, J. 1976. *Family and inheritance*. Cambridge: Cambridge University Press.

Hertz, R. 1960. *Death and Right Hand*, pp. 27–86. New York: Free Press.

Humphries, S. C. and King, Helen, eds. (1981) *Mortality and Immortality: The Anthropology and Archeology of Death*, Academic Press, London.

Huntingdon, R., and P. Metcalf. 1979. *Celebrations of death: The anthropology of morturay ritual*. Cambridge: Cambridge University Press.

Kalish, R. A. 1985. *Death, grief and caring relationships*. 2nd ed. Monterey, California: Brooks/Cole Publishing, p. 214.

Lamm, M. 1969. *The Jewish way in death and mourning*. New York: Jonathan David Publishers.

Lifton, R. J. 1979. *The broken connection: On death and the continuity of life*. New York: Simon & Schuster.

Malinowski, B. 1948. *Magic, Science and Religion*. New York: Free Press.

Neusner, J. Death in Jerusalem. In J. Reler (ed.) *Jewish Perspectives On Death*. New York: Schocken, 1974.

Palgi, P. and H. Abramovitch. 1984. Death: A cross cultural perspective. *Annual Review of Anthropology* 13:385–417.

Rosenblatt, P. C., R. Walsh and A. Hackson. 1976. *Grief and mourning in cross cultural perspective*. New Haven: Human Relations Area Files Press.

Scholem, G. 1965. *Tradition and new creation in the ritual of the kabbalists: On the Kabbalah and its symbolism*. New York: Schocken.

Trachtenberg, J. 1974. *Jewish magic and superstition: A study in folk religion*. New York: Atheneum.

Tuchinski, Y. 1948. *Bridge of life*. 2nd ed. (Hebrew). Jerusalem: Jerusalem Burial Society.

4

Tradition and Innovation in
Jewish Religious Education in Israel

MORDECAI BAR-LEV

INTRODUCTION:

Religious education has been perceived in all societies in the past and in most societies today as "that process of teaching and learning by means of which religions have sought for their transmission and self-perpetuation" (Hull 1984b). In all religious schools, religious education was a holistic activity, one that demands that educational principles line up with religious values in terms of the teachers' personal commitments, instructional material, and the school's apparent and hidden objectives and agendas.

With the growth of modern national educational systems, a struggle began in many countries between church and state regarding the control of these school systems, affecting the status and scope of religious education. These struggles, often carried out in legal forums (Brubacher 1947) as well as in politics and in the media—brought about four major arrangements:

1. Religious education, full or part time, is forbidden in all public and other educational institutions (Nationalist China).

2. Religious education, full or part time can not take place in public educational institutions but is permitted in private

*This chapter has been prepared under the sponsorship of the Eliezer Stern Institute for Research and Advancement in Religious Education, School of Education, Bar-Ilan University.

educational institutions, or departments thereof (United States, Japan).

3. Religious education (part time—2 hours weekly) is provided by public educational institutions. It is optional and requires prior parental agreement. Adult religious education requires the consent of the students themselves. In private educational institutions, the guidelines for religious education are not under state jurisdiction (West Germany, Australia, Great Britain).

4. Religious education, full time, is mandatory in all public educational institutions. Private educational institutions as well must set aside a few weekly sessions for religious instruction (Pakistan, Iran).

The third arrangement placed religious education in the respective countries in a "market situation" (Berger 1967) that stressed the significance of religious education over religious activity. According to this new outlook, contemporary religious education must legitimize itself by emphasizing educational considerations and criteria more than theological ones. This educational viewpoint was initiated primarily in Great Britain in the late 1960s, under the influence of the writing of Cox (1966) and Smart (1968), where new instructional programs for religious education were brought into the school systems.

These programs were to a large extent anchored in educational philosophy and sociology and in modern theories regarding curriculum development. This new approach to religious education represented a radical break with traditional religious education and was even seen as a "secularization . . . of religious education" (Hull 1982). Whereas the traditional notion of religious education stressed religious activity, which differentiated significantly between Catholic religious education and Islamic religious education for example, the new approach stressed educational activity, which blurred the distinctions between religious groups. This led to the development of pluralistic curricula that included a heavy dose of studies based on comparative religion (Hull 1984a).

Traditional Jewish religious education in the diaspora and in Israel saw its essential function in religious activity. This approach had been dominant for many generations, as long as Jewish society had been all encompassing. According to this outlook, the goal of religious education was to mold the student's entire personality, and it was the educator's task to seize the student's soul "to enter it under the wings of the Holy Spirit." The principal educational objective was thus to bring the student under the dual yoke—the "yoke of Heaven," accepting the religious beliefs and ideas on an ideological level, and the "yoke of mitzvot," willingly undertaking to perform the precepts of the Law (Enoch 1981).

From the 1870s through the early years of the state of Israel, the belief that the role of religious Jewish education was to promote religious activity became the focus of many bitter conflicts and debates. Elements from the religious community, on the one hand, claimed, at least until the London Agreement of 1920, that public educational institutions in the Jewish Yishuv (community) of Eretz Yisrael (The Land of Israel) were responsible for continuing the tradition of compulsory religious education. Militant elements from the nonreligious community, on the other hand, claimed that as part of their campaign to restructure Jewish society, the schools must be "conquered,"and a new and modern educational model must be created.

Most conspicuous among the many sides to this prolonged controversy were the political parties. The Mizrahi party was founded in 1902 as a result of the ideological-political controversy between the democratic faction headed by Ahad Haam who demanded nationalist involvement from the Zionist Congress in Jewish education in Eretz Yisrael, and the religious faction headed by Rabbi Reines, who opposed this demand.

The intense political involvement and the split of the religious community into subgroups with completely different goals and interests did little to help crystallize a compromise. In the early 1950s, a model for public religious education in the state of Israel was established. This model did not in any way resemble any of the four arrangements described above but, in fact, split further into three or four alternative models: religious state schools, independent educational institutions, and "exemption" institutions. A fourth Sephardic model has since emerged, supported by a new religious political party, Sephardic Guardians of the Torah.

RELIGIOUS STATE SCHOOLS

With the State Education Law of 1953, elements in the religious community faced a dilemma. Should they maintain quasi-private frameworks for religious education, or find new structures and arrangements that allowed for integration into the state framework?

After much deliberation, two of the four religious political parties, Mizrahi and Hapoel Hamizrahi, decided to integrate—with the assurance that religious education was the right of any individual who so desired and that they would be guaranteed educational autonomy, similar to that provided in the London Agreement, in their school system. At the start of the 1954 school year, all schools previously aligned with Mizrahi merged into the religious state schools, along with 84 "religious extension" schools, some 20 Agudat Israel schools, and all of the Habad schools (Kill 1977).

Religious state education as an educational model available to every parent interested in a religious education for his children had to be fashioned on both an organizational and educational level. On the organizational level, religious state schools were to be set up with the help of the Department of Religious Education of the Ministry of Education and Culture. They were also helped by the Religious State Education Council, a body with the public and legal authority to approve supplemental curricular material and to effectuate the autonomy of the religious state schools, in addition to the usual tasks of hiring and firing school staff.

On the educational level, religious state education does not limit itself to the instruction of religious subjects, seeing its role as much more comprehensive. It emphasizes its state status as equal to that of the state school and disassociates itself from any particular political party. Its nursery schools, elementary schools, junior and senior high schools are clearly religious in nature: the educational staff is religious as is the content of the curriculum and the inherent values and life-style put forth.

As a state school system, religious state education had to show openness to the expectations and the wide range of traditions of the heterogeneous parent population. This was reflected in time, both in the extensive specialization and differentiation among the various educational institutions, particularly in the high schools, and in the controversies with parents regarding goals and social and educational priorities. In addition, state status required that religious schools adapt to the economic and technological changes that Israel experienced over the years, and that they develop tracks that responded to the challenge of religious education in a modern society.

After some 35 years of religious state education, it is possible to point out a number of quantitative and qualitative changes. The number of students has stabilized after a significant leap in the 1950s and 60s and a decline in the 70s, a considerable decline in the dropout rate during the transition from elementary to high school. Academic achievement has increased in the major areas, such as reading comprehension and mathematics, in elementary and secondary schools for the privileged and underprivileged alike. There is intensive cooperation between the religious state schools and the religious youth movements, which are permitted to use school facilities. The system has been exposed to systematic researched criticism (Langerman 1986). Planning and development continue in accordance with the changing needs, giving rise to the military boarding school, to the prestigious technological school, and to a yeshiva track in a comprehensive day high school for boys and girls. Religious aspirations of the students and graduates have risen, and there is critical openness to change.

Nevertheless, religious state education today faces a crucial decision with political, social, and religious ramifications: should an alternative separate-sex school be set up in response to the demand of parents who seek more intense Torah education for their children, schools which would be unaffiliated with those for families whose religious demands are less intense? Such a move could create internal and external accusations that religious state education is rejecting integration and turning inward, becoming extremist and elitist. This decision will force religious state education to scrutinize its ideological underpinnings and to rethink its philosophical goals, objectives, and methods.

It can be assumed that a decision to establish a separate school system within the state religious trend would cause a shift back to the traditional emphasis on religious activity. The opposite decision would symbolize the continuing dialectic tension between religious particularism and universal educational activity. This latter course could, paradoxically, aggravate the ideological struggle of religious state education that, because of the gravity of the present problem, ignored three major complex educational issues over the past 15 years:

1. The position of religious state education regarding the secular world and its values: the issue of a Jewish majority vis-a-vis an Arab minority; secular studies in general and humanistic studies in particular integrated harmoniously with religious studies; identification and socializing with nonreligious Jews; acceptance of Western culture and its spiritual contributions without adopting its permissiveness.

2. The position of religious state education regarding the non-Zionist ultra-Orthodox and their value system: legitimization of the basic concepts of religious Zionism as central to the physical and spiritual building of the state and the rejection of the ultra-Orthodox stand; strengthening the social and educational status of women, which is challenged by contra-

dictory messages from ultra-Orthodox society; separating ideological differences with ultra-Orthodox from acceptance of them as fellow Jews and human beings.

3. The position of religious state education regarding ethnic tensions: new solutions to the problem of absorbing students from different ethnic backgrounds; continuing efforts to improve the academic achievement of underprivileged students, primarily of Afro-Asian descent and including Ethiopian immigrants, many of whom enter religious state education; sensitivity to the traditional life-style of the Eastern ethnic groups and to the inherent pedagogic values in these differences.

"INDEPENDENT EDUCATION" INSTITUTIONS

The religious Agudat Israel party removed itself from the political and educational framework of the Zionist Organization during the Yishuv period (1919–1948). In the early years of the state, however, it joined the first government and therefore was able to join the state system as one of the four educational streams. In 1949, Agudat Israel's educational institutions and staff fell under the jurisdiction of the government and of the local authorities, thus becoming the fourth educational track. State law granted them legal status with rights and obligations equal to those of the other three tracks.

When the track system was abolished and state religious state education was introduced in 1954, the Council of Torah Scholars in Jerusalem decided that the Agudat Israel elementary schools, which included some 15,000 students, would not join the religious state school system. The Council decided on a separate educational framework known as the Center for Independent Education for Students of Torah, and for Agudat Israel and Nonaffiliated Schools in Eretz Yisrael. The government decided in 1954 to designate these independent schools as "recognized but nonofficial" educational institutions. A written request from two-thirds of the parents was necessary for a particular school to be recognized as part of Independent Education. This privilege, however, was limited to parents of students individually and not to any group or organization using their names; only later was the Center for Independent Education recognized, de facto, as an umbrella organization for these institutions.

Since its establishment, Independent Education sees its central task to be imparting of basic Jewish faith and knowledge of the Torah, Prophets, Mishna, and Talmud. While secular studies are taught in these schools, no attempt is made to integrate Jewish and secular studies and certainly not to teach broad, general culture. The purpose of secular studies is "to teach the student those subjects—such as reading, writing, mathematics and some foreign language—necessary for him to know in order to make a living.... It is also worthwhile for him to be familiar with scientific achievements in different fields... on condition that he does not study from books which teach heresy or in places of study where heresy is taught, and on condition that this does not become a permanent and central area of study, but rather remains secondary and casual, like reading a letter..." (Karlbach 1964, 45).

These goals and methods as applied in all stages of education require very careful selection of teachers and guidance of the students. Boys are to continue after elementary school in a lower yeshiva, then in an advanced yeshiva. Girls are to continue in a Beit Yaakov seminary after high school. The final goals are a young man learned in Torah; and a young woman, Beit Yaakov-educated, married to a learned young man, and permitted to work in specific fields, particularly teaching in religious schools, to allow him to continue in Torah study. The entire educational framework—from nursery school through seminary for the women and advanced yeshiva for the men— is so structured as to inculcate and effectuate these role models (see Bernstein 1987).

Unlike religious state education, which is a unified system, Agudat Israel education is split into many networks and frameworks. Even among these various divisions, however, the Center for Independent Education stands out in its scope and organizational ability.

Independent education is presently administered on a government-supported, nationwide basis. The district administrator of Independent Education is also the Ministry of Education administrator of its schools, and the supervisor is the department director for the Organization of Elementary Schools. The Center for Independent Education presents its budget proposal that is, in effect, its yearly program. After the Organization of Elementary Schools and the Budget Department give their approval, the Center may carry out the proposal. From this point on, administration of the departments of Independent Education is carried out according to the stipulations of the proposal and is reviewed periodically by the controller from the Ministry of the Treasury, who must sign every payment order. The Center for Independent Education must also submit a monthly budgetary balance, signed by the treasurer of Independent Education and the Ministry of the Treasury comptroller, to the Ministry of Education. These guidelines greatly reduce bureaucratic procedures and the threat of strikes. They reflect not only the signigicant changes Independent Education has undergone since 1954 when it received only 60 percent of its expenses per student, but also certain trends toward modernization. While Independent Education is ostensibly perpetuating traditional Jewish education, whose primary goal is to protect traditional values from contemporary trends, it has in fact introduced into its own school system, in recent years in particular, much that is new and modern.

Characteristic examples of change include: modernization on the administrative level, with computerized budgetary and organizational administration, administrative guidelines regarding hiring and firing, etc. Greater attention is paid to detailed and systematic planning of curricula. Teacher training and advanced study have increased, and the number of noncertified teachers was reduced to only 13 percent. Hebrew is now the language of instruction, and there is beginning awareness of need for special education and informal education, with early preparation for computerized instruction. It is no coincidence that these trends toward modernization are accompanied by protest and withdrawal on the part of more extreme religious groups.

Nonetheless, the prominence of religious activity as Independent Education's center of gravity does curb educational activity in other vital areas such as planning detailed curricular material for other subjects and increasing the books available. It limits the response of Agudat Israel youth movements to the expressive and social needs of youth and the individual attention and cultural sensitivity to students from Sephardic families or from newly religious families. It blocks flexible alternatives for male graduates for whom continuing studies in lower yeshivot is not appropriate and for female graduates who do not see their future in teaching: it impedes creating new models for cooperation between Independent Education and other sectors in the Israeli Jewish community (Bar-Lev, in press).

EXEMPTION INSTITUTIONS

In 1949, shortly after the establishment of the state, a compulsory education law was passed requiring all parents to register children aged 5-14 in a recognized school and to enforce their regular attendance. Talmudei Torah, Old Yishuv schools (pre-Zionist settlement), which operated primarily in Jerusalem since the 1840s, known also as heder, accepted children aged 3 through 15-16, after which they continued their studies in lower and then advanced yeshivot. These were all private, nonrecognized institutions, and Talmud Torah students were therefore not fulfilling the Compulsory Education Law. A special clause in the educational legislation authorized the Minister of Education and Culture to publish a directive in *Reshumot*, the official gazette of the Israeli Government, to the effect that parents of students and the students themselves who study regularly in an educational institution described in the directive, which was not officially recognized, were exempt from the obligations of the 1949 compulsory education law. Twenty-one institutions (some 2,500 students, only 400 outside Jerusalem) requested that the regulation be implemented in their regard. These have been exempt ever since. During the 1950s, the situation did not change. In the 1960s and particularly in the 70s, however, there was a significant increase in both the number of exemption institutions and in the number of students attending. In 1975 a number of the new institutions requested exemption status along with financial support. Relying on the 1949 precedent, it was decided to respond positively to this request if the following conditions were fulfilled:

1. The physical security of the children must be provided for.

2. The school budget must be administered in an organized fashion and authorized by an accountant.

3. Teachers were qualified, and equipment, minimal furnishings and decorations, and cleanliness provided, all subject to the judgment of a supervisor from Independent Education.

4. The program of studies must not come out in any way against the state.

5. A class in the city must have at least 25 students; in a development town there must be at least 25 students in two jointly taught classes.

This arrangement was renewed in 1978 and has since been renewed yearly—always following the same model.

Aside from institutions receiving formal budgetary recognition (20 in Jerusalem, 19 in B'nei Brak, and 13 scattered from Yeruham in the south to Tiberias in the north), a number of additional heders and Talmud Torahs have been set up since the founding of the state. These receive no financial support whatsoever and have not even requested formal exemption status. According to our calculation, they have some 2,000 students in Jerusalem and a few hundred in other areas, particularly in B'nei Brak. These institutions exemplify traditional religious education resembling the heder of the Old Yishuv, with its emphasis on religious activity reflected in the following areas:

- Daily schedule from 8:30 A.M. until 6:00 P.M. for older children.

- Program of primarily religious studies; for children over 6, with up to an hour and a half in the afternoon for secular studies such as Hebrew writing and grammar, arithmetic, Jewish history, and geography of Eretz Yisrael.

- Language of instruction is Yiddish in the majority of schools.

- Background of teachers: *melamdim*, traditional schoolmasters who are usually Talmud Torah graduates.

- Teaching methods, including teaching of reading, the social rituals and customs, and traditional methods of motivation and encouragement, are not supplemented by technologies like TV, video, and computers, nor enhanced by modern psychology of learning theory.

The exemption institutions for girls are much smaller than those for boys. Girls' schools include Old Beit Yaakov, founded in 1926, and Daughters of Jerusalem, founded in 1949, both of which were afforded exemption status in 1949. In the past 20 years, additional schools for girls have been founded, most of which are aligned with the *haredi* (ultra-Orthodox) community. More than 3,000 girls study in these schools, and the exclusive language of instruction and conversation is Yiddish. The curriculum differs from school to school regarding the scope of such subjects as history, geography, mathematics, nature, geometry, and the Hebrew language, and regarding the teaching methodology for *Tanach* (Bible) and Yiddish. Mishna (Oral Law) and foreign languages are not taught in any of these schools (see Bar-Lev, in press; Schneller 1980).

THE YESHIVOT

For many students, yeshiva represents the high point in their intellectual and religious experience. Therefore, despite the fact that the yeshiva school system accepts older male students who are generally graduates of compulsory education, we include it in this discussion of religious institutions.

There are two principal tracks in Israel's yeshivot, and since the 1970s, a third track has begun to operate as well:

1. The traditional track—three levels:
   a. Lower yeshiva (or *mechina*) for students aged 14–18;
   b. Advanced yeshiva or higher yeshiva, for students over 18;
   c. *Kollel* college, half or full day for married, advanced yeshiva students.

This track has diversified with yeshivot founded for different communities: Jerusalem yeshivot (old Yishuv yeshivot), Lithuanian, Hungarian, Hassidic, Kabbalistic, Sephardic, nationalistic yeshivot, and even yeshivot for foreign students.

2. Modern track—three levels:
   a. Yeshiva high school and vocational yeshiva for students aged 14–18;
   b. *Hesder yeshiva (five years) for graduates of yeshiva high school, vocational yeshiva, and religious high school; recently a parallel model, the integrated yeshiva (shiluv* yeshiva), was established for high school graduates from religious kibbutzim. These also accept graduates from other religious state high schools.
   c. *Kollel* or *Machon*, half or full day for married students.

This track is characterized by the combination of traditional yeshiva study with theoretical secular studies and/or technology studies or with army service.

3. Track for *baalei tshuva* (those who have recently become observant)—generally for high school graduates and modeled on the advanced yeshiva. A *kollel* framework, full or half day, for married students is developing as well. There is a parallel track for women (Aviad, 1980; Shaffir 1983).

The *baalei tshuva* track, founded in 1967, has also diversified into at least six streams: Lithuania, Hassidic, Kabbalistic, and Sephardic yeshivot, yeshivot for delinquent youth and ex-convicts, and nationalistic-Zionist yeshivot. This last type of yeshiva is experiencing dynamic growth and must be taken seriously as an emerging institution.

The three yeshiva tracks rest on different ideological underpinnings, in relation to some or all of the following issues:

1. Should the conservative approach to innovation and change in such areas as technological and secular studies be made more flexible?

2. What should be the attitude toward the state of Israel and its institutions, including army service, and toward the values and institutions of the Zionist movement?

3. How can the modern track legitimize the institutionalization and integration of the new and the old in its curriculum material and in its timetable?

4. How can the yeshiva tracks be brought together to create social and religious pluralism in the yeshiva world?

5. How should the issue of governmental financial support and an equitable distribution of funds be dealt with?

6. Should Torah institutions remain apolitical to avoid formal identification with any particular political party?

7. Should yeshiva institutions be decentralized away from the centers of Jerusalem and B'nei Brak? In 1986, over 70 percent of lower yeshiva students and some 65 percent of *kollel* students studied in Jerusalem and B'nei Brak. On the other hand, in the modern track and particularly in that of the *hesder* yeshivot combining Torah study with military service, the schools were scattered throughout the country.

8. What should be the minimum number of students in new institutions? This issue is most obvious in the *kollel;* in 1986, 39 percent of the kollels accepted 15 or fewer students, 38 percent accepted between 16 and 30, 14 percent between 31 and 60, and only 9 percent accepted at least 61 students.

In addition to the structural differentiation between the various religious educational institutions in Israel, there are as well significant curricular, ideological, and social differences. The second part of this chapter will analyze tradition and change in yeshiva education on four different levels: the structural, the ideological, the curricular, and the social. Detailed case studies will be taken from one of the four religious educational frameworks—the modern model of the *hesder* yeshiva—to exemplify the process of preserving tradition while welcoming change and innovation. The following section opens with a conceptual and historical perspective on the yeshiva institutions and continues with an analysis of the central dilemmas facing them today.

THE YESHIVA IN ISRAEL

The classical yeshiva was a Jewish institution of scholarship, education, amendment of the Law, and communal leadership. The earliest use of the term 'yeshiva' to denote a Jewish institution of biblical and Talmudic learning dates back to the first century C.E. The multipurpose structure of the Palestinian yeshiva reflected both the needs and the aspirations of traditional Palestinian Jewish society. These yeshivot acted as agents of continuity in a traditional context. According to some scholars, the term *yeshiva* (sitting) reflected the transition from studying Torah in a standing position to seated study. In the yeshiva the students sat before their teachers in rows within a fixed seating arrangement. During the twelfth and thirteenth centuries, the yeshivot of Europe and North Africa became primarily educational institutions; and the Palestinian yeshivot retained the multiple functions they had fulfilled since ancient times.

In contrast to their original role as agents of continuity, various yeshivot are now attempting to transform themselves into agents of social change. The analysis is focused on the hesder yeshiva, founded after the establishment of the state of Israel. The hesder yeshivot are of special importance because their graduates are now a recognizable subgroup within the new elite of modern religious Israeli society. "Modern religious" is understood as those religious Israelis who are genuinely interested in significant contact and interaction between Jewish religious tradition and modern society. (Regarding the differences between the main types of Israeli religious society, see Liebman and Don-Yehiya 1984.) Moreover, the students and graduates of hesder yeshivot are prominent among the supporters of *Gush Emunim,* the movement that, since the Yom Kippur War (1973-74), has called for massive Jewish colonization of Judea and Samaria (the West Bank) and for Israeli legal sovereignty over all territories conquered by Israel's army in the Six-Day War in June 1967.

To sum up, we can define the hesder yeshiva as an institution of elite education dominated by Israeli modern religious society. The institution operaties as an agent of socialization for the elite groups, preparing them in the halachic (Jewish Law) spirit to initiate gradual processes of social change.

ATTEMPTS AT SOCIAL CHANGE DURING THE PRESTATEHOOD PERIOD: A HISTORICAL PERSPECTIVE

In Palestine, the yeshiva became an exclusively educational institution for young people only when the Askenazi community in Jerusalem had become consolidated, during the nineteenth century. in 1862, members of the Ashkenazi community in Jerusalem founded the Etz Haim Yeshiva to provide a framework of further study for children who had completed their studies at the Etz Haim Talmud Torah, a primary school. In this framework, education is for boys only, and the central if not the exclusive studies are the sacred as opposed to secular subjects.

These parents and children, who had only recently arrived in Palestine from Europe, could not accustom themselves to the multi-functional structure of the Sephardic yeshivot and, consequently, set up a single-purpose yeshiva in Jerusalem modeled after the Lithuanian yeshiva familiar to them. This new framework, which seem to have been the most important educational institution in nineteenth century Jerusalem, came to be known as the Jerusalem Yeshiva. It was large and well organized, and at its height it taught several hundred students. The main purpose of Yeshivat Etz Haim was not to award certification for rabbinical posts but to provide Torah education for young people. Following Etz Haim, other single-function Ashkenazi yeshivot were established until the outbreak of World War I. In 1890, a Sephardic Yeshiva was established, and run on such lines.

In Jerusalem Ashkenazi Old Yishuv circles, such innovation was considered sufficient, and they deliberately avoided any further changes. 'Old Yishuv' might be defined as the communities of the four sacred cities of Jerusalem, Safad, Tiberias, and Hebron. Since the nineteenth century, these communities had been founded on a philanthropic base, and they depended upon *halukka* money (charity). Jews in these towns belonged to the religious Orthodox community and their lives centered around yeshivot, *kollelim* and *halukka* distribution. They formed the majority of the Jewish population in Palestine, at least until the beginnings of the New Yishuv (1882). The leaders of this community paid no heed to the innovations attempted at this time by certain yeshivot in Europe. They violently resisted attempts to introduce any subjects other than the Talmud and its commentaries, or to change their language of instruction, Yiddish. Their resistance stemmed from their view that their sole role in the holy land was to fulfill the central religious and social values of Jewish society as a whole, such as prayer and Torah study. These leaders maintained that Jews living in the land of Israel should not spend their time building a rational economic base: they should devote all their time to maintaining the central religious values of Jewish society. They felt the Jews in the Diaspora should be responsible for the economic and physical needs of the Yishuv in Palestine.

It is thus not surprising that the normative system of the Old Yishuv accorded no legitimacy to secular studies and rejected the need to prepare young people systematically for entry into the occupational world. It is also easy to understand why many older students, who were married and heads of families, flocked to the Jerusalem yeshivot, as the city offered a livelihood in addition to the *halukkah*. This structure was based on artificial economic support of all the families in the community; support that was never enough for decent existence and so roused social, economic, and political tensions and scandals. The Jerusalem Yeshiva thus gradually lost much of its distinctiveness as a single-function institution.

This society, based on *halukkah* and enabling both young and old students to pursue studies without any productive purpose, could maintain itself as long as traditional Jewish society in the Diaspora and in Palestine was prepared to give it both ideological legitimacy and material support. When the leaders of the Ashkenazi Old Yishuv lost their spiritual hegemony over Jewish society in Palestine and especially over Diaspora Jewry, and when economic difficulties and pressures mounted during World War I, the Jerusalem yeshivot found themselves in ideological and economic crisis. In 1918, immediately after the war, there were only 478 students in yeshivot in Palestine: of these, 343 were married men with families. During the war years, the yeshivot had been divorced from their sources of aid and support and their situation became desperate.

Their continued existence after the war depended on the aid proffered them by the Zionist Aid Committee. It was the Zionist movement, which controlled most of the aid funds, that saved the yeshivot from extinction. This aid was provided even though the members of the New Yishuv had already come to view the Jerusalem yeshivot students as an alien element.

The reservations felt about the yeshiva students became sharper after the British occupation and the Balfour Declaration (1917). Not only did members of the New Yishuv in the colonies and cities object to the employment of rabbis who were graduates of the Jerusalem yeshivot: the leaders of the Zionist movement took a strong political stand against the entire political and social structure of the Old Yishuv. In an attempt to overcome this division and to bring the Old Yishuv closer to the Zionist movement, Dr. Chaim Weizman, heading the Zionist Commission in 1918, presented a proposal for far-reaching reform in the Jerusalem yeshivot:

1. The rabbis should cooperate with Zionism in establishing the national home.

2. The language of instruction in the yeshivot should be Hebrew.

3. The students should adhere to a fixed and organized curriculum.

4. Only young people should be entitled to study at the yeshivot.

5. Only the gifted should be students, and that those below a certain minimal level of achievement should enter the labor market.

Weizmann's negotiations with the rabbis of the Old Yishuv were not successful, and the rabbis insisted that the situation in the yeshivot could not be touched.

With political domination of Zionism over institutions of the Yishuv, and the dynamic development of practical Zionist activity in settlement, economy, defence, and education, secularization in Palestine was intensified and Jewish religious society was further eroded. Many religious youths were attracted by what they saw as the idealism of the pioneering ideology of secular groups within the Jewish community of that period. They also imagined that the economic future envisaged by these groups was more realistic and secure. In this process of secularization and social erosion, the veteran yeshivot suffered further setbacks. Religious youth, particularly those of the New Yishuv, began to reject the yeshivot ideologically and came to regard them disparagingly as economically unproductive institutions.

In this period, heterogeneous patterns appeared for the first time within the yeshiva in Palestine. The attitude toward the Zionist movement and its institutions, and the attitude toward social and economic change, gradually emerged as the main dimensions of differentiation among yeshiva institutions.

Yet, even in this period, yeshiva institutions continued to follow the traditional model, taking a neutral or even hostile stand toward the values of the Zionist movement, its institutions, and other expressions of social and economic change. At the other end of the social spectrum, new yeshiva institutions emerged during the last decade of the British Mandate and adopted innovative models. They sought integration with the economy and society by including secular studies in the curriculum, took a positive and sympathetic sttitude towards values and institutions of the Zionist movement, and spoke Hebrew, the "new" national language. The new yeshivot displayed varying degrees of openness and willingness to adopt innovations in values, structures, contents, methods, and social features. Prominent within this trend were the first attempts at shaping an institution that would eventually become the yeshiva high school.

These heterogeneous trends in yeshiva education in the latter part of the Yishuv period continued and developed further in the state of Israel. In the following section, we shall discuss the major dilemmas confronting the new trends, dilemmas that deepened social differentiation.

MAJOR DILEMMAS CONFRONTING THE YESHIVOT IN ISRAEL SINCE STATEHOOD

Two events of profound significance occurred in the life of the Jewish people in the 1940s: (1) the Holocaust, decimating Jewish society in Europe and destroying its institutions; and (2) the creation of the state of Israel, fulfilling the aspirations of the Zionist movement by establishing a national home for the Jewish people.

These two events, affecting all of Jewish society, created ambivalence for the religious Jewish community in Israel. The Holocaust wiped out large segments of traditional Jewish society that might have formed a reserve pool for religious society in Israel. Moreover, centers of Torah learning and yeshivot, the glory of religious Jewish society, were destroyed and most of their students and teachers killed, and the tiny remnant dispersed all over the world. Naturally, therefore, the Holocaust survivors, with their traditional brethren in Eretz Yisrael, sought to perpetuate the memory of their loved ones by "setting a yeshiva on their graves," similar to the traditional yeshiva destroyed in the Holocaust. At the same time, the emergence of the state of Israel confronted the entire young Jewish generation there with new challenges. As anticipated, the new state offered them paths for advancement in defence, economic life, science, politics, and higher education. In Europe prior to World War II the social mobility of Orthodox Jews had been minimal. This intensified the challenge facing the young Orthodox generation virtually for the first time to seek out these paths of advancement and admission to institutions of learning that could serve them as appropriate socialization agents. These cross pressures, underlying the process of development of yeshiva institutions in Israel, confronted these institutions with dilemmas related to values, the social sphere, and questions deriving from the overall climate of the system.

Value Dilemmas

Those who shaped yeshiva education in Israel had to make a value choice—either to adhere to the traditional conception of the yeshiva's role or, in light of the economic and social changes since the establishment of the state, to formulate a new conception of its role. This choice posed dilemmas.

1. The traditional educational ideal of the yeshivot, based exclusively on Torah study for its own sake, molded the *talmid hacham*, the scholar. Should the yeshiva adhere exclusively to it, or should it adopt a new educational objective based on pluralism of educational ideals, which would include the traditional approach? Must the traditional idea find expression only in the figure of the *talmid hacham?*

2. The traditional ideal operated without external incentives and without a graded course of study, and ended formally without the receipt of some certificate or diploma. The question that now arose was whether this approach should be retained in an achievement-oriented society. Could antipragmatic education be preserved? Is the testing of the achievements of the student and the granting of diplomas unavoidable? Given Israel's pragmatic tendencies, should the yeshiva retain its antipragmatic conception of its role, or should that conception be broadened, particularly with regard to syllabus? Should study in the yeshiva continue to focus exclusively on antipragmatic study of the Talmud and Talmudic commentaries, or should the curriculum expand to include Bible and Jewish philosophy as well as secular studies? Should the changes and diversification of subject matter merely conform to economic pragmatic constraints, or meet the needs and principles of a synthetic curriculum?

The shapers of yeshiva education in Israel also had to decide on their position toward the basic values of the Zionist movement and its institutions, positions regarding the importance of defence, economic productivity, and modern Hebrew for everyday speech. Decisions revolved primarily around whether yeshiva students should segregate themselves and withdraw from the rest of Jewish society in Israel, and disregard their civic duties to state and society, or should they seek integration. This dilemma was expressed practically in attitudes toward compulsory military service, toward productive occupation, and toward political part membership. Moreover, should Yiddish, the everyday language of the Diaspora, remain the language of instruction and speech in the yeshivot, or should Hebrew be adopted?

Social Dilemmas

After the establishment of the state of Israel, the pool of potential candidates for yeshiva study grew considerably. The decline in the religious behavior of the children of religious families in Israel was reduced, fertility rates of these families stabilized at a high level, and large waves of immigration arrived. At the same time, the differences between the potential candidates from the veteran sectors of the Yishuv and those from the immigrant population made the prospective students a heterogeneous group. This intensified the problem of the social composition of the student body in the yeshivot.

In earlier periods, the yeshiva abroad, and particularly the Lithuanian yeshiva, had been highly selective. Its elitist conception was usually unrelated to economic status, the yeshivot demanding only that candidates display intellectual distinction and achievement. Students without sufficient intellectual abilities had to be satisfied with basic studies in Talmud Torah or heder. Now these intellectual demands created pressing problems. Should the yeshivot adhere to an elitist approach, or should they make their admissions criteria more flexible in view of the egalitarian values and conceptions widely accepted in Israeli society in general and in the educational system in particular? Should the yeshivot continue to select candidates of intellectual achievement, or should they accept more or less any candidate? Should the yeshivot invest the bulk of their educational efforts in outstanding students, devoting less attention and resources to the others, or should they treat every student equally? Should the same intellectual criteria for admission be applied to candidates from the Sephardi communities, or should the yeshivot take into account the spiritual leadership crisis of most Sephardi yeshivot in Palestine and in the Diaspora in the past few generations?

Should the yeshiva maintain its traditional goal of homogeneous student body, or should it accept the prevailing social imperative and contribute its share toward social integration? Should separate Ashkenazi and Sephardi yeshivot be maintained, or should ethnic considerations be eliminated when planning new yeshivot?

Dilemmas Related to the Climate of System

The yeshivot in Palestine and the Diaspora had operated within a traditional society where the prevailing system was authoritarian. In this climate, the yeshiva also developed a certain monolithic quality where obedience, insularity, and centralism were manifested in normative guidance and social control of the students. The state of Israel confronted the yeshivot with an acute dilemma, for its declared values were democracy, equality, liberty, pluralism, and openness. Thus, the yeshivot had to decide whether to maintain an authoritarian climate in the interaction between student and teacher, or to allow for more democratic relations. For example: should the head of the yeshiva continue to be an unchallenged authority in all domains, or should the student be allowed to express an opposing personal view? Should the yeshiva introduce greater egalitarianism in the relations between students differing in level of achievement, age, or seniority at the yeshiva? Should the yeshiva students be educated toward total obedience to a specific rabbinic Halachic authority, or should the yeshiva allow a more pluralistic approach?

Should the yeshiva supervise leisure time by dictating to students a particular style of conduct and consumption? For example, should the yeshiva interfere with regard to newspapers and books, listening to radio and watching television, outings, dress, membership in religious youth movement, and relationships with girls? Should the yeshiva forbid or restrict their students' access to representatives or bearers of the values of secular Jewish society? In other words, should the yeshiva be prepared to grant a measure of legitimacy to the pluralistic pattern developing in Israel? Within the system, the yeshiva faced yet another dilemma: Should all institutions operate at a single centralized system in form, framework, and context, or should each be conducted as an administratively and educationally autonomous unit?

These dilemmas, related to the social and value spheres and to the climate of the system, have led to diversification and heterogeneity. Practical responses have encouraged forces within religious society to develop new types of yeshivot, some more traditional and some more innovative.

THE HESDER YESHIVA: A HISTORICAL SETTING

In the 1940s the two youth movements—B'nei Akiva and Noar Ha'Mizrahi—founded institutions for their members, and these developed into the yeshiva high school. It was assumed then that graduates would aspire to further religious education. Indeed, many graduates of the yeshiva high school turned to the Lithuanian yeshivot. These young men had to decide whether to continue their Torah study at the higher yeshiva and not do their compulsory military service, or to report for military service and give up their higher Torah studies.

Upon entering the higher yeshiva, they had to adopt different dress norms and use Yiddish as the language of everyday speech and of study.

The problem of adapting also touched upon ideology and emotions. The attitude in the higher yeshivot was often hostile, estranged, or indifferent toward the new state and the Zionist movement, their institutions, and their values. The graduates of the yeshiva high schools found the values imbibed in the youth movement and the yeshiva high School challenged by the values they now encountered. Graduates and their parents pressed the youth movement and the adult political movement for a solution.

The national leadership of the youth movement understood that one of its main responsibilities was the further education of its members, and in 1954, in cooperation with the adult political movement, the National Religious Party, it set up its first yeshiva. This was followed after the Six-Day War (1967) by the development of a broad network known as the *hesder* yeshivot.

CHARACTERISTICS OF THE HESDER YESHIVA

In contrast to the Lithuanian yeshiva, with its exclusive goal the anti-pragmatic one of educating scholars who study Torah for its own sake, three primary, conspicuously pragmatic goals came to be defined in the hesder yeshiva:

1. Educating young men of Torah and scholars with a positive attitude towards the national renaissance and the state of Israel, in the spirit of religious Zionism;

2. Requiring students to serve in the Israel Defence Forces;

3. Contributing to the settlement of Israel and to its religious character by locating hesder yeshivot in rural, border, or socially deprived areas.

Following this shift in educational orientation, a new image of the yeshiva student developed. This image, sharply different from the traditional elitist image of the scholar, stressed the conception of religious Zionism about "the Land of Israel for the People of Israel in the spirit of the Torah of Israel."

The new value orientation was reflected in the arrangement between the yeshivot, the Ministry of Defence, and the Israel Defence Forces. Its essence is to divide the hesder yeshiva student's time between yeshiva study and military service. This contrasts sharply with other yeshivot where students are exempt form military service as long as they maintain their status as yeshiva students, and they frequently do not serve at all.

This combination of yeshiva study and military service is seen by students and teachers alike to derive from a religious outlook according to which service in Israel's army, just as Torah study for its own sake, is a mitzvah, a religious injunction. Defence of the homeland is a religious imperative in the true sense of the word. Yeshivot notions of the sancity of the Land of Israel, holy war, and other notions are bound up in this outlook with the duty of military service.

Until 1974, *hesder* yeshiva students served within the *Nahal* (Combat Pioneering Youth). A yeshiva Nahal was then established similar to the agricultural Nahal. Yeshiva students did six months' basic training, followed by advanced training in a paratroop unit. Whereas after their advanced training other Nahal soldiers went to work for a period of unpaid service in farm settlements, the yeshiva students resumed their studies for a mandatory 48 months from the date of their recruitment. Some yeshivot required one year's study prior to enlistment, and some 7 months.

The following arrangement went into effect, beginning with the 1986-87 school year:

12 months' study at the yeshiva prior to enlistment
9 months' basic military training
12 months' study at the yeshiva
6 months' advanced military training
21 months' study at the yeshiva

The gradual shift from six months in Nahal paratroop units to 15 months of military training created a demand for yeshiva students in command and officer training courses. Students who signed up for armored corps officers' training extended their military service to 21 months and agreed to lengthen their period of study at the yeshiva by six months.

The yeshiva's unique structural arrangement, the essence of which is the division of time between study and army service, influenced structural aspects of the yeshiva itself. The pool of potential students was restricted to those who support and justify the obligation of military service. Consequently, in all the years of the existence of the *hesder* yeshiva, they had admitted almost exclusively graduates of yeshiva high schools. Following the 1977 coalition agreement, the pool of potential hesder yeshiva students was broadened to include graduates of vocational yeshivot and graduates of the Torah studies section in religious secondary schools, now in the Torah study track.

The yeshiva found it difficult to maintain a strictly stratified authority structure. Because the students acquired strong feelings of personal responsibility when they served in the military, they tended no longer to accept unquestioningly the authority of the head. This led to a situation in which the hesder yeshiva generally tried to accommodate the students' inclinations rather than counter them.

Another reason for the flexibility of relations is apparently the homogeneous social background of students and staff. The students come from youth movements and yeshiva high schools and have internalized democratic and egalitarian concepts and values. Many heads of yeshivot—particularly those who are relatively new in their positions—grew up in a similar social climate.

Shouldering its share of the defense burden and making its contribution towards achieving national goals, the hesder yeshiva forcefully demanded that the state and its institutions share in financing it. Heads of the yeshiva were unwilling to rely exclusively on fund-raising campaigns and other contributions like the traditional yeshivot.

Hesder yeshivot funds come from three major sources:

1. contributions by parents;
2. overseas fund-raising;
3. government aid.

The yeshivot are demanding that the Ministry of Education budget for them as it does for universities. Until recently, the state, through the Ministry of Religious Affairs, financed only about 10 percent of the expenditure of the yeshivot, a share since increased to about 20 percent. The hesder yeshivas are now demanding a considerable increase in this allocation.

The influence of the classic yeshiva on the curriculum and daily schedule of the hesder yeshiva is clear, although the link with the army also influences the program of studies. Anticipating the encounter with secular youth, the heads of the yeshivot have tried to influence the worldview of their students, and so introduced the regular study of Jewish philosophy. Up until now no fixed mode of study or uniform curriculum has been developed. In some yeshivot, study circles and courses in Jewish philosophy are compulsory; at others they are optional. This teaching of the subject clearly distinguishes the hesder yeshiva from the Lithuanian type.

The students of the hesder yeshiva begin Jewish philosophy in many yeshiva high schools either as a matriculation or optional subject. There is considerable similarity in the mode of instruction between the hesder and the Lithuanian yeshivot. The *Va'ad* (Committee) and *ha'vruta* (the practice of two individuals studying as a team) are institutions in the overwhelming majority of the hesder yeshivot, and tests, grades, and diplomas are absent.

The hesder yeshiva, however, is confronted with an acute methodological-educational dilemma: the disolcations that might be caused when an entire class leaves for the army. How can the institution prevent the military atmosphere from invading the religious atmosphere of the yeshiva? How can it limit the impairment of scholastic accomplishment resulting from military service?

A reasonable solution to these problems is essential. Were military service to cut the student off from the religious influences of the yeshiva, and were it not to leave him time for his Torah studies, many would gladly proclaim the impossibility of combining Torah study with the duty of defending the country, and that therefore the hesder yeshivot need not and should not exist. In 1974, following the Yom Kippur War, their students had to be mobilized for very long periods. Although the heads of the yeshivot appreciated the gravity of the situation, they informed the defense establishment of their worry lest the yeshivot, by going beyond a "red line" in this regard, be deprived of their legitimacy. How did the yeshivot handle this problem?

Unlike the traditional yeshivot, students in the hesder yeshivot are not organized in multiage groups on the basis of scholastic achievements. The study group is composed instead of individuals who will enter the army together, so students of more or less the same age study together.

The hesder yeshiva stresses the method of studying the literal meaning of the Talmudic text and subjects components of the Talmudic problem to logical analysis. The hesder yeshiva, similarly to Sephardic yeshivot, de-emphasized Talmudic casuistry (*pilpul*) and focused instead on the early rabbinic jurists (*poskim*). This has deepened the familiarity of the students with the Talmudic text, in spite of the limited time available to them.

The major achievement of the hesder yeshiva has been shaping the outlook of the students. On this score the head of one hesder yeshiva said:

> The period which the young men devote to military service is not what counts. What is important is that they are young men who are at peace with themselves.... Leaving the yeshiva for periods of military duty does not mean leaving it psychologically. The young man has a deep feeling that he is performing mitzvot, that

he is doing what is required of him for the security of the people and the country. It is hard to believe with what fervor the boys reintegrate into the yeshiva even after a lengthy period of service in the army...

A sense of mission and a high level of motivation are cultivated during military service. The heads of the yeshiva and the teachers visit their students, with the consent of the military authorities, and boost their spirits with a Talmud lesson or a friendly conversation. The students themselves, aware of the danger of drifting away, sometimes set aside moments for Torah study. When the students return from military service to the yeshiva, they have no sense of estrangement and, as a rule, resume their studies enthusiastically.

These students are socially distinctive. Their joint studies at the yeshiva high school, membership in the religious youth movement, and the army service together all intensify social cohesion and influence the climate of the yeshiva. This climate is reflected in conduct considered acceptable. For instance, there is no strict supervision of the student's leisure, and he can freely pursue hobbies and cultivate his own tastes. Many students spend vacations together, on trips and outings, and many act as senior escorts at camps, seminars, and excursions of the religious youth movement. Relationships with girls are not rigidly supervised or prohibited: corresponding with and dating a girl friend is quite acceptable. There is thus no need for the marriage broker, an institution that these students regard as old-fashioned and unnecessary. They tend to dress simply and to speak a slangy, sabra Hebrew.

These details reflect the social impact of military service and, perhaps even more, the extent to which the values and norms of the youth movement have been internalized. The hesder students stand out among all yeshiva students in Israel as a group with very distinct social characteristics in terms of both their ideological positions and their behavior.

The hesder yeshiva leaves its imprint on its students even after they leave it. The students' direct contact during his stay at the yeshiva with the social and security problems of border villages and of settlements in the occupied areas, or with the social problems of disadvantaged communities, heightens his inclination to become socially and politically involved with Israel society. Military service together with nonreligious soldiers promotes an openness and sense of responsibility towards the nonobservant too. Refraining from sectarian isolation is part and parcel of the sense of social and religious mission that the yeshiva fosters. The hesder yeshiva's imprint has also been evident in the occupational patterns of some students. A considerable number turn to education in development towns and in border areas. Others find their place in settlements, mostly in those set up by the Gush Emunim movement. Recently, graduates have also begun to take up rabbinical positions. A number of graduates are already on the teaching staff of the hesder yeshivot and are fanning the spirit of change. The majority, however, are entering the academic professions.

We shall now examine the responses of the hesder yeshiva to some of the major dilemmas that have confronted all yeshivot since the establishment of the state. In many substantive respects their pattern is still being shaped.

Even at this stage, however, trends and processes that represent full or partial responses can be discerned.

THE HESDER YESHIVA: RESPONSES TO MAJOR DILEMMAS

Value Dilemmas

1. The hesder yeshiva, like the other yeshivot, holds to the traditional ideal of Torah study for its own sake, but with at least two innovations. The ideal does not have exclusive status, and it must combine with other, essentially pragmatic conceptions. The ideal is embodied in the scholar who combines the book and the sword, rather than in the traditional figure whose world is totally circumscribed by Torah study.

2. Some institutions are still hesitant about broadening the curriculum to include additional religious studies. While a considerable portion of the yeshiva students study Jewish philosophy, it has not been institutionalized nor made compulsory, suggesting profound doubts about its legitimacy.

3. The yeshivot are also reluctant to grant full legitimacy to the strikingly new conceptions they represent. The heads of yeshiva and senior teachers advocate the combination of yeshiva studies and military service as a matter of principle. However, some regard the pattern as an unavoidable necessity and would prefer to see their students in an ordinary yeshiva. This hesitant attitude and the doubts about the sources of the legitimacy are apparently the reason that until recently the hesder institutions have not formulated an unambiguous educational philosophy.

4. The relationship of these yeshivot, in principle and practice, to the basic values of the Zionist movement and its institutions has been fully resolved. The rift between the world of Torah and the values of Zionism, which characterized the traditional yeshivot in Israel for a long time, has almost entirely disappeared in the hesder yeshivot. Here the students are educated towards positive identification and integration with Israeli society. This shows in their basic outlook and attitudes toward Zionism in general and religious Zionism in particular, and in their conduct during military service, particularly in the extent to which they volunteer for combat units and serve as officers. This basic stance is also reflected in the fact that studies at the yeshiva are conducted in Hebrew and not in Yiddish. This position of principle, which essentially is identification of hesder yeshiva students with representatives of Israel secular society and its political and Zionist institutions, seems to stem from two factors. First, the yeshiva educates toward a positive attitude toward Israeli society as a whole. This, of course, rests on earlier education in the yeshiva high school, in the religious youth movement, and in the home. Secondly, many secular people have a positive attitude toward *hesder* yeshiva students, which grew stronger following reports about tehir combat performance in the Six-Day War, the Yom Kippur War, and the Lebanese War. This attitude has enhanced students' self-confidence and self-image and has reinforced their sense of solidarity with other segments of the population.

Social Dilemmas

The hesder yeshivot, like the traditional yeshivot, have been characterized by elitist conceptions. Candidates for admission as well as veteran students met very strict intellectual requirements. However, these new yeshivot did not emphasize the cultivation of the *ilui* (boy wonder) as did the Lithuanian yeshivot. As the number of hesder yeshivot grew, admission requirements were relaxed. In 1967 there were two such yeshivot. In 1968, there were five; and at the end of 1985, there were fourteen. Heads of the yeshivot had to consider supply and demand. In the 1970s and 1980s the yeshiva high schools produced about 900 to 1,000 graduates each year. To meet the demand of this large population, the heads of the yeshivot had to lower their admission requirments. As a consequence of muting the elitist policy, more Sephardi students have been admitted. This has generally not been accompanied by interethnic tensions. The hesder yeshiva is not guided by ethnic considerations, and no new yeshiva has been opened to serve students of a particular ethnic group. Nevertheless, the rate of admission of students from Sephardi backgrounds is still lower than their percentage within the population of yeshiva high school graduates. This might be because many Sephardi youths seeking social advancement perceive regular service in combat units to be a better expression of social status and potential for social advancement than service within the hesder yeshiva.

Dilemmas Related to the Climate of the System:

1. The egalitarian tenor of social relations is manifested in the attitude of the students towards the heads of the yeshiva and the senior teachers, as well as in the relations among the students themselves. Involvement of the heads of the yeshiva in supervision of the leisure time is minimal.

2. The climate of the system encourages the granting of legitimation to the pluralistic pattern gradually emerging in Israeli society. This refers to the encounter with secular Jewish society and to the subjection of all students to one central rabbinical-halachic authority.

3. The climate of the system encourages the institutions to shape autonomous educational frameworks.

The Dilemma of Legitimation

The hesder yeshiva had in 30 years become an autonomous, unique yeshiva pattern, but it has not as yet received unequivocal legitimation. Legitimation of the existence of the hesder yeshivot has been gaining ground in secular circles. In traditional religious society and in the circles of the traditional yeshivot, by contrast, there is latent opposition challenging the justification of the hesder yeshiva to be considered a yeshiva at all. The ultra-Orthodox circles neither helped in its creation nor are they prepared to welcome it today. Initially they feared that the arrangement with the army would become binding for students at other yeshivot. Once they realized that the army had no intention of imposing such an arrangement on them, however, these circles refrained from waging open battle against the new type of yeshiva. They merely created a social climate among their own students conducive to the view that: "the studets of the hesder are to be regarded as soldiers studying Torah and not as yeshiva students who serve in the army, and we have no objection to a soldier studying Torah."

The general feeling within modern religious circles about the hesder yeshiva is one of satisfaction, and members of this community regard it with full legitimacy. Most of this religious public sees the students as tough fighters. Moreover, the parents of these students contribute heavily to their sons' studies, a practice less frequently encountered in traditional yeshivot. The students of the hesder yeshivot have high social status within the modern religious community, as is attested to, inter alia, by their rating as potential marriage partners.

The political leadership of this public considers the combination of Torah and military service an extension of the tradition of *Torah v'Avoda* (Torah and Labor), and hence has given it full legitimation. The National Religious Party has, through the government and the Israeli parliament, given full support to the hesder yeshivot.

CONCLUSION

In traditional society the main role of the educational institution was to perpetuate the existing society and to transmit its values. In modern society there are two types of educational institutions. The main role of the first is the perpetuation and preservation of the existing society, and the second is to promote social change. Yeshivot, the oldest institutions of higher Jewish education, had as their primary social role in the course of many generations, the preservation of the structure and the values of traditional Jewish society. Even yeshivot such as the Lithuanian, which emerged in modern times and seemed to be the main reference group of Jewish society throughout the nineteenth century, served in many respects as agents of preservation.

In this chapter the unique characteristics of a new Israeli type, the hesder yeshiva, were presented. This type is characterized by pragmatism, democracy, and social cohesion and has become, in fact, an agent of socialization. Its role is mainly the social change of contemporary, modern religious society. Likewise there is no doubt that elite groups—persons of comprehensive education, religious and secular, and of collective and individual self respect—like the hesder yeshiva graduates, are gaining influence outside modern religious circles: their involvement in the *Gush Emunim* movement is not the only model of general activity and influence. These institutions have absorbed many graduates into their own staff. They have increased their number of Sephardi students. The social control of the religious Zionist public over the activities within the institutions has deepened. All this might stimulate the continuation and the completion of the social change processes initiated in the hesder yeshivot, and might also strengthen the status of these yeshivot as the central socialization agents of modern religious society in Israel.

The first religious army boarding school, the religious kibbutz yeshiva, the yeshiva within the religious university, and the female yeshiva-style college all provide significant evidence of the continuation of these social change processes and their effect on modern religious society in Israel.

REFERENCES

Aviad, J. 1980. From protest to return: Comtemporary tshuva. *The Jerusalem Quarterly* 16. 71–82.

Bar-Lev, M., ed. 1986. *Religious education in Israeli society* (Hebrew). Jerusalem: The Hebrew University of Jerusalem.

Bar-Lev, M. Values: "Israeli yeshivot 1948–1984," "Religious state education," "Independent education and different frameworks for religious education." In *The Hebrew Encyclopedia—Israel 1948–1984*, vol. 2, Tel Aviv: Sifriat Poalim, in press (Hebrew).

Berger, P. L. 1967. *The sacred canopy: Elements of a sociological theory of religions.* New York: Doubleday Anchor Books.

Bernstein, F. 1987. The socialization of girls in an ultra-Orthodox institution." In *Residential settings and the community: Congruence and conflict.,* eds. Y. Kashti and Arieli. London: Freund.

Brubacher, J. S. 1947. *A history of the problems of education.* New York: McGraw Hill.

Cox, E. 1966. *Changing aims in religious education,* London: Routledge and Kegan Paul.

Enoch, H. Z. 1981. *Studies in education and instruction* (Hebrew). Jerusalem: Jewish Agency.

Friedman, M. 1977. *Hevra Vedat.* Jerusalem: Yizchak Ben-Zvi Memorial 4–5 (Heb.).

Hull, J. 1982. *New directions in religious education.* London: Palmer.

Hull, J. 1984a. *Studies in religion and education.* London: Palmer.

Hull, J. 1984b. Nature of religious education. In *A Dictionary of religious education,* ed. J. M. Sutcliffe. London: SCM.

Karlbach, S. 1964. *Our way in education.* (Hebrew) B'nei Brak. Or Habalin

Kill, Y. 1977. *Religious state education—Its roots, history and problems.* Jerusalem: Israel Ministry of Education and Culture.

Langerman, S., ed. 1986. *Research in religious education in Israel.* (Hebrew). Jerusalem: Henrietta Szold Institute.

Liebman, C. S., and E. Don-Yehiya. 1984. *Religion and Politics in Israel.* Bloomington: Indiana University Press. 3-8.

Schneller, R. 1980. Continuity and change in ultra-Orthodox education. *The Jewish Journal of Sociology* 22:35-46.

Shaffir, W. 1983. The recruitment of baalei tshuva in a Jerusalem yeshiva. *The Jewish Journal of Sociology* 25(I). 33-46.

Smart, N. 1968. *Secular education and the logic of religion.* London: Faber & Faber.

Part II

Dissent and Religious Alternatives

—————————————— 5 ——

The Identity Dilemma of Non-Orthodox Religious Movements:
Reform and Conservative Judaism in Israel

EPHRAIM TABORY

Religious movements must develop plausibility structures that are responsive to the needs of the target population if they are to remain viable organizations in a pluralistic society (Berger 1967). This chapter analyzes the manner in which liberal religious movements that developed and flourished in a pluralistic environment cope and respond when they establish new branches in a society in which their original forms and structures are seen to be discordant with mainstream religion. The case analyzed deals with the manner in which the organizational movements of Conservative and Reform Judaism in Israel respond when they encounter apathy on the part of the general population and, in addition, are depicted as deviant and as "inauthentic" forms of religion by the dominant Orthodox Jewish establishment. The central focus is on the efforts of the movements to clarify their religious identity when they encounter, in effect, a hostile environment, and the dilemmas that emerge from their reaction to the pressures of the external environment.[1]

The thesis of this analysis is that the problem of identity for reli-

*The analysis presented herein is based on interviews with national and local leaders in the Reform and Conservative movements in Israel conducted on a regular basis from 1978 to the present. I would like to acknowledge the financial support of the Memorial Foundation for Jewish Culture and the National Institute for Mental Health, United States Public Health Service, during the course of this study.

gious organizations is analogous to that of the individual. It is necessary for organizations, as for individuals, to formulate a concrete identity in order to regulate and regularize interaction with others. A clear and focused identity is also important for the way individuals, and organizations, relate to their internal needs and for the establishment of a concrete sense of self.

The group identity of an organization relates to its cultural orientation, that is, its shared patterns of thoughts, beliefs, feelings, and values. Without some degree of shared culture, there is no group but only an aggregate of people. The shared, consensually validated, set of definitions that comprises the group culture and that is passed on as the correct way to define the situation can be grouped into an external and internal set of issues. External issues relate to the manner in which the leaders and members define then determine how to survive in the environment. The internal issues relate to the definition of how to organize relationships among members of the group to permit survival in the specific environment through effective performance and the creation of internal comfort (Schein 1985).

The problems of external adaptation, according to Schein (1985), relate to the definition of the core mission and strategy of the organization, the specification of the goals that derive from the mission, the development of consensus regarding the means to achieve the goals, and agreement on how to measure the group's performance and how to correct faults that might emerge. The internal-external distinction generally corresponds to Mintzberg's (1983) focus on the publics that the organization must consider in its power game.

There are similarities between personal identity and between the collective identity of a group or organization. Personal identity is "a typified self at a stage in the life course situated in a context of organized social relationships" (Weigert, Teitge, and Teitge 1986). Individuals have more than one facet to their identity, and multiple identities are communicated through displays of appearances, behavior, and language.

While classical symbolic interactionist theory emphasizes the interactive process in the mirror theory of identity, it focuses specifically on the identity that results from the reflected image. McCall and Simmons (1978) elaborate on this by pointing out that identities are also affected by counter-role models. These models serve as a backdrop or framework against which identity is defined and demarcated. The perception of who one is is affected by the cognitive orientation as to who one is not. This is more than a complementary role model. The counter-role of a teacher is not only a pupil, for example, but also peers who are not teachers, and even teachers in other types of shcool systems.

The case of Reform and Conservative Judaism illustrates how religious leaders who focus on external factors in analyzing the success or failure of the group they head can get caught up in a dilemma relating to their identity. Their focus on an external explanation for their limited success leads them to adopt an identity that is based on the counter-role of Orthodox Judaism. Reacting to the charges of Orthodox Judaism against their own legitimacy deflects from their primary goal—presenting themselves as an alternative for the non-religiously identified public. By focusing on the external environment in their power game, leaders are also jeopardizing the loyalty of those members who are only interested in the internal needs of the movements and the personal satisfaction that they might obtain from their membership.

THE REFORMATION OF JUDAISM BY THE REFORM AND CONSERVATIVE MOVEMENTS

The development of the Reform movement involved a radical redefinition of the nature of Judaism as a religious collective (Philipson 1967). Jewish communities in Western societies, prior to the Emancipation, were politically isolated from the larger social environment, the Jews constituted not just a religious entity, but a supranational peoplehood. Jews in all counties were united by a religious system that emphasized responsibility for the deeds of others and a common allegiance to the redemption of Zion as a territorial and spiritual entity. Some Jews felt that the nationalistic and peoplehood components of Judaism might support the charge that they owed political allegiance to an entity other than their countries of residence and serve as justification for denying them citizenship. By limiting the scope of Judaism to ritual, the Reform Judaism that started in Germany in the nineteenth century enabled its members to be accepted as equal citizens with non-Jews, and yet to retain a Jewish identity.

Reform Judaism was totally rejected by the adherents of Orthodox Judaism, who saw it as a complete abrogation of Jewish law (*halakah*). Halakah represents an internal legal culture characterized by its complete enclosure, and insularity to change, on a conscious level (Friedman 1975). Change in sacred law systems, such as Orthodox Judaism, takes place primarily through slow reinterpretation, or through legal fiction. Reform Judaism did not seek to introduce changes through religious reasoning. It rather sought to abolish the system by saying that it was no longer binding. This orientation undermined the legitimacy of halakah and Orthodox Judaism.

The Conservative movement in Judaism developed as a reaction to what some saw as the excesses of Reform, on the one hand, and the intransigence of the Orthodox, on the other. In contrast with the Reform movement, the positive-historical school, developed by Zecharia Frankel, believed that Jewish law is binding, although subject to change. In contrast with the Orthodox movement, it believed that the conscious development of Jewish law is acceptable and to be encouraged. This school became formally known as Conservative Judaism when it was brought to the United States in the latter part of the nineteenth century (Waxman 1958; Davis 1963; Sklare 1972).

If Reform Judaism was the movement of Europe, and of German immigrants to the United States, Conservative Judaism thrived in an environment that was more tolerant of religious diversity and less sensitive to charges of dual loyalty. The success of both movements can be attributed to the degree to which they developed plausibility structures that allowed Jews to have greater contact and intercourse with non-Jews who were willing to interact with them in the nineteenth and twentieth centuries. Statistically, Orthodox Judaism has become the minority denomination (Lazerwitz 1979), although it is the denomination that attracts "returnees" to Judaism (Danzger, forthcoming) and ideologically views itself as the only authentic and legitimate form of Jewish life (Feinstein 1985; Grunblatt, 1986).

THE REACTION TO THE MOVEMENT IN ISRAEL

One way of judging the reaction to the movements in Israel is by looking at the number of congregations they have established and their rate of growth. While Reform and Conservative Judaism had an institutional presence in Israel before statehood (1948), their modern history in that country dates to the 1950s and 1960s. Early members came from Europe. The number of Conservative congregations grew at a more rapid pace in the late 1960s, with an increase in migration from English-speaking countries, but its development in the late 1970s and 1980s has been fairly static. The congregational growth of the Reform movements has virtually ceased since the late 1960s.

The Reform movement, in 1987, has about 15 congregations that meet fairly regularly on weekends, and there are about 30 Conservative congregations that hold regular Sabbath services. A survey of the movements in 1979 found that the average age of the members was 59 years in the Reform movement and 53 years in the Conservative movement (Tabory 1988). According to the vice president of the Reform movement, the average age in 1987 is older, inasmuch as gogues are not attracting new young members. The Conservative congregations seem to be somewhat more successful in this regard. They are attracting more immigrants, mainly from English-speaking countries, as well as some native Israelis who are either married to Conservative Jews or who learned about the movement when they spent time abroad.

There are between 3,000 and a maximum of 5,000 families in the 45 Reform and Conservative congregations, and these account for less than one-half of one percent of Israel's Jewish population. It is not that the general population wants to affiliate actively with Orthodox Judaism. While there are an estimated 7,000 Orthodox synagogues in Israel (Don-Yehiya 1975) only about 15 to 20 percent of Israel's Jews are Orthodox. The feeling of many nonreligious Israeli Jews appears to be that while they do not wish to attend synagogue services, it is an Orthodox service that they wish to refrain from attending. Reform and Conservative synagogues are not a salient part of their frame of reference. As Liebman and Don-Yehiya (1984) argue, most nonreligious Jews in Israel do have a positive orientation toward Jewish tradition; they simply draw the line at observing the religious commandments. Many Israelis, especially Sepharadim, or Jews from an Oriental background, accept Orthodox assumptions about the nature and requirements of Judaism, and issues of religious conscience do not arouse Israelis (Liebman and Don-Yehiya 1984).

Mintzberg (1983) notes that the compatibility of social movements and organizations with the system of social norms and ethics operating in society can have an impact on their success. Reform and Conservative leaders argue that their movements are in harmony with the religious norms of native Israelis. Indeed, they argue that most non-Orthodox Jews in Israel are de facto Reform or Conservative Jews, as far as religious practice goes. This claim is based on the fact that the majority of non-Orthodox Israelis do observe some Jewish religious practices (Ben Meir and Kedem 1979). The practices that are observed are the same ones that Reform, and especially Conservative Jews, follow. Given this situation, the fact that persons who should or who might find the movement useful, nevertheless do not join, is particularly challenging because such individuals indicate the relative weakness of the association by symbolizing the apparent dubiousness of its values and its services (Merton 1976).

Movement leaders are concerned about the discrepancy between the norms and shared symbols that relate Judaism and Israeli society and that appear to be discordant with the way that Reform and Conservative Judaism is portrayed in Israel. As Liebman and

Don-Yehiya (1984) argue, state and nationality cannot be separated in Judaism, and the very definition of Israel as a Jewish state means a preferred status for the Jewish religion. Jewish and Israeli identities seem to be intertwined for many Israelis (Herman 1971, but see Segre 1980 for his analysis of how Israel faces the challenge of traditionalism without losing the benefits of its acquired Westernization). In a national study of Israeli university students Bar-Lev et al. (1981) found that 87 percent of the respondents say that they identify with the Jewish people. The biblical concept of a "nation that dwelleth alone," and the words of a popular song, sung to an incongruent jolly tune, that "the whole world is against us," fit in with the popular perception of Orthodox Judaism as being the spirit around which the unity of the Jewish people has been maintained in the past. This is the spirit that characterizes Israel as well, surrounded, as it is, by enemies on all sides. By comparison, the Reform and Conservative movements appear to be legitimizing assimilation inasmuch as they allow their adherents to mingle more easily in the secular world. This picture is encouraged by Orthodox leaders who deny legitimacy to these denominations and often refuse to use the Hebrew term (*rav*) for "rabbi" when referring to their clergy. They prefer, instead, the English term ("rabbi"), in quotes, to indicate that they are not real rabbis and that they are foreign. The Orthodox do not portray Reform and Conservative Judaism as mere errant interpretations of Judaism. They are not perceived to be religious movement at all, but rather "counterfeit" (Rosen 1987). A former state chief rabbi (Goren 1987) has gone so far as to claim that Judaism and Christianity have more in common with one another than with the Reform movement. Particular care is taken to differentiate between nonobservant Jews and the movements that represent non-Orthodox Judaism. The non-Orthodox movements are presented as antireligious movements that undermine Jewish identity, not just alternate religious movements (see Plate 1).

Formal constraints also limit the ability of organizations to function in their environment (Mintzberg 1983). The Orthodox political and rabbinic establishments in Israel have constantly sought to obstruct the development and expansion of the Reform and Conservative movements in a variety of spheres (Abramov 1976). Public institutions have been threatened with the cancellation of the certificates testifying to the kosher (observing dietary laws) status of their restaurants if they were to agree to allow non-Orthodox services to be held on their premises. One Reform congregation was told by a municipality that it could not build a synagogue in a residential area because it would disturb the neighbors. The complaint was later changed to the fear that the synagogue would disturb passersby when it was

ב"ה

באזני צירי הועידה
של התנועה הרפורמית!

היהדות הנאמנה אינה לוחמת
ביהודים שאינם שומרי תורה,
אך תילחם עד חרמה
בכל מי שרוצה להפוך

(כמו, למשל, התנועה הרפורמית)

את האנטי-דח - לדת!

לא נסבול כל פגיעה

בזהותו המקורית

של עם ישראל!

הועד למען שלמות העם
רח ציון-על-כה 20, ת"א טל. 282098

Plate 1 Handbill distributed at the 1980 Reform movement convention in Jerusalem. For the Ears of the Delegates of the Reform movement convention! Loyal Judaism does not fight Jews who do not observe the Torah, but it will fight to the death all those who want to turn (as does, for example, the Reform movement) ANTI RELIGION TO RELIGION! We will not tolerate any infringement on the original identity of the People of Israel!

pointed out that the building site was in a recreation area. Another congregation was refused use of the local school building because Reform services there might lead to a disturbance of the public order, inasmuch as Orthodox Jews would demonstrate against them. The irony is that attempts to prevent Jews from building a synagogue abroad would be attacked in Israel as a mainfestation of anti-Semitism (see Plate 2).

Plate 2 Source: *The Jerusalem Post*, March 7, 1977.

At times more specific and focused campaigns have been carried out against Reform and Conservative activities. For example, the Jerusalem rabbinate annually publishes a newspaper advertisement warning that one who attends High Holiday services in a Conservative or Reform synagogue will not fulfill the religious requirement of hearing the blowing of the ram's horn (see Plates 3 and 4). A political campaign, replete with derogatory wall posters, has been waged against Conservative parents who sought to introduce a non-Orthodox religious syllabus into their children's schools.

הרבנות הראשית לירושלים והמחוז

THE CHIEF RABBINATE OF JERUSALEM DISTRICT

המועצה הדתית ירושלים

HALACHIC RULING

Many people have asked us the question: Is it permitted to participate in the High Holyday services arranged by the Movement of M'sorati Judaism ("Conservative"), which have been advertised in the Press. We wish to express our opinion — halachic ruling — (as we did in the press on the eve of Rosh Hashana, last year) that the Holy Tora forbids participation in these "prayers," and that one cannot fulfil one's obligations to pray by going to a Conservative congregation, either on the High Holydays or during the year.

In the same way, one cannot fulfil one's obligation to hear the blowing of the shofar, at the "prayer" houses of the Conservative Movement.

We therefore issue this only appeal to the public not to be tempted by the propaganda of this movement, not to participate in any of their activities and not to associate with them. Everyone can find a place at a synagogue where the form of prayers is the form used from generation to generation; there he may devote himself to the Creator of the world, and pour out his heart to Him who examines the hearts of all.

And may the Almighty bless us, hear our prayers, give us salvation, and with compassion and favour accept our prayers and grant the blessing of peace on all Israel and on Jerusalem,.

May you be signed and sealed for a good year.
May it be a year of redemption for us and all the House of Israel.

Shalom Mashash   Chief Rabbis of Jerusalem   Yaacov Bezalel Zolti

Plate 3 Source: *The Jerusalem Post*, September 5, 1980

Perhaps the most problematic issue for the Reform and Conservative denominations in Israel is the lack of state recognition for their rabbis. They may not conduct weddings or divorce proceedings. One of the perennial issues in Israel is the question of the legal definition of who is a Jew for registration purposes on state forms and identification papers. The question is whether a civil or religious definition should prevail. As Samet (1985, 1986) notes, however, the real question is who is a rabbi, inasmuch as it is the validity of conversions conducted by Reform and Conservative rabbis that are specifically called into question.

Dry Bones

Plate 4 Source: *The Jerusalem Post*, September 19, 1978

The latter point raises the question of who is most affected by the problems that the movements face in Israel. It appears that the national leaders, and especially the rabbis, are most sensitive to the external environment, while the members at large are much more interested in matters affecting their local congregations. The lack of official recognition for the movements and the rabbis affects the clergy first and foremost.

The movements serve an important religious function for many members, a moral and spiritual function for others, and perhaps even an ethnic function for some, permitting them to associate with other immigrants in a setting that might seem to them to be more legitimate (religious groups) than a purely "immigrant" organization (Tabory and Lazerwitz 1983). Only the exceptional, ideologically motivated individual member, cares more about the success of the national organization than the effectiveness of his or her local congregation. The question of the national success of the movements is less important for these persons. Many of the national leaders complained, in their interviews, that their members do not really recognize a movement but rather see themselves as belonging to a congregation that is, at best, part of a federation of synagogues. The inability of the rabbis to function as such with regard to extra-congregational issues constantly reminds them of the limits of the external environment.

The significance of this point is that the goals of the movements are determined by the national leaders. The policies that they formulate have led to institutional dilemmas in the long run because as they are out of line with the internal needs of the members.

THE ADAPTATION OF THE MOVEMENTS

How has the leadership of the movements, then, adjusted to the hostile environment that they have encountered in Israel? The two primary activities that each of the movements has undertaken relate to their external environment. They attempt to identify just who they are and what they stand for, and to fight the restrictive actions of the Orthodox rabbinate and political institutions.

Attempts at Identification

Each of the movements has argued that the non-Orthodox population in Israel is its natural audience. Religiosity in Israel is denoted by use of the terms *dati* (religious, which corresponds to Orthodox Judaism), *mesorti* (traditional) and *lo dati* (nonreligious). The Conservative movement in Israel has changed its name to the "Movement of Traditional Judaism" with the specific intention of signifying that it is a suitable and appropriate movement for traditional, but non-Orthodox Jews. An additional reason for changing the name of the movement from the Movement of Conservative Judaism was to indicate to the Israeli public that their movement was different and independent of the parent movement abroad. In this way it would be able to counter the claims that it was merely an imported movement and a continuation of a movement that was oriented to assimilation.

Fear of the charges that the movement was an imported entity also led many congregations to prefer an Orthodox prayer book for their services rather than the American Conservative prayer book. The main drawback of the American prayer book was that it included an English translation. It was felt that the use of such a prayer book would support the claim that only immigrants were worshippers in and members of the Conservative congregations.

The Reform movement in the early 1980s was much more

attached to its American counterpart than was the Conservative movement. The Conservatives could symbolically break off from the Americans because they received only limited financial support from them. The Reform movement received, and still receives, much more support from its American counterpart. However, the movement was particularly sensitive to the charge that it was just an "Orthodox minus" movement, meaning that its main feature was the permission granted to members to refain from performing all the rituals required by Orthodox Judaism. Leaders felt that it was necessary to concentrate on issuing a platform that would state the goals and aims of the movement in Israel. In sessions that lasted from 1978 to 1983 it sought to formulate what its director called "a positive calling card," that would state what they are and not what they are not.

Efforts were also undertaken by the Israeli movement to issue an Israeli prayer book that the leading rabbi of the Reform movement hoped would be "fat, like the Orthodox prayerbooks, and not a thin one, like the Reform prayer books in the United States."

An additional endeavor undertaken by the Reform movement was the establishment of several kibbutz settlements in Israel. The initial impetus for this on the leadership level was to counteract the claim that the Reform movement is non-Zionist and that it is a foreign, imported entity alien to Israeli Jewish life. The kibbutz enabled the movement to claim in a brochure publicizing the first kibbutz that "Reform Judaism in Israel is rooted in the land" (Tabory 1985).

The Conservative movement has attempted to make its stand in Israel more clear in a series of publications that it prepared in the middle 1980s (Hammer n.d.; Golinkin n.d.; Pearl n.d.), but in general, Conservative leaders in Israel feel less pressure to issue a formal platform because they perceive themselves to be more successful than the Reform movement in Israel. They have established more congregations than have the Reform and attracted a younger public, notwithstanding the fact that the majority of the members are immigrants.

Efforts to Gain Recognition

Movement leaders realize that they have still not succeeded in attracting large numbers of native Israelis despite the formal preparation of a platform in the Reform movement and brochures clarifying that Conservative Judaism is about. Their limited success has been attributed, by some leaders, to the success of the Orthodox establishment in labeling them as inauthentic and illegitimate movements. As a result, the movements have undertaken activities to challenge the Orthodox rabbinate directly in recent years.

This is not the only reason for the decision to meet the Orthodox establishment head on. The latter does appear to have become more extreme in its criticism and intolerance of non-Orthodox denominations. Efforts were exerted in the 1980s by the ultra-Orthodox religious parties in Israel's parliament to alter the law regarding the definition of who is a Jew and to make it explicitly clear that Reform and Conservative conversions are not recognized by Israel. This affects not only Jews in Israel, but seriously undermines the legitimacy of non-Orthodox Judaism everywhere. Indeed, this was perhaps the primary reason why the Orthodox brought up the issue in Israel (Samet 1986).

Despite the implications for Reform and Conservative Judaism outside of Israel, it is the Israeli leaders who have undertaken greater efforts to seek recognition. The Reform and Conservative movements have held public demonstrations for their rights in front of the Israeli parliament. They have also joined forces and formed an umbrella organization with other organizations in a Council for Freedom of Science, Religion and Culture whose purpose is to fight against discriminatory legislation and to argue for tolerance of religious pluralism.

Not all Conservative leaders are happy about fighting the Orthodox establishment, and especially about cooperating with the Reform movement. These persons seek to distance themselves from the Reform as much as they can because they also view the Reform as a movement that is not based on halakah, and that is therefore an illegitimate religious movement. From a pragmatic viewpoint, these persons also hope that the Orthodox establishment will eventually recognize their own movement. Cooperation with the Reform would undermine such a possibility.

The Reform movement is aware of the hesitation of the Conservative movement. Having little hope of peaceful accommodation with the Orthodox, the Reform movement has been particularly active in fighting the Orthodox establishment. It has submitted a legal brief against the government for the right of their clergy to function as rabbis with regard to state sanctioned activities. (The case has been pending before the Supreme Court, sitting as the High Court of Justice, since 1983).

There are additional reasons for the more militant stance of the Reform. In its efforts to create a more "Israeli" movement, it has encouraged native-born Israelis to enter the Reform rabbinical program. The first graduates are assuming positions of national leadership in their movement. These persons are more willing than many immigrants to challenge the Israeli religious establishment in the courts, and thus play the game according to Israeli rules. A debate in 1987 between the American-born director of the Conservative movement and an Israeli-born advisor to the (non-Orthodox) foreign minister and former prime minister serves as an example. The advisor recommended that the movement seek recognition and legitimization "in the legal system, according to the rules by which the game of politics is played in Israel."The Conservative leader was livid with rage because, as he insisted, "Conservative Judaism is not politics. Israel needs Conservative Judaism as a religion, and it has to adjust to it if it wishes to remain a Jewish state at all. The problem is not the future of Conservative Judaism but the future of Israel."

An additional reason for the more militant attitude of the Reform is that they are aware that their movement is particularly unsuccessful in attracting young Israelis, even relative to the Conservative movement. One of their responses has been to ask whether their movement in Israel should forego the synagogue as a center of religious life in Israel and, instead, try to attract new followers through a youth movement. At the same time, they have sought to attribute much of the blame for the lack of interest in their movement to the actions of the Orthodox establishment.

DISCUSSION

The Reform and Conservative movements in Israel have expended much energy in reacting to their social environment. In their formative years, Reform and Conservative Judaism were positive options for those persons who wished to retain a Jewish ethnic identity, while loosening the bonds of ritual that had limited the possibility of greater participation in the non-Jewish world. The counter-role of the Reform and Conservative Jew was the totally assimilated Jew, no less than the Orthodox Jew. This discussion will focus on the implications of the movements' actions in Israel with regard to their counter-roles, given the fact that almost by definition there can be no assimilated Jew in Israel.

Gamson and Modigliani (1987) argue that changes in the careers of policy issues can depend on their sponsorship and how they resonate with larger cultural themes. The focus of the religious problem in Israel relates to freedom *from* religion: not freedom *of* religion (Rubinstein 1967), or on how one relates to a non-Jewish majority, as is the case in Diaspora. The concern about Jewish survival in a non-Jewish society, on the public agenda in such countries as the United States (Cohen and Fein 1985), is irrelevant in Israel. The resource mobilization perspective of social problems (McCarthy and Zald 1977) suggests that groups that focus on issues congruent witht he priorities of established institutions are likely to obtain support from outside sources in producing a social problem. The cultural package regarding religion that resonates as a social problem in Israel is religious coercion, not the quest for more religious involvement.

In focusing on the Orthodox establishment as a primary explanation for the lack of success of the movements in Israel, Reform and Conservative leaders have won support among others who argue against the religious monopoly held by the Orthodox. Secular Jews have thus joined Reform and Conservative leaders in viewing Orthodox Judaism as their counter role. The problem that the Conservative and Reform movements face in Israel is that the secular Israeli might identify and sympathize with those movements only because they share similar counter-roles as opponents and not because they are interested in more Jewish involvement. The dilemma for the movements is that the admiration expressed for them might be based on their being perceived as *antireligious* organizations. This is most clearly seen in parliamentary debates and newspaper editorials when support for the rights of the Reform and Conservative movements is related to the negative practices of Orthodox Judaism, rather than to the needs of a modern society for alternative and more suitable religious expressions. The Citizen's Rights party, for example, supports the Reform and Conservative movements as part of a larger civil rights package.

In fact, though, the movements are not antireligious but only anti-Orthodox. They are actually interested in greater religious involvement in the state, and their challenge is to evolve a religious identity that can be presented in a positive manner to attract persons who are interested in more religion. The movement makes no attempt to attract Orthodox Jews or persons who are interested in less religion to their ranks.

The movements face an additional dilemma. National leaders, including the clergy, who focus on the external environment and who take it as their reference point in formulating movement goals and activities, might, as a result, alienate local members and leaders. Persons not interested in the fundamental issue of official recognition of the movement of which their synagogue happens to be a part have expressed discontent with actions that have led them to be perceived as members of illegitimate and, indeed, even nonreligious movements. For many local members, the official recognition of their rabbis with regard to the functions that he or she can perform outside of their synagogue is a moot question. They are primarily interested in the services provided to them, rather than in the question of the reaction to external forces, and the quest for a larger share of the market.

The case of the Reform and Conservative denominations in Israel demonstrates the dilemma of movements that evolve in line with the needs of a changing population (in Europe and the United States) but that later became entrapped when those needs do not prevail in another setting (in Israel). The effort to redefine Judaism and restrict its ritualistic practices was acceptable and even desirable for Jews who lived in a religiously pluralistic society. This enabled the Jews to compartmentalize their religious life from their involvement in secular society and focus on the ethnic aspect of their Jewish identity. These same denominations, however, become entangled in a series of dilemmas when they are transposed to a society in which the nature of religious identity is intertwined with nationality. In such a situation, they must again seek to redefine their identity, but this time by expanding their definition as religious entities. The question then is whether persons who do not wish to follow religious tradition need to join a movement that legitimizes such an option, when in any case it is legitimate to behave religiously as one chooses.

REFERENCES

Abramov, S. Z. 1976. *Perpetual dilemma: Jewish religion in the Jewish state.* Rutherford, NJ: Fairleigh Dickinson Press.

Bar-Lev, M., A. Hareven, and P. Kedem. 1981. *The Jewish world of Israeli students.* Jerusalem: The Van Leer Institute.

Ben Meir, Y., and P. Kedem. 1979. Index of religiosity of the Jewish population of Isreal. *Megamot* 24:353–62 (Hebrew).

Berger, P. L. 1967. *The sacred canopy: Elements of a sociological theory of religion.* Garden City, New York: Anchor Books.

Cohen, S. M., and L. J. Fein. 1985. From integration to survival: American Jewish anxieties in translation. *The Annals of the American Academy of Political and Social Science.* 480:75–88.

Danzger, M. H. 1989. *Returning to Tradition: The Contemporary Revival of Orthodox Judaism.* New Haven: Yale University Press.

Davis, M. 1953. *The emergence of conservative Judaism: The historical school in 19th century America.* Philadelphia: The Jewish Publication Society of America.

Don-Yehiya. E. 1975. *Religion in Israel.* Jerusalem: Israel Ministry of Information.

Feinstein, M. 1985. *Igrot Moshe, Even Ha'Ezer* Vol 4: Responsa 59; 75 Hebrew.

Friedman, L. M. 1975. *The legal system: A social science perspective.* New York: Russel Sage Foundation.

Gamson, W. A., and A. Modigliani. 1987. "The changing culture of affirmative action." Pp. 137–177 in *Research in Political Sociology,* edited by R. D. Braungart. Greenwich, CT.: JAI Press.

Golinkin. D. n.d. *Halakah for our Times.* Jerusalem, The movement of Masorti Judaism in Israel (Hebrew).

Goren, S. 1987. Israel needs its religion. *The Jerusalem Post,* (13 February).

Grunblatt, J. 1986. Unity, legitimate wish, unrealistic hope. *Sh'ma: A Journal of Jewish Responsibility* 17/321:5–6.

Hammer, R. n.d. *The belief in God.* Jerusalem, The movement of Masorti Judaism in Israel (Hebrew).

Herman, S. M. 1971. *Israelis and Jews: The continuity of an identity.* Philadelphia: The Jewish Publication Society of America.

Lazerwitz, B. 1979. Past and future trends in the size of American Jewish denominations. *Journal of Reform Judaism* (summer):77–82.

Liebman C. S., and E. Don-Yehiya. *Religion and politics in Israel.* Bloomington: Indiana University Press.

McCarthy, J. D., and M. N. Zald. 1977. Resource mobilization and social movements: A partial theory. *American Journal of Sociology 72:1212–41.*

McCall, G. J., and J. L. Simmons. 1978. *Identities and interactions* (revised edition), New York: The Free Press.

Merton, R. K. 1976. *Sociological ambivalence and other essays.* New York: The Free Press.

Mintzberg, H. 1983. *Power in and around organizations.* Englewood Cliffs, NY, Prentice Hall, Inc.

Pearl, H. n.d. *The substance of the Torah.* Jerusalem, The movement of Masorti Judaism in Israel (Hebrew).

Philipson, D. 1967. *The Reform movement in America.* New York: Ktav Publishing House, Inc.

Rosen, I. 1987. No confidence in Amnon's platform. *Hatzofe* (National Religious Party Daily), (14 February) p. 8 (Hebrew).

Rubinstein, A. 1967. Law and religion in Israel. *Israel Law Review* 2:380-414.

Samet, M. 1985. Who is a Jew? (1958-1977). *The Jerusalem Quarterly* 36:88-108.

Samet, M. 1986. Who is a Jew? (1978-1985). *The Jerusalem Quarterly* 36:109-39.

Schein, E. H. 1985. *Organizational culture and leadership.* San Francisco: Jossey-Bass Publishers.

Segre, D. V. 1980. *A crisis of identity: Israel and Zionism.* Oxford: Oxford University Press.

Sklare, M. 1972. *Conservative Judaism: An American religious movement.* New augmented edition. New York: Schocken Books.

Tabory, E. 1973. Reform and Conservative Judaism in Israel: A social and religious profile. *The American Jewish Yearbook* 81:41-63.

Tabory, E. 1985. Pluralism in the Jewish state: Reform and Conservative Judaism in Israel. In *Conflict and Consensus in Jewish Political Life,* ed. S. A. Cohen and E. Don-Yehiya, 170-193. Ramat Gan: Bar-Ilan University Press.

Tabory, E., and B. Lazerwitz. 1983. Americans in the Israeli Reform and Conservative denominations: Religiosity under an ethnic shield? *Review of Religious Research* 24 (3):177-87.

Waxman, M. 1958. *Tradition and change: The development of Conservative Judaism.* New York: The Burning Bush Press.

Weigert, A. J., J. Smith Teitge, and D. W. Teitge. 1986. *Society and identity: Toward a sociological psychology.* Cambridge: Cambridge University Press.

—————————————————————————— *6* ——

Back to The Fold:
The Return to Judaism

BENJAMIN BEIT-HALLAHMI

Religion in Israel means Judaism, and more specifically, Orthodox Judaism. Eighty-five percent of the population in Israel is defined as Jewish, and this definition is legally made by the state. The involvement of religion and state in Israel has two aspects: first, there is no separation of state and religion; second, there is a relationship between religion and political and legal rights. Laws respecting the establishment of religion have been made in Israel, and in this it is like many European countries. What is almost unique in Israel is the officially sanctioned relationship between religion, nationality, and political rights. Being Jewish in Israel accords certain privileges, defined by law, as Jews constitute not only a religious group but a national group as well. Whether one belongs to the privileged group or not is clearly marked in the personal identity card issued by the government.

Every resident of the state of Israel over the age of 16 is required to have in his possession (and if he is male to carry it at all times) an identity card. This identity card lists, among other items of personal identification, the individual's nationality. For Jewish residents, nationality is defined as "Jewish" and not "Israeli." The term *Israeli* appears only in passports, where it defines citizenship. The boundaries of the Jewish group are kept by the system of religious courts as well as by civil authorities, and marriage between Jews and non-Jews is rare. The question of membership in the privileged group is not easily settled in cases where individuals want to separate religion and nationality (for example, by being a Catholic Jew). Israeli secular courts have ruled that one cannot be a Jew by nationality and a

Catholic by religion. This unique historical feature of Judaism has been preserved in Israel.

The religious system in Israel today is a continuation of religious traditions in the two main areas of origin for Jewish immigration to Israel: Eastern Europe and the Arab world. In both areas, though separated by geography and history. Jews carried on similar or identical rabbinical traditions for hundreds of years. Several features of historical Judaism have left their mark on Jewish culture all over the world. One such feature is the existence of a religious consensus without the existence of a central authority. This paradoxical tradition can be related to intellectual independence and the lack of respect for authority for which Jews have become known. A lack of respect for authority together with a national consensus have been a feature of social and political life in Israel.

Religion is very much tied to national ideology in Israel. Zionism is both a continuation of Jewish history and a rebellion against it. While Zionism in earlier years defined itself in secular terms, in recent years it has come to rely more on religious arguments and symbols (Beit-Hallahmi 1973). Religion is very much part of everyday political discourse in Israel, as well as a factor in group cohesion and division. Within the Jewish population there is a clear dividing line between two subcultures, the religious and the secular. The nature of Judaism as a religion of practice makes this division public and visible. While the two subcultures cannot be defined as castes, intimate contacts across the dividing line are rare. Members of the two groups can identify each other immediately by distinctive cues, such as dress, and expectations for public behavior are quite clear. The taboos concerning the Sabbath in Orthodox Judaism can serve as the best example of behavioral divisions. Driving on a Saturday (except for a real life-and-death emergency) is out of the question for members of the religious subculture, as is watching television or using the telephone. Making decisions about public activities on the Sabbath is a complicated matter in Israel. By force of tradition, created through constant political struggles between the two subcultures, a curious set of rules governs such activities. Public transportation in Israel does not operate on Saturday, except for a skeleton bus service in Haifa, but soccer games are allowed. Most movie theatres are closed on Friday night, but government television and radio stations operate for the benefit of those who are not religious. Raising pigs and selling pork are forbidden by law, representing a symbolic victory of millenia of Jewish dietary taboos, but the nonreligious can easily get around these limitations. These are just a few examples of the special role of religion in Israeli public life.

The Jewish population in Israel (those individuals whose government identity cards show them to be members of the Jewish people) is divided into an Orthodox minority, known in colloquial Hebrew simply as "religious" and a secular majority. Sizes of the respective groups and respective subcultures can be reliably estimated. The dividing line is the practice of Orthodox Jewish prescriptions, specifically covering one's head at all times, for males. Only a minority of Israelis do that. The state school system in Israel for Jews (there is a separate system for Arabs) is divided into two parallel subsystems: one religious and the other secular. Children of the religious subculture, raised according to Jewish Orthodox beliefs and practices, attend state religious schools. There is also an independent Orthodox system that is state financed but directed by the ultra-Orthodox community. (It should be remembered that even the secular state schools give their students large doses of Old Testament, Jewish history, and even Orthodox law.)

Ben-Meir and Kedem (1979), following the basic Glock and Stark (1965) model, have developed two reliable indices, for religious beliefs and for religious observance. The indices were based on a survey of a stratified random sample of the urban Jewish population in Israel. The belief scale includes six items, which meet the requirements of a Guttman Scale, and the observance scale includes 20 items, similarly scalable. The belief scale starts with the belief in the immortality of the soul (29 percent agreement in the sample), then goes on to the belief in the coming of the Messiah (36 percent, to belief in the Jewish people as chosen (57 percent), and to the final item, belief in God (64 percent). When it comes to the 20 items of the observance scale, a similar picture emerges. Only 11 percent of the men cover their head at all times, and 14 percent lay phylacteries every day. Only 22 percent do not drive on Saturday, and 44 percent report keeping to the dietary separation between meat and milk. Seventy-four percent claim to fast on the Day of Atonement, 88 percent light Hanukkah candles, and 99 percent take part in the Passover meal. There is undoubtedly an element of social desirability and conformity here, as becomes evident when we compare the two scales. Thus, only 64 percent believe in God, but 74 percent fast on the Day of Atonement. Nevertheless, the important finding here is that of the continuum of religious belief and observance, reflecting the social and historical realities of Judaism in Israel, the range of individual differences is much greater on religious practice than on religious beliefs, again in keeping with Jewish historical traditions. Judaism in Israel remains a religion of practice, rather than dogma. A survey of a representative sample of the adult Jewish population in Israel (1153 individuals), conducted in July 1983, found that the population could be divided in terms of observance into four groups: complete observance (14.3 percent), largely observant (19.5 percent), some observance (41.1 percent), and completely nonobservant (24.5 percent) (Shye 1983).

The varying levels of religiosity among Israelis are reflected in the following lables: *haredi,* denoting the very Orthodox; *dati* (literally *religious:ehp1*), denoting Orthodox, *mesorti* (literally *traditional:ehp1*), denoting those who are partially observant; and *hiloni* (literally *secular:ehp1*), denoting the non-Orthodox majority. These Hebrew terms are in everyday use, in both spoken and written language.

Judaization is defined here as the process through which secular, nonobservant, young (and not so young) Israelis who have grown up in Israel, within the majority culture, have become practicing Orthodox Jews, and have joined the minority subculture of Orthodoxy. "Israeli baalei teshuvah [returnees] are quite clear and forceful in defining themselves as having been secular, meaning that their life was not determined by the commandments of the Jewish Law and that their actual behavior violated aspects of it" (Aviad 1983, 8). Such a transformation obviously means leaving behind a secular identity and a secular life-style. The return to Judaism is known in Hebrew as *hazarah betshuvah* or *teshuvah,* and the returnees as *hozrim betshuvah* or *Baalei teshuva.* These terms, taken from the Orthodox Jewish vocabulary, used to be heard only in the Orthodox community. Since the 1970s, they have become part of everyday language in Israel. Judaization in Israel since 1973 should be regarded as a personal and collective renewal movement. It does not involve a complete change of identity. Nominally speaking, all returnees used to be regarded as Jews even before their transformation. The question before them, and before the majority of Israelis, is the kind of Jewishness they wanted to espouse. Judaization means accepting the assumption that being Jewish means a close continuity with historical Judaism.

The "return to Judaism" occurs when an individual, who has grown up in Israel as a nonpracticing Jew, like the majority of Israeli Jews, joins the minority of Orthodox Jews by beginning to practice the prescriptions and proscriptions of Judaism. Orthodox Judaism is a religion of practice, and joining it means clearly visible changes in behavior: covering one's head and other changes in dress for men and women, growing a beard, avoiding forbidden foods, etc. The "born again" individual is immediately recognized as belonging to the Orthodox subculture in Israeli society. For those who have known him before, the change is dramatic. Practicing Orthodox Judaism also means curtailing one's social activities and intimate contacts because one can no longer share one's family's food or their entertainment habits on weekends.

Unlike some of the other studies of the return to Judaism (for example, Aviad 1983) our discussion here will be limited to returnees who are Israeli born and raised. The phenomenon of Judaization among Diaspora Jews is, I believe, a separate issue, with different parameters. The problem of Jewish identity in the United States or Great Britain, where Jews are a minority, is totally different from the problem of Jewish identity in Israel. Israeli-born returnees start their return to Judaism at a different point on the religious-secular continuum, not only with a different identity from that of Diaspora Jews (Israeli Jew as opposed to American Jew), but also at a different level of practice. All of them know Hebrew, their native language, and have been exposed to Orthodox Judaism in a variety of ways. Many of them know quite a bit about Judaism at a cognitive, intellectual level. This is not always the case with Diaspora Jews.

JUDAIZATION: INDIVIDUAL

The mass media possess a powerful instrument of legitimizing or delegitimizing popular roads to salvation by presenting positive testimonials or negative case studies. In the case of the return to Judaism, the media in Israel have been most active in presenting numerous and powerful case studies, many in the form of testimonials. There have been thousands of media reports on the Judaization movement. The vast majority are exemplary tales of return. The exemplary tale, like the salvation tale, follows a stereotype: the returnee used to be secular/antireligious/Marxist/criminal/suicidal, and now, following the return, is devout/happy/productive/a rabbi. Almost without exception, portrayals of born-again Jews in the Israeli media are extremely positive. They follow the formula of search and salvation: a former life characterized by restlessness, confusion, and failure, and a new life filled with joy and peace.

Women's magazines are filled with touching stories of returnees from elite families, who found their happiness in Judaism, individually and collectively. Yotam Shoham, son of a physician who retired from the Israeli Defense Forces (IDF) active duty with the rank of brigadier-general, married Shahar Prihar, the daughter of a Haifa tveterinarian. Both are young, attractive returnees, and their wedding made headlines (Ben-Ari 1986). Returnees usually get married to other returnees tbecause the strictly Orthodox will not intermarry with the newly observant.

The media have given prominence to cases where the returnees are children of leaders and famous personalities. General Rafael Eitan, chief of staff from 1979–1983 and M.K., General Rehavam Zeevi, a distinguished military man and newly elected M.K., General Abraham Tamir, director general of the Foreign Ministry since 1986 all have returnee children.

A public opinion survey dealing with the return to Judaism was carried out in November 1978. The results showed that 68 percent believed that Israel needed a "strengthening of religious values," 51 percent believed that the return was the way to do it, 46 percent believed that Israel needed a "strengthening of religious values," 46 percent believed that the return movement had a positive influence on Israeli society, and only 4 percent thought it had a negative effect. Fifty-eight percent thought that the returnees were happy, and only 7 percent thought they were unhappy; 53 percent thought they were balanced, and only 14 percent thought they were unbalanced; 48 percent thought they were courageous, and 14 percent felt they were weak (Aviad 1983). This positive valuation of the return movement and the returnees is reflected in media reports and in everyday conversations.

There are two classes of stars among the returnees: those who were artists before their return, and those who were combat officers and fighter pilots in the Israel Defense Forces. Public appearances staged with the aim of gaining more returnees often feature either the former or the latter. Having members of IDF elite units as returnees changes the image of the Orthodox as unmanly and as as outsiders to the Israeli elite. The IDF has several commando units, whose reputation is legendary. When a returnee states "I served in Unit X," his audience will gasp, especially when the speaker displays the typical Orthodox appearance of long beard and long, black clothing. Such returnees will arouse understandable admiration among most secular Israelis. Another admired group are combat pilots. Reserve Colonel Noah Hertz is a former combat pilot who lost a leg in action and was a prisoner of war in Syria in 1973. Colonel Hertz's search for meaning started in the Syrian prison, and ended up in Orthodox Judaism. Colonel Hertz has a brother who is a member of *Emin*, the new religion. As of 1987, Noah Hertz is a returnee superstar, who appears in public to proselytize (Genossar 1986).

Present and former fighter pilots have been the stars of mass rallies for Judaization, and are often quoted in the media. One air force colonel, a squardron leader, is quoted as saying: "I am a model returnee. Nothing traumatic has happened to me. I wasn't a prisoner of war ... Suddenly I saw the light ... I started thinking and saw the light. I started thinking that the state of Israel is a passing episode. In the Declaration of Independence the Holy Name is not mentioned. The heart knows what the mouth will not dare to say"(Artziely 1984, 15).

Another returnee star, whose name has been mentioned in the press, is Shmaria Harel, a reserve captain who had served in the most celebrated commando unit of the IDF. Mr. Harel was born in 1951 in Kibbutz Kissufim and went on to become the epitome of the new Zionist man, a farmer and a fighter. Since his return to Judaism, he has been a member of the *Lubavitcher* movement and has continued to serve as a reserve officer.

Nothing has symbolized the success of individual Judaization like the cases of famous artists and bohemians who have become tOrthodox. When the painter Ika Israeli returned to Judaism in 1971, he was a unique and rare case, greeted by disbelief. His conversion at the age of 39 represented an anomaly, but by the late 1970s, the movement was there, and its stars were indeed the actors, directors, and painters who now appeared in front of their shocked audiences wearing long, black coats, black hats, and long beards. These famous cases of return to Judaism do indeed represent significant cultural victoriestfor Judaism within Israeli society. When a famous artist, or athlete, or military officer surrenders to the ancient tradition, he admits publicly the failure of secularism.

Uri Zohar is the undisputed hero of the Israeli Judaization movement, its prized possession, its beloved emblem. He symbolizes more than anything else, the victory of old Orthodox Judaism over Zionism, and the abject defeat of the latter by history and tradition. There could not have been a better example of the prototypical *sabra*, the Israeli-born new man, embodying the free spirit and the lack of respect for tradition, characterizing the new Jewish sovereignty in Israel. Uri Zohar was born in Tel Aviv, the first Hebrew-speaking modern city in Palestine, and he represents in every way the spirit and the experience of that city, the center of Israeli reality. What Uri Zohar embodies now is the greatest victory of Orthodox Judaism over mainstream Israeli culture. Zohar first attracted attention in the late 1950s as a stage comedian, and as a stand-up comic. He was an idol to thousands quite early on.

Born in November 1934, he graduated from high school in 1952 and went into military service, where he was a member of a military entertainment team. By 1956, as a civilian, he was a comedy star. His first marriage to a budding singer, the daughter of Israel's greatest actress, ended in divorce. Later on, in 1960, the popular comic surprised everybody with his serious approach to film criticism and turned to philosophy studies at the Hebrew University. He also gained

publicity and stature by his active participation in political demonstrations in support of better treatment of Palestinians. Zohar found
his true calling in films and became the leading film director in Israel.
The early 1970s saw a burst of artistic creativity in Israel, and Uri
Zohar was at the center, directing television shows and films. Zohar
was known as an exceptionally intelligent entertainer, the intellectual
among actors, the great hope of Israeli cinema. He was the first person
ever to be given the Israel Award, the highest civilian honor in Israel,
in recognition of work in the cinema in 1976. It was the first time that
an Israeli contribution in cinema was deemed worthy of such attention. Uri Zohar, in characteristic fashion, turned down the Israel
Award, an act reminiscent of Sartre's refusal of the Nobel Prize. This
was the first time in Israel that anybody turned down such an honor,
and it increased Zohar's standing as an independent artist, and as an
enfant terrible. Before winning the Israel Award he was convicted of
marijuana possession and spent three months in jail, under most
favorable terms.

At the age of 40 he started his search. Before that time, he had a
"wave of faith" at age 12. He had always believed in a God that created
the world but did not believe in the giving of the Law at Mount Sinai.
The process of Judaization for him meant examining, and accepting,
Orthodox claims about the Law being the absolute and only truth.
Once he became convinced of that, he had to start following the Orthodox life style (Nevo 1981).

He started his Judaization process as a television star in 1977. He
then starred in a popular game show, and the viewers were shocked
one day to see him wearing a skullcap, the familiar badge of the Orthodox. This gesture was first dismissed as a passing phase, an experiment. But Uri started looking more and more Orthodox on the screen,
and then dropped out of television altogether and moved to Jerusalem. By 1977, Zohar had his own radio program, a call-in broadcast
after midnight. While his viewers on television were shocked to see
him in his Orthodox garb, his listeners were even more surprised to
hear him preach and urge them to join the return to Judaism movement.

Telling his own story (Zohar 1983), Uri Zohar speaks of age 40
as the starting point of his quest. He was a successful artist, but
without any real belief or mission in life. "Socialist Zionism, humanism,
and the love of children all turned to dust" (Zohar 1983, 5). There was
a feeling of emptiness and estrangement, which reached its climax
during a trip to Scandinavia with his wife. He decided to interrupt the
trip and returned home. During a visit to Jerusalem he ran into a
former colleague, now a returnee to Judaism, and was struck by the

dramatic change in the man, who used to be depressed and depressing, and now was glowing with an inner light.

Like all Israelis of his background, Zohar had acted with disdain towards the Orthodox, and expressed it on many occasions. They looked to him primitive and repelling, a relic from the Middle Ages and the dark ghettoes of the past.

A chance encounter with an Orthodox man at a party led to the beginning of the return for Uri Zohar. That man claimed that the giving of the Law on Mount Sinai was a proven historical fact. He strongly impressed Zohar as a man who was not only intelligent and well educated, but also without visible personal flaws or deficiencies. His Orthodoxy could not be explained away as the result of some frustration or ignorance. He presented a challenge that could not be answered.

The search from that point on, as described by Zohar, was mainly intellectual. The question to be examined was whether Judaism represented the sacred truth. Through reading the Old Testament and the rudiments of the Oral Law, Zohar reached the conclusion that the whole edifice of Jewish tradition, created over thousands of years, is based on devine revelation and divine election. "What have we gained? Actually only one thing: the knowledge, which is not based on any experience ... that there is a purpose to our existence, and there is a reward for our actions" (Zohar 1983, 111).

Batya Lanzett, one of Israel's leading actresses in the 1950s who used to be involved in left-wing political activities, returned to Judaism in the late 1970s when she was over 50 years old. In her new life as an Orthodox woman in Jerusalem, she would not dream of entering a theatre or even watching television.

Rutti Navon was a rising singing star in the early 1970s in Israel. Today she is an Orthodox married woman, who sings only before female audiences. In a newspaper interview, she mentioned two events that pushed her toward the return to Judaism. The first was a road accident in which she was injured and her driver killed. "Then, after the accident, the Yom Kippur War broke out. I started asking, what's happening in this country? Such a tragedy. Why isn't the nation waking up? I felt that spirituality was missing in my life, that the pioneers who built this country did it without a spiritual foundation" (Quoted in Maimon 1986, 20).

Irit Bulka was a rising entertainment star, singing, writing, and composing her own songs. Her name kept popping up in the gossip columns. She was married twice and divorced, and started her search for meaning. She first discovered naturopathy, and then Judaism. Today she is an Orthodox married woman who appears only before audiences of Orthodox women like herself. (There have, it should be noted, been several cases of artists who have become returnees only to go back to secular life-styles.)

Another category of returnee celebrities is former star athletes. Several leading soccer players now grace yeshivot that specialize in returnees. Soccer players are heroes to young people in Israel, and when they return to Judaism, they become models, promoted by the Judaization organizations.

The Judaization of former criminals is the source of exemplary tales of salvation. Since 1980, the media in Israel have reported on hundreds of cases in which convicted criminals or defendants in criminal trials have turned Orthodox. The "change of heart" claim, common in criminal cases everywhere, has a special kind of evidence to support it here. The defense can point to real and dramatic changes in behavior: "He has been studying the Talmud 12 hours a day and keeps all prescriptions and proscriptions." Everybody in court can observe the changed appearance of the person involved: a long beard, covered head, face in a religious book throughout the proceedings. There is an obvious utilitarian aspect to this change of heart. Judges have been impressed quite often, and leniency has been the rule. In some cases, the defense has been tried more than once, since the bornagain Jew has reverted to criminal behavior. In other cases, this religious rehabilitation has worked and the former criminals now lead new lives, free of their former bondage, and bonded to religion as their calling and vocation.

The Israel Prison Authority started sponsoring the Judaization of prisoners in 1985, when 300 inmates took part in what was called "religious rehabilitation" (*Haolam Hazeh* 1986). There are three ye-shivot in Israeli prisons, each with 20 students. In 1985, the Israeli interior minister, Yitzhak Peretz, a member of the ultra-Orthodox Shass party, proposed a general pardon to all convicted criminals who have returned to Judaism. This proposal was not adopted by the government (Rabi 1985).

The Orthodox campaign has the effect not only of gaining new members for the Orthodox minority but of also invigorating regular members, especially when they act as recruiters. Returnees have been recruited through study meetings that are advertised widely and through mass rallies. In the mid 1980s, the organizations working to promote return started to distribute cassettes with sermons about the evils of secular life and the benefits of Judaism. The Judaizers raise the question of Jewish identity directly. If secular Israelis claim to be Jews, representatives of Orthodoxy can challenge them on the Jew-ishness of their Judaism. Individual sponsors of returnees show sincere concern, love, and care to the persons who come to them in a state of crisis. The environment of the yeshiva is as supportive as that of other religious groups and does have a clear psychotherapeutic effect on the returnees joining it. Returnees with serious psychological problems show a clear improvement as a result of yeshiva life. The yeshiva often becomes the last stop for seekers after a long career of search and experimentation. (Many of the Israeli returnees have tried various new religions.)

A secular young Israeli, whose life is basically an empty search for material security, is offered a meaning for his individual existence that ties him to a cosmic journey. He becomes part of the Jewish people, ordained as the Chosen People, through a direct tie to the Almighty, to keep holiness alive here on earth. For the first time, life has a meaning, and a serious one, within a community of faith, supportive, coherent, and united. Compared to the demoralized emptiness of secular life in Israel, always in the shadow of annihilation, Orthodox Judaism offers real salvation. Accepting Orthodoxy gives life a clear meaning, as the individual adopts an explicit life goal: being a Jew, part of a community with the mission of carrying on the communal worship of God, which replaces the emptiness and selfishness of secular existence. "I would return to secular life, if there were something to return to. There are only shambles there" (quoted by Kisslev 1984 7). Returning to Judaism means joining a long, impressive historical tradition, a comprehensive structure that covers every aspect of human life with rules and rituals. It supercedes self-actualization with divine demands from the individual. (In conversations with numerous returnees, the 1973 War was mentioned as the starting point in the questioning process, which led to the eventual return to Judaism.)

The return to Judaism is an admission that the Zionist attempt to create a secular Jewish identity has failed. Other roads to private salvation express the same admission. Many of the returnees have left Zionism behind as they have become more and more Orthodox. This has caused more concern and criticism in public. As long as the Judaization movement was seen as revitalizing Zionism, no such concern was experienced or expressed. Once Judaism is recognized as a challenge to Zionism, which it might be to a majority of the returnees, then Orthodox Judaism becomes only slightly better than the new religions in terms of the state of Israel and its goals. The rejection of Zionism by many of the returnees (Meislisch 1984) and their return to pre-Zionist Orthodoxy is, on a political level and on a family level, a dramatic rebellion. Zionism has failed, and on its ruins, old Judaism is being rebuilt. The rejection of Zionism by returnees is part of the overall rejection of secular values. Zionism, a secular national movement, is regarded as an element of the failed secular experiment of the Jews, a passing phase destined to be soon forgotten as have other non-Orthodox experiments in Jewish history (Meislisch 1984). After all, as many of the returnees say, Judaism has a history of millenia, whereas Zionism might be only a passing historical episode. The returnees' parents, "normal" secular Israelis, have called themselves Jews but do not take Judaism seriously. Their children are exposing their hypocrisy by going all the way, back to real Orthodox Judaism, and not to any of the modern non-Orthodox varieties. This is clearly a challenge and a rebellion. Returnees denounce their parents by their mere actions. They show their parents, who claim to be Jewish while not taking Judaism seriously, to be hypocrites and, in general, show that they are serious about their declared ideals, unlike most of their parents.

In terms of majority opinions, there is no doubt that switching to a non-Zionist Jewish identity is seen as preferable to switching to a totally non-Jewish identity, such as that of ISKCON or Jehovah's Witnesses. The cultural continuity, if not closeness, and the overall common identity of Jewishness, which is accepted by most Israelis, override other factors in forming an attitude towards the returnees.

A clear indication of moving beyond Zionism is the refusal to serve in the Israel Defense Forces. While conscientious objectors are not recognized in Israel, and they end up in prison, Orthodox Jews can refuse to serve with immunity. Those who have returned to Judaism while in regular military service, or under reserve obligations (all men under 55), are released from duty if they ask to be. Members of the Knesset have quoted stories according to which the Israel Air Force has lost a significant number of trained pilots, who had become returnees and stopped flying (Margalit 1986). According to IDF sources, the number of such cases was no more than 30 in 1985.

Zionism has failed, or at best produced ambiguous results. The Orthodox are confident in their eternal truths. Among the moderately religious, the religious Zionist camp, pressure is felt from two opposing directions: the more Orthodox side and the secular side. What we can observe as a result of cross pressures, are two kinds of personal changes, greater Orthodoxy and individual secularization.

Organized Judaization activities are financed by the Israeli government, which officially supports religious schools at all levels. Between 1967 and 1973 there were several yeshivot in Jerusalem catering to returnees, but the latter were all non-Israelis (Kramer 1972). Machon Meir, a yeshiva whose mission is Judaizing secular Jews, was founded in the summer of 1974 in Jerusalem. As of 1984, it had 100

Israeli students and 100 foreigners. Its school for women, Machon Ora, had a dozen Israeli women and twice as many foreigners (Kohn 1984). It was estimated that in 1986, Or Sameah, a yeshiva catering to returnees in Jerusalem, had 1,000 students, not all Israelis.

Meislisch (1984) estimates the number of Israeli returnees as 8,200 individuals as of 1983, not including family members, who have become returnees in some cases. Here we are not including those Jews from other countries who have become returnees. The estimate (Meislisch 1984) is that there have been about 5,000 of these. The phenomenon of the return to Orthodox Judaism among Diaspora Jews, though related to its parallel in Israel, is not our concern here. In a survey of returnees who were active students at yeshivot, Meislisch counted 1,460 students in 1983. They were either returnees in the early stages of their personal transformation, who are engaged in full-time study of rabbinical literature, or veteran returnees, who have made study their way of life and sole occupation.

One can speak today of a Judaization industry, which includes 230 yeshivot, and in 1984 had 4,400 returnees attending. As of 1984, there was a total of 80 organizations involved in recruiting returnees (Kisslev 1984). Forty percent of the budget for these groups comes from the Israeli government. The various organizations ranged from ultra-Orthodox and non-Zionist to nationalist, addressing a variety of audiences and suiting the message to the intended public. A central role in these efforts has been played by former scientists, who specialize in debunking evolutionary theory and proving the rationality of religious faith.

The Belsz Hassidic movement started offering evening lectures and weekend retreats in 1979, and has reached thousands of Israelis. The Habad movement, better known as the Lubavitcher Hassidim, has been extremely active in the Judaization campaign. It has 56 branches in Israel, and its members are busy recruiting non-Orthodox Israelis into Orthodoxy. Because of their nationalist stance, they have had no difficulties with the Israeli establishment and are a favorite with the media. Returnees that have joined Habad espouse a worldly way of life, most of them continuing to be gainfully employed. They also continue military service.

Several of the Judaization groups have offered weekend retreats devoted to "Jewish education" and "Jewish values." Participants are expected to pay, but the prices are heavily subsidized. Thousands of Israelis have taken part in these retreats, oriented towards whole families. The Judaization organizations publish a variety of pamphlets and leaflets. They are addressed to secular readers and try to reach them with references to common problems and the emptiness of secular life. Several publications, and many lectures, attack the theory of evolution, with claims familiar from similar sources in Western countries. Of course, the majority of participants in lectures, rallies, and retreats organized by various Judaization groups have not become Orthodox, and should not be counted among the returnees.

One organization offers the public what it claims are kabbalah (Jewish mysticism) courses. Rabbi Shraga Berg, who came to Israel in 1971 from the United States, has been operating the "Kabbalah Research Institute" since 1975. The Institute offers popular classes on such topics as "kabbalistic astrology" and "kabbalistic reincarnation." Orthodox rabbis and organizations express their open disapproval of Rabbi Berg, but his organization does serve as a recruiting agency for returnees to Judaism. It promotes the notion that the Age of Aquarius hails the early coming of the Messiah.

An organization, Parents Against The Return to Judaism, was started in 1984, and its members have been visible in the media. Activities of parents whose children had returned to Judaism started taking on a more militant and bitter tone, as a group calling itself Victims of the Return of Judaism, which started vigorous media campaigns in 1985. One of the main arguments used by the group was that the returnees had become non-Zionist and stopped serving in the military. The organization had 100 members as of 1986. Some of the parents decided to tell their personal stories in the media and started debates with their own children, with rebuttals and counter-rebuttals. The parents' complaints were against the Judaization process, which was compared to brainwashing, and against the final product, described as a return to the ghetto (Meller 1985).

The question of a tradition of interest in religious experimentation or in Jewish mysticism in Israel before 1973 is often raised. Isn't it possible that the recent wave of Judaization grew out of a broad base of such general, more muted, interest? The evidence shows that there was no such broad base and that religious experimentation was quite limited. Weiner (1962, 1969), who went searching for it, shows us that those *9 1/2 Mystics*, as his book is titled (1969) were indeed the last saving remnant of a great tradition, with no prospect of a great awakening in sight.

The process of individual and collective secularization in Israel is still going on, and there is still an Orthodox minority and a secular majority. Apostasy continues to be a major problem for Israel's Orthodox community.

The history of the Jewish people over the past ten generations is one of the consistent and thorough secularization. The return to Judaism, as an individual and social phenomenon, goes against this historical trend. The Orthodox community is still a minority, and its members feel that they are surviving under a constant threat, as they are. Writing about Israel before 1967, Friedmann could quote an unnamed Israeli sociologist, who stated: "There is no people on earth less religious than the people of Israel" (Friedmann 1967, 216). Indeed, the Israel elite, which created the state of Israel and has been in control since, is mostly atheist and nonobservant, and this is still true. If we look at the Israeli government of 1987, most of its leaders, including Yitzhak Shamir, Shimon Peres, Yitzhak Rabin, Ariel Sharon, Ezer Weizman, and others, are totally secular people whose life-style bears no signs of influence by Judaism and its commandments.

The process of personal secularization, through which the Orthodox minority in Israel has been losing members, has been continuing despite the appearance of movement in the opposite direction. It has been estimated that 10 percent of the moderately Orthodox (national-religious) youth leave the status of "observant" behind at age 18. This is marked by taking off the habitual skullcap for men. What Liebman (1984) observes is that there has been an increasing overlap between Israel and Jewish identity since 1973, "But whereas religious symbols play an increasingly important role in Israeli public or collective life...There is no evidence...that the level of religious observance has increased, that more people refrain from violating the Sabbath or eating bread on Passover, or that more people pray" (p.6). Orthodox Jews are today, and have been at least for three generations, a minority among Jews all over the world, and a minority among Israelis. This situation has not changed and is not likely to change in the future.

MESSIANIC POLITICAL MOVEMENTS

Since 1973 in Israel, there have been several religious-nationalist groups of a messianic nature. The best known in Gush Emunim. All of these groups share a messianic vision of the coming redemption of the Jewish people in Israel. Although some individual members of these groups are returnees to Judaism, the groups themselves do not offer or promote private salvation because they are political movements whose goal is to change the world, and not individuals.

The creation of messianic Zionism in Israel after 1976, and its growth after 1973, is documented by Liebman and Don-Yehiya (1984). The crisis that led to the development of messianic movements is described by a national-religious (not nationalist) Labor party member as follows: "As the Zionist era is fading we realize that our hopes were not realized. The Jewish people has not changed. Society is not healthier, and the state of Israel only added new troubles to the old ones. So the messianics have replaced the Messiah of hope with the Messiah of despair" (Burg 1984, 7).

Here and there, one could find in Israel over the years small groups of individuals, who indeed represent a messianic faith. These groups, and these individuals, are on the margins of the Judaization movement. There are those who dream of building the third Jewish Temple in Jerusalem, and there have been those who have engaged in practical activities to that end. Some have been weaving special clothing for the priests of the Third Temple and making exact plans for the altar on which regular daily sacrifices of two sheep are to be made. All those individuals believe that the building of the Temple, through divine intervention or by human hands, is to occur shortly. We might consider their ideas and their actions strange, but they are not involved in private salvation but in what they consider a collective, or even universal, one.

While messianic interpretations of events in the Middle East started after 1967 War, it was limited to a few fringe groups and individuals. This trickle became a stream only after the 1973 war, with the founding of Gush Emunim on January 30, 1974. There are those among the religious-nationalist group Gush Emunim (and outside the group) who believe that the state of Israel is but a preparatory stage for the coming of the Kingdom of Israel. These religious-nationalist activists, small in numbers (equal to the number of members in new religions), enjoy broad influence thanks to their political vision and political actions. They offer the demoralized majority hope and vitality. The new messianic ideologies have led to the creation of several violent underground groups, which carried out attacks against Arabs and plotted the bombing of the Temple Mount in the early 1980s.

A MESSIANIC CULT

Through informants, I have been able to locate a small messianic group, led by one charismatic woman, and run as a cult. The leader, H.R., is in her late thirties, well educated and well respected in her community, where she works as a teacher. She is intelligent, articulate, and relaxed. She is also attractive but has never had any relations with men, as far as could be ascertained. One informant suggested that there might be a lesbian relationship between H.R. and her second in command, D.M. Around H.R. and D.M. a small group of adepts gathered. The group meets at least once a week. The meetings are wholly devoted to the teachings of H.R., which are presented as messages from two spirits, J. and G. These two spirits speak through H.R. only. The small group of followers range in age from 19 to 56. There is a majority of women, most of whom are married, who pursue this activity without their husbands. The teaching includes "unconventional thinking," expressed through new definitions for familiar terms, such as "ambition" and "education," and the development of "spiritual consciousness."

The most important teachings, dictated by the two spirits, deal with the destiny of humankind and the special role of the Children of Israel. According to the teachings, humankind is about to enter a new age in which human beings will change their behavior completely. There will be first a human harmony with nature, which is filled with "positive radiations," and should be treated with love. The most important change to take place in the New Age has to do with the two sexes, which will become one. Physical ability will lose its meaning as humankind learns to use gravity and move objects by "telecosmic" means. The two elements, feminine and masculine, are separate and unequal in this world, but this will change. The feminine element creates harmony in nature and correlations among nature's laws. The masculine element is expressed through cosmic creation, planning, and changing. The feminine element is the Shechina, and the masculine element is God. The feminine element was subordinated to the masculine one because of the Garden of Eden affair, but this will change in the New Age.

The Children of Israel were created in order to show all of humanity the way to a correct utilization of all psychical and physical forces, in harmony with humankind and nature. Israel's wars are ordained by God, who specifies their dimensions and goals. These wars are always aimed at destroying evil and aggression emanating from other human groups. Pagan nations beyond redemption were destroyed by the Children of Israel, when no other choice was left. People who refuse to change their evil ways have to be destroyed, and the Children of Israel should not flinch from their duty to God to carry out this task. In most cases, however, other peoples in the Middle East showed themselves ready to accept Judaism, and no war was mandated against them. Those who resist the true faith will be subjugated.

Wars between the Children of Israel and other peoples occur for three reasons:

1. Other peoples cannot accept the existence of the Children of Israel, who remind the former of their inferiority.

2. Peoples in the Middle East want to prove that they are chosen by God, through their control over territory.

3. Humanity still fights against the need to become better and to accept cosmic laws through the Children of Israel. They still resist the divine order.

For these reasons, more trials and tribulations can be expected, and the 1973 War was but the first example. In addition to the teachings of the spirits J. and G., which are recorded and mimeographed, members of the group are supposed to read contemporary messianic and nationalist literature. An example of the former is a book published by a Jerusalem technician, who has been predicting the coming of complete redemption (that is, the Messiah) since 1967. The first edition of his book predicted redemption in 1968. In several editions since then, the date has been moved forward.

H.R.'s interpretation of Jewish history, which might seem bizarre and chauvinistic to many, is actually not that uncommon among Israelis. We have to keep in mind that in secular Israeli schools, starting in second grade, Old Testament stories are taught as history and are accepted as such by the vast majority of Israelis. The Old Testament story of the creation of the Jewish people, with the Patriarchs, the exile in Egypt, the Exodus, Joshua's wars, etc., are treated by most Israelis as history, not mythology. Analogies are sometimes drawn between Joshua's conquest and contemporary events (Zweig 1969). Israeli archeology is guided by a desire to confirm this outline of ancient Jewish beginnings. Connecting the Old Testament Children of Israel and contemporary Jews is, of course, one of the cornerstones of Zionism.

Thus, H.R. is a deviant because she claims to receive knowledge from two spirits and because of her ideas about the New Age, masculinity, and feminity. These universalistic ideas are not often heard in Israel, and in this sense, H.R. represents a new religion. Her historical-religious-political message, however, nationalistic as it might be, is not that much different from what one can read in the writings of leading Israeli nationalists after 1967 and 1973 and what can be read every day in most Israeli newspapers.

The tiny group around H.R. represents a classical collection of seekers. They range in age from 19 to 56. There is a 56-year-old respectable grandfather, seeking peace of mind, and a 19-year-old soldier whose parents are separated. There is a 32-year-old former political activist who has been disheartened by the failure of the peace movement. There are three divorced women, burdened with worries about finances and children. There are two married women who do not share their search with their husbands. There is a teacher who has been involved in a variety of groups and actually started his own at one point, following the deterioration of his marriage. All of these individuals have found some meaning and support in H.R.'s group, which is quite secretive and elitist. Told by their leader that they are among the elect and the select, this experience of belonging obviously does something for them. Membership in the group, unlike that in a new religion or returning to Judaism, requires little in the way of investment, commitment, or change in life-style.

SUMMARY

The individual Judaization movement reached its upper limit in 1986 and, since then, has been stable or stagnating. A significant minority of the returnees have reverted to a secular life-style, but the majority have persisted at a rate higher than that of those who have joined new religions. The reasons for this are quite clear. Return to Judaism means moving into the bosom of a strong, coherent, nourishing community with much material and social support. The returnees do not feel persecuted, like those who have joined new religions. They feel loved and supported because they are loved and supported by the immediate community and by the society at large.

The Judaization movement in Israel is a rebellion that, paradoxically, is institutionalized and supported. At the level of individual family units, it is usually a rebellion of children against parents. On the ideological level, it is usually a rebellion against Zionism. At the same time, it is perceived as conformist because its end goals are still within the framework of collective Jewish identity. Compared to other salvation movements, and especially new religions, it is less threatening to Jewish identity and Zionism, and thus it is not only tolerated, but sanctioned. And it is certainly preferable to self-destructive responses to crisis, which are always recalled as alternatives ("Do you want your son to be a follower of some guru, or a drug addict, instead of a yeshiva student?"). This distinction is realistic and understandable.

REFERENCES

Artziely, M. The Judaization offensive. *Haaretz*, November 30, 1984 (Hebrew).

Aviad, J. 1983. *Return to Judaism: Religious renewal in Israel.* Chicago and London: University of Chicago Press. 1983.

Beit-Hallahmi, B. Religion and nationalism in the Arab-Israeli conflict, *Il Politico*, 1973, *38*, 232–243.

Ben-Ari, D. 1986. A wedding dawn. *Laisha*, 26 May (Hebrew).

Burg, A. 1984. Followers of the Messiah. *Davar*, 22 May (Hebrew).

Friedmann, G. *The End of the Jewish People?* Garden City, NY: Doubleday, 1967.

Genossar, S. 1986. How soldiers are returned to Judaism. *Davar*, 5 February (Hebrew).

Haolam Hazeh 1986. Religious rehabilitation for prisoners, 9 April (Hebrew).

Kisslev, R. 1984. Who organizes the road to divine truth? *Haaretz*, 19 March (Hebrew).

Kohn, M. 1984. Teaching tolerance. *The Jerusalem Post*, 8 July.

Kramer, M. 1972. The returnees. *The Jerusalem Post Magazine*, 18 May.

Liebman, C. S., and E. Don-Yehiya. 1984. Separation of religion and state in Israel: A program or slogan? In *Religion and Politics in Israel.* ed. C. S. Liebman and Don-Yehiya. Bloomington: University of Indiana Press.

Maimon, S. 1986. Rutti Navon: A new Jewess. *Yediot Aharonot*, 13 June (Hebrew).

Margalit, D. 1986. Returnees—the questions. *Haaretz*, 7 February (Hebrew).

Meislisch, S. 1984. *The Return to Judaism.* Tel Aviv: Masada (Hebrew).

Meller, D. 1985. I lost a son. *Maariv*, 18 October (Hebrew).

Nevo, A. 1981. Uri Zohar—Enlightenment. *Maariv*, 6 November (Hebrew).

Rabi, A. 1985. Interior minister: Parson to all returnees. *Hadashot*, 29 May (Hebrew).

Weiner, H. *The Wild Goats of Ein Gedi.* Garden City, NY: Doubleday, 1961.

Weiner, H. *9½ Mystics.* New York: Holt, Rinehart & Winston, 1969.

Zohar, U. 1983. *Therefore choose life.* Jerusalem: Hamessorah (Hebrew).

Zweig, F. *Israel: The Sword and the Harp.* London: Heinemann, 1969.

7

Conversion Experiences:
Newcomers to and Defectors from Orthodox Judaism (hozrim betshuvah and hozrim beshe'elah)

WILLIAM SHAFFIR

The 1960s and 1970s witnessed the emergence of a variety of fundamentalist groups that sociologists examined in terms of their recruitment tactics (Davis and Richardson 1976; Gordon 1974; Lofland 1986; Zygmunt 1967), the individual characteristics of the converts (Catton 1957), and the social conditions favorable for the emergence of potential recruits (Glock and Bellah 1976; Harrison 1974). In contrast to the many studies about conversion to religious sects or cults, the sociological literature contains comparatively few analyses of disengagement from religious communities. Since Mauss (1969) commented upon the paucity of available research literature on the subject of religious defection, several studies that give a fuller picture of the phenomenon have become available (Albrecht and Behr 1983; Beckford 1978; Brinkerhoff and Burke 1980; Jacobs 1984; Peter et al 1982).

Religious revival and defection have also characterized Israeli society, the former achieving far greater prominence than the latter. As Cohen et al. have written: "in Israel, the phenomenon of renewal of traditional religion is reflected in the internal strengthening of Orthodox Judaism, and in the attraction of this particular form for Jews from secular backgrounds, seeking a path, known as *tshuvah*, of return to Judaism" (1987, 320). *Baalei tshuvah*—represents or returnees to Orthodox Judaism, or newly Orthodox Jews as they are sometimes called—include Jewish men and women who become attracted to the idea of transforming their secular way of life into a mode of living based on the precepts of the Torah. Since 1967, a variety of institutions for facilitating such efforts have been established in Jerusalem alone, while others are present elsewhere in Israel, Europe, the United States, and Canada. Describing the *baalei tshuvah*, also identified as *hozrim betshuvah*, Aviad writes that they are

> The Jews from the Diaspora and Israel, who have "returned" to Orthodox Judaism. Their presence is felt in the city [of Jerusalem]. As individuals, they may be noticed by the mixture of traditional and modern they display in their dress, manners, style. As a group they are visible through the many yeshivot established for them and planted in Orthodox neighborhood. (1983, 2)

In contrast to the academic research generated by the baalei tshuvah phenomenon (Aviad 1983; Cromer 1981; Shaffir 1983), the defection of *haredi*—ultra-Orthodox—Jews from their communities in Jerusalem and B'nei Brak—the two largest concentrations of haredim in Israel—has, so far, failed to generate scholarly research. With the execption of one treatment of the topic (Shaffir and Rockaway 1987), reports and articles about the defection of haredim, popularly designated as *hozrim beshe'elah*, or "returning to the question," have appeared only in the Israeli press, radio, and television.

The adoption by former *haredim* of a secular way of life is seemingly the obverse of the experience encountered by baalei tshuvah. In fact, there are significant parallels in the respective experiences. Broadly speaking, when conceptualized as a process, each involves a transformation resulting in the adoption of a radically different lifestyle affecting relationships with significant others. In this respect, both experiences can be characterized as conversion in that each "involves the adoption of a pervasive identity which rests on a change at least in emphasis from one universe of discourse to another" (Travisano 1970).

This chapter highlights a number of similarities and differences in the transformation experiences of *baalei tshuvah* and *hozrim beshe'elah*. I begin by briefly examining the explanations individuals offer for embarking upon the radical change and, conceptualizing the transformation as a status passage (Glaser and Strauss 1971), examine the specific context within which it develops. The particular context, I suggest, is directly related to how the transformation is negotiated, and I focus on the individual status of one experience in contrast to the collective status of the other. I then attend to selected components of the negotiated transition and conclude by offering some avenues for further research.

The data constitute two separate research projects and were gathered in different years. Both the *baalei tshuvah* and hozrim beshe'elah studies, conducted in 1978-1979 and 1986 respectively, relied upon participant observation and informal interviews. I spent seven months in two Jerusalem yeshivot for *baalei tshuvah* and participated in the full ranges of the students' activities —attending classes, taking meals with them, and engaging in informal conversation. The *baalei tshuvah*, of whom 50 were interviewed ranging in age from 18-30 years, were from predominantly middle to upper middle class families in the United States (a minority were from England and Canada), and a majority were in the midst of their university studies. Their length of stay ranged from one month to four years. The *hozrim beshe'elah*, of whom 35 were interviewed over a seven-month period, during 1986 and 1989, ranged in age from 24 to 43 years and included 30 men and 5 women. Upon leaving their *haredi* communities, six persons chose to become modern Orthodox Jews, while the remainder ceased practising completely.

SEEDS OF DISCONTENT

Both in the cases of the *hozrim betshuvah* and *hozrim beshe'elah*, the individuals decide to embark upon a course of action to alter their life-style radically. While the newly observant and former haredim arrive at their decision differently, both are propelled by a series of experiences convincing them to investigate and, ultimately, to adopt an alternate way of life.

Whereas the two groups of individuals might be characterized by a desire to search for something different and more meaningful in their lives, both the circumstances surrounding the search and the pace at which it is conducted are radically different for each. In the case of the *hozrim beshe'elah*, the decision to exit from haredi society is accomplished through intense internal debate and reflection extending over a period of years. Typically, motivation to leave results from experiencing intense discomfort within haredi society. Though this discomfort manifests itself in various forms, a common theme revolves around the confining nature of the haredi life-style. As one haredi maintains: "It is geographically a prison, it is socially a prison, it is emotionally a prison. You are not allowed to do so many things." By contrast, while reevaluating their past retrospectively and concluding that they have long, albeit unknowingly, searched for 'authentic Judaism', *hozrim betshuvahs'* decision to investigate and embrace Orthodox Judaism is reached rather suddenly, followed by a rapid identification with and commitment to Orthodox Judaism.

Despite the few *hozrim beshe'elah* who trace the source of their disaffection with *haredi* society to psychologically oriented considerations—two, for example, spoke of specific incidents in their childhood that made them feel resentful and rebellious—over half claim they felt fundamentally different from their *haredi* peers as long as they could remember. They stress that they have been aware since childhood that they were deviants—set apart from the mainstream of their society. One 42-year-old man, for example, speaks unhesitatingly about his early disenchantment and says that by the time he was 12 or 13 he had come to the conclusion that Orthodox religious teachings were nonsensical and that he had learned to detest and despise the piety of his schoolmasters. But, as he recalls, his initial doubts occurred even earlier:

> I remember myself as a boy of ten, a member of an orthodox family in B'nei Brak. I don't think I was ever religious. I think I was a boy who was nonreligious. I wasn't a boy who was God-fearing. I was compelled to be a religious boy in a religious society and did what I was told to do.

A female, from a Hassidic family near Mea She'arim, reflects on her attitude toward the imposed life-style: "I was never friendly with the girls. I didn't like the education, I didn't like the customs, and I remember this from when I was young." Another respondent also was rebellious from an early age and comments: "I always stood out. The rest of the friends did what they were told. I questioned."

The majority of the respondents, however, do not refer to their childhood years as a period when unhappiness or awareness of being different had afflicted them, or when they felt estranged from their peers. Virtually all, though, become deeply resentful as their attempts to discuss and query religious tenents are frustrated by their elders. Moreover, they are reprimanded for even raising such issues. As two individuals recall:

> I asked difficult questions... I showed them that there wasn't any logic [in religion]. There's a contradiction. On the one hand they say that God exists and, on the other hand, they don't know what this is.... They say: "Look, you get up in the morning. There must be a God." And I asked: "What does He look like?" "No, [they said] you can't know and you mustn't think about such matters and you mustn't ask about Him."

... it's not that at the beginning I asked, "Is there or isn't there a God?" In God for sure I believed. With all the education I received, there wasn't a doubt that there was a God. It's forbidden to even suggest that there isn't a God. So it began with little things, like praying, like putting on tefillin, like Shabbat, like Torah. What is it? I wanted to know what I was doing.... So I went to the principal of the yeshiva. He tried to explain it to me but I couldn't accept it. And then I began to ask myself even more difficult questions on the foundations of the religious beliefs. And I went to the Rav)Rabbi) and I said, "Listen, I have problems, and I can't work them out." And everyone gave me the same answer basically. Basically, the answer was that I wasn't to think about such matters. The *posek* [verse] I was quoted was "What you can't understand, don't try to understand." Asking the questions, I was told, was wrong. I should wait until I'm married and I would then see things differently.... I finally got to the question, "Is there or isn't there a God?"

The majority of the ex-*haredim* become increasingly angry when what they sincerely believe to be reasonable queries or arguments are either ignored or dealt with in vague pious terms. Several became gradually disillusioned by the superficiality of the religious convictions of the members of the group, who automatically and unquestioningly behave as they are expected to behave. As two individuals recall:

It was, "This is our way of life. This is the way we want to on living." And any ideology or idealism becomes trivial, becomes subservient to the way of life. [The focus is] more on the external aspects of religion.... The ideal is not to think; the ideal is to conform. The ideal is just to do, to be, and not to think. It was this complete absence of thinking that was disturbing to me.

It's as though you begin to lose sight of why religion is meaningful and you do what you do because everyone does it. You see, you can ask questions providing that you ask the kinds of questions that people find acceptable. But if you should start to think for yourself, and there are people who do it but give up when they realize what's involved, you run into problems in the world. Conformity is what is expected and you haven't any room to deviate.

In the case of two other respondents, it is a war that raises fundamental doubts about their commitment to *haredi* precepts and triggers off their decision to leave. For one, it is the Six-Day War of

1967. A moral justification has to be found for killing the enemy in war, for shooting another human being; and all one's values have to be reassessed. Another claims that the Yom Kippur War of 1973 aroused in him passionate feelings of Israeli nationalism, which could not be reconciled with the anti-Zionist attitudes fostered in him by his up-bringing; and so he decides to leave.

If the *haredi* defectors are disillusioned by the confining nature of *haredi* society, they are not in a position to distance themselves from it immediately. As we shall see, the decision to leave the haredi framework evolves over a period of time and is deliberately executed. In most cases, the seeds of discontent and frustration reach matura-tion over a period of years, and as the individual is influenced to react increasingly against the teaching and life-style, he embarks upon a series of steps consistent with that decision that typically involve deception and impression management.

By contrast, however, the process by which the *hozrim betshu-vah* land in the yeshiva is unplanned. In a very real sense, the world of Orthodox Judaism is stumbled upon by chance. Typically, the indivi-duals do not appear on the yeshiva doorstep eager to advance their understanding of Torah Judaism but are either recruited by students of the yeshiva or arrive searching for a friend enrolled in the program.

The unplanned nature of their decision to attend the yeshiva is evident by the convoluted paths by which the *hozrim betshuvah* reach the institution. Their arrival is shaped by the confluence of unrelated circumstances. Two typical examples follow:

> Had you told me I'd be studying in a yeshiva in Jerusalem, (and I've been here for three years), I would have said, "Impossible." I never even thought of a yeshiva, I didn't even know what it really was. The fact is that I planned a trip to Israel to visit some friends staying on a kibbutz. I stayed there for about one week and then decided to travel a little because this was my first time in the country. A few months earlier, I received a letter from a friend who was in the program and I decided to look him up.

> I never planned to come to Israel in the first place. I was set to travel through India with a friend, but she cancelled at the last minute and I wasn't prepared to go alone. At the same time, my aunt took sick, and so my uncle suggested that I join him. It was a good offer, so I accepted. The tour came to Jerusalem and the guide took us through the Old City. That's where I met Baruch and his friends who were explaining to passersby what the yeshiva was about. What they said was interesting, and I planned

to stick around for the three days that the tour was here. It's now been close to two years [since I came].

Despite the absence of a planned agenda, the baalei tshuvah are of the general view that their travel and decision to visit Israel are deeply motivated by a search for meaning that would provide greater order and direction to their lives. Their search, they feel, is best understood within the context of overall dissatisfaction and uncertainty characterizing their lives in North America. They express feelings of discontent concerning, in their words, the "degenerate" or "empty" nature of North American society and with the impact that this is having on their lives. An American, aged 21, expresses the general views of many when he says:

> I was doing well. I had a job that paid well, had all the material things I could possibly want. But I just wasn't happy. I mean, inside I wasn't satisfied. The material things didn't mean a lot and I just felt there had to be something more. And I found myself thinking about these things more and more.

For a large majority, the need to understand themselves is connected to their weak and tenuous relationship to Judaism. Two examples follow:

> I was taking this aesthetics class in school... and I was bothered by particular points the teacher was making. We got down to questions about life, what it was, and I wasn't really getting any answers. I heard myself asking, "What is life? What am I living for?" One evening I was in my apartment, minding my own business, reading the five books.... about Moses and his relationship with the Jewish people. Moses is not allowed to go into the Promised Land and I kind of looked at that as someone who doesn't really get the ultimate reward in this life.... I just had a moment of incredible realization. I just had the transcending experience and I realized what I had been searching for, understanding what it meant to be alive, what Judaism was. And I realized that the Torah was true. It was actually God's word, and that there is a God, and I am chosen to do whatever I'm supposed to do as a Jew.... In the next few days, I saw God's hand in the world.

> I was beginning to ask myself questions about Jews, about the religion and the history. I mean Jewish history is absolutely

incredible. We survived against all odds. Well, why did we survive? How did it happen? And then I asked myself about Jewish life today, questions about assimilation and Jewish identification. I didn't have any answers, but I just felt that Jewish history didn't unfold as it did just for Jews to assimilate. I didn't really know much about orthodoxy because it wasn't part of my life or my family's. But somehow I felt that it was the direction at least to explore.

Unlike the *hozrim beshe'elah* for whom the final impetus to sever ties with the haredi community provided some dramatic event in their lives—the proverbial straw that breaks the camel's back—the hozrim betshuvah's decision to be drawn to Orthodox Judaism is typically unaccompanied by any experience of dramatic proportion. For the majority, were it not for their fortuitous contact with the yeshiva, they would not have embarked upon a path to Orthodox Judaism. Encountering Orthodox Judaism, then, is both sudden and unexpected. Reflecting the astonishment of many, one person remarks: "I sometimes can't believe that I'm here and it's been close to two years. My parents still have trouble understanding what has happened to their son and my friends are still shocked that I'm at a yeshiva." In this sense, then, the *hozrim beshe'elah* exercise more control over their pace or tempo of the ensuing transformation than is the case for their newly observant counterparts.

While both sets of individuals embark upon processes that eventuate in dramatic changes in their lives, the context within which the process unfolds, as well as the consequences awaiting the individual both during and following the transformation, differ significantly. I now turn to an examination of these matters.

THE CONTEXT OF THE TRANSFORMATION

As much of the literature suggests, the process of religious identity transformation can be conceptualized as a conversion experience (Travisano 1970) or status passage (Glaser and Strauss 1971). Both the shape and structure of any status passage are fashioned by the context within which they occur, the latter providing the guidelines that influence both the form and content of the transition. While both experiences involve a dramatic transformation, their respective unfolding and management are critically related to their differing social contexts that both channel and guide the individual's movements. In contrast to the *baalei tshuvah's* resocialization, which occurs in the highly structured setting of the yeshiva, the *hozrim beshe'elah's* proceeds in the absence of any formalized supports.

At the time of the research, the two yeshivot for *baalei tshuvah* have developed an elaborate system for acquiring recruits. For instance, while they do not systematically deploy their students as recruiters, they have a highly structured curriculum in place in addition to a well-rehearsed approach for encouraging the newest arrivals to remain for an extended period. A brief description of one of these yeshiva's study program is in order. The medium of instruction is English because the majority of the students are unfamiliar with Hebrew. A short introductory program lasts for three months, with courses on the *humash* (Pentateuch), the Commandments, the divine authorship of the Torah, Jewish laws and prayer, and a specially designed class entitled "the Forty-eight Ways to Wisdom." There is also an introductory class on Jewish history. This program is regarded as a prerequisite for the more intensive four-year course of study that follows.

The first-year program is divided into two segments. During the first six months, the curriculum includes courses on the Mishna (an introduction to the concepts of the Oral Law), Halakah I (a class on Jewish law in which the daily observance are taught), *humash* I (a survey course designed to cover the general scope of the entire Pentateuch), Hebrew Ulpan (instruction in Hebrew grammar and conversation), and *Mussar* (a course emphasizing different aspects of ethical conduct). The second six-month program is mainly a continuation of the preceding six months, but at a more advanced level and with the addition of an introductory course on the Rambam (Maimonides) and the Gemara (commentary on the Talmud). In the second and third years, the curriculum consists of increasingly advanced courses on the various areas of Jewish law. In the fourth year, the study of Gemara is continued, including a reexamination of "The Forty-eight Ways to Wisdom" and of "Proofs of Torah from Sinai."

The format of the curriculum is modeled partially after the university system of teaching, a format with which the students are familiar. Classes begin at 9 A.M. and end at 10 P.M., with breaks for meals. However, it is not unusual for the majority of students to start the day at 7 A.M. with preparations for the morning prayers and to end at 11 P.M. with a review of the day's studies and the preparation of assignments for the following day's classes.

Upon arrival at the yeshiva, the individual can depend on a warm reception in an attempt to draw him into a lively discussion that will convince him to stay on. As one senior student explains:

In the short amount of time that you are going to deal with him,
you are going... to show him that to spend a little time here is a
better opportunity for him than what he's doing now... You have
to get hold of a guy... whatever it takes, with all honest means.
It's like a salesman, he knows he has to make a sale.

In the initial encounter, the newcomer is asked about his future plans
and about how he intends to achieve them. He is also likely to be asked
about his belief in God and about his views on the meaning of life. Then
a central question is put to him, "What are you living for?" The visitor
soon discovers that the student body includes young men whose backgrounds and recent histories resemble his own, and they use all their
persuasive powers to convince him that it is in his best interest to join
them.

The newcomer who agrees to remain for three months has a
structured curriculum to introduce him to Jewish laws and traditions; he is taught by sympathetic tutors in a friendly atmosphere that
encourages him to consider changing his life-style permanently.
Through the presentation of a series of carefully coordinated arguments, rooted in Torah principles, the yeshiva hopes to effect a conversion in the student's outlook: the alteration to a religious frame of
reference from a secular one.

By contrast, *hozrim beshe'elah's* transformation is characterized by the absence of any such formalized support. In fact, a feature
common to all in this category is their extreme reluctance to confide
their thoughts about leaving to anyone else, this despite the fact that
their defection eventually becomes common knowledge. They maintain that it is impossible to talk with any other members of their group
about religious doubts, doubts about the existence of God, or about
their growing dissatisfaction with the confining nature of *haredi*
society. As one respondent comments sarcastically:

The sin you're commiting can't be shared with anyone. You feel as
if you're sinning, transgressing. It's a crime. You become paranoid
about this and you're too ashamed to discuss it.... No, no, it can't
happen. It's more taboo than sex.

Another ex-*haredi* has a similar experience: "It's just impossible to let
others know how you're feeling. Can you imagine mentioning it to a
rav? And you can't even mention it to your closest friend. No, it
remains a deep dark secret, and that's what makes it so difficult."

Existing away from *haredi* society, then, becomes a difficult
undertaking both because of the absense of formalized supports as

well as the inability to share any misgivings about the *haredi* life-style with others who might react similarly. Not only is the transformation undertaken secretly, but it must be managed alone. Reflecting upon his experience, an individual draws the following analogy: "It's like living in a Communist country. To speak out to someone against the government, you don't know if he is loyal to you or if he's going to give you away to the counselors and teachers." Contrasting his experience with that of a *baal tshuvah*, a *haredi* contemplating departure remarks:

> Look, there's a world of difference. If somebody wants to become a *hozer betshuvah*, I'm not saying it's easy, but he knows where to go. He can go to one of many places and each of them is thrilled to accept him. He receives instruction, he'll have a place to sleep and eat. The point is there's support and encouragement. I can leave [*haredi* society] in the sense that I can get to a number 54 bus and I pay 80 agorot, and I come to the central bus station. But where do I go from there? There's no place to go, and there's no place that's ready to help me. So I have to do it all alone. I have to plan it by myself and I have to manage it by myself.

As the above remarks suggest, the differing contexts within which the resocialization occurs bear directly on how the experience itself is evaluated and managed. While both groups of individuals embark upon the acquisition of a new perspective and identity, the *baalei tshuvah's* resocialization provides them access to a subculture that offers sympathetic understanding and support. By contrast, the *hozrim beshe'elah* initiate their exit in the absence of any guidelines on either the mechanics of the disengagement or the emotional consequence resulting from separation from family, friends, and a lifestyle steeped in Torah observance.

MANAGING THE TRANSFORMATION: INDIVIDUAL VERSUS COLLECTIVE STATUS

When a person moves into a new interpersonal setting, he faces a major problem of understanding the setting and coming to terms with its demands. He must develop a workable definition of the situation to guide his actions. The newcomer might be assisted along this line by others who either have already experienced this transition or currently share a similar situation. Of critical importance, then, is whether the individual experiences the new situation alone or in the company of others; in other words, the individual or collective status of the recruits. As Goffman (1961) has shown, much socialization is organized so that a large number of persons are introduced to the new setting simultaneously. Under these circumstances, adaptation is likely to proceed much differently from those instances where a person enters alone because the recruits can arrive at a collective solution to the problems presented. A second and related aspect is whether the individual has been preceded by others who have experienced the same transition and who can "teach him the ropes." This distinction is between a serial pattern of socialization and a disjunctive pattern where the recruit is not following in the footsteps of predecessors (Wheeler 1966). As I have suggested, the socialization of the *baalei tshuvah* is characterized by its collective status and serial pattern.

The structure and organization of the yeshiva setting are connected to two important features affecting the transformation experiences of *baalei tshuvah*. First, because the yeshiva processes newcomers, it thereby maintains a measure of control over the direction and shape of their socialization experiences. Second, and following from the collective status and the serial pattern of the resocialization, there emerges the formation of a yeshiva subculture—a set of perspectives and understandings about what the *baalei tshuvah* experience is like and how to deal with it, and a set of routine activities based on these perspectives. Alongside this subculture is a vocabulary of motives (Mills 1940) that explains, justifies, and answers questions about the behavior in question.

The newcomer who agrees to remain in the yeshiva for a three-month period follows a structured curriculum that introduces him to Jewish laws and traditions. He is taught by sympathetic tutors in a friendly atmosphere that encourages him to consider changing his life-style permanently. At this particular stage, it is felt by those responsible for processing the newcomer that only appeals to the person's logic will be effective in ensuring a conversion. As one of the rabbis explains:

> You know, the majority of our students are either university educated or are completing their university training. It's difficult to convince them to change if your arguments aren't persuasive. But overpowering the individual with logic in your first or second discussion with him won't necessarily do the trick. Success isn't achieved so quickly. No...he has to come to the realization that...what we are asking of him makes sense.

In assisting them to arrive at this realization, each of the students attends the same core of basic courses, exposure to which is considered central towards shaping newcomers' attitudes and behavior. Moreover, the content is coordinated to appeal to the students' intellect, and the instructors are selected because of their charismatic appeal. For instance, in the case of "The Forty-eight Ways of Wisdom" class, the students are unanimous in asserting that the manner in which Rav Noah, the instructor, taught the course is the main reason for which they stay on. As one of them explains:

> The class is really basic.... More than any other class, this one sets the pace. This is the one that really makes you think.... The thing about this class is that everything is presented so logically. You are constantly challenged to point out where the arguments don't make sense. Many times people stay on for three months just to complete this class.

In referring to another one of the basic courses on "Proof of the Divine Authorship of the Torah," a senior student remarks:

> The proofs have been organized so carefully. A lot of guys figure that they'll be able to refute the arguments. After all, what do rabbis know? They [the newcomers] have studied philosophy, religion.... First of all, they realize that they're up against some very bright and sophisticated teachers. Second, and this is what they find even more confusing, the arguments seem to make sense. Many of the guys have tried challenging them, but then they realized they [the arguments] might be right. For sure, they're convincing enough not to dismiss them.

An integral feature of the yeshiva's curriculum lies in convincing students that their presence there cannot be attributed to chance factors but, rather, that they have been guided by Divine Providence. Students are continually encouraged to reflect on the series and timing of events that led to their initial encounter with the yeshiva and to assess the likelihood that the requisite circumstances could happen on their own accord. As one of the rabbis offers in reply to a student's query:

> What do you think? Do you think you're here by chance? Think about the things that had to happen, according to a particular sequence, for you to have made it here. Really, does it make sense to believe that this is due to luck or chance? No. You are here

because God wanted you here. This is an opportunity that Ha-Shem [God] is offering you. It's now up to you to take advantage of it.

Both formally and informally, the message conveyed to students is that their decision to remain in the yeshiva is a reasonable one. For those choosing to remain, their decision is mainly attributed to the yeshiva's distinctive approach to challenging their intellect. As one of the students observes:

> Before I knew it, they proved to me there was a God with logical proofs. There is none of this belief or faith....Everything is 'think'.... If you show us a hole in the proof, you can walk away. But if you can't...you have to accept it.

Although the yeshiva's program does not demand that students sever extra-group ties, as so many radical sectarian movements do (Bittner 1963; Kornhauser 1962), the activities at the yeshiva are structured to consume most of the students' waking hours. When he is not attending classes or studying, he is usually in the company of other students engaging in informal conversation during which the subject of religion is the central topic. One student observes:

> It's really quite remarkable. Wherever you turn, someone is talking about religion or something that's connected. At lunch, for example, someone raises the point brought up in class, or someone else tells about a conversation he had with someone to get them to come to the yeshiva. No one talks about baseball, or if someone talks about sports, it'll be directed to a conversation about religion.

Although the yeshiva's formal curriculum aims to appeal to the students' logic and reason, it also affords them opportunities to relate their yeshiva experience at the affective level. The friendships established with others, the pairing of students for purposes of study, and the numerous informal opportunities for sharing feelings and concerns provides an invaluable support system. Such a supportive environment enables them to compare themselves to others, both peers as well as more senior students, to assess their progress, evaluate their deepening identification and commitment to Orthodox Judaism, and to seek solutions to problems resulting from their changed life-style.

Many studies focusing on new religious movements show that friendship and a sense of community play an important part in the recruitment-commitment process (Barker 1984; Harrison 1974; Kanter 1972). The students who elect to pursue their studies at the yeshiva claim to be attracted not only by the logical arguments but also by the sense of community that prevails in the yeshiva and by its communal rituals. Many admit to having been influenced by the affectionate attention directed towards them during and after classes, and say that they are prepared to trust the yeshiva because the student body impresses them as being sincere and contented.

What is most impressive about the yeshiva environment for students is that those around them take a special interest in their personal situation. Fellow students and faculty are not only prepared to listen to the individual's concerns and answer his questions about Judaism and related matters, but they are also willing to reciprocate and speak about their own feelings and reactions. As a result, the students conclude that people do sincerely care about them. As one of them remarks:

> The thing about this place is that it's genuine. People here are interested in you and that comes across right from the start.... I've been involved in a number of religious groups. The affection showered on you in those groups was contrived. It's not like here. People here care about you in a real and sincere way.

However, the peer group atmosphere extends beyond the offer of sympathetic understanding. More significantly, as the students' bonds of friendship widen, they are able to learn how others chart and manage their course toward Orthodox Judaism. In time, students discover that their particular problems are not unique but are, instead, typically shared by others who proceded them. One individual sums up this view as follows:

> Becoming an orthodox Jew isn't something that happens immediately. There are a lot of things you think about, questions that you wrestle with, and it's important to get feedback. That's where the students help you most, especially those who have been where you're at now. They really understand and their advice helps a lot.

Indeed, the student culture becomes helpful in suggesting ways of coping with the problems accompanying the transition and, particularly, in forecasting the typical problems that the individual will encounter. A student illustrates this point by drawing upon his own situation:

Look, from what I can gather, my case was typical. You run into different kinds of problems when you decide to stay. I was in the middle of university and decided to take a break. My parents were really upset. Well, a number of the guys understood because this is what happened to them as well. An approach has developed to dealing with this problem with parents and family. It's a very common problem that has been worked out at the yeshiva. You can draw upon other guys' experiences and it makes you realize you're not alone.

In extreme contrast to the *baalei tshuvah*, the resocialization experience of the *hozrim beshe'elah* is both individual and disjunctive and, as a result, is accompanied by feelings of loneliness and abandonment. They are suddenly utterly isolated in the secular society without knowing to whom to turn for help or comfort. Reflecting on his own travails in exiting from haredi society, one person says:

A person can really go mad from such an experience. It's a terrible loneliness and you become really alone. You cut off everything that you had and are by yourself. And nobody cares about you and that's it. Nobody cares about you as a person.

Another *hozer beshe'elah* echoes this reaction:

You feel an emptiness, a very deep emptiness, and there's also confusion. What makes it all so difficult and terrible is that you have nobody to talk to, nobody who really understands what you're going through. The loneliness can be overpowering. You're cut off. The close friends you've had since childhood, you never see again.

Although some individuals might find the closeness of *haredi* life suffocating, they are nevertheless aware that such closeness means that no member of the community is allowed to go hungry or ill clad or unattended in ill health. As one *hozer beshe'elah* puts it: "The most difficult thing about leaving is that you're leaving a community, a really strong community, very close, very family-like.... You see, it's leaving a whole way of life and starting a new life on your own."

As we have already seen, the yeshiva environment provides individuals with a ready-made group of persons with whom they can establish ties of friendship. Although their decision to remain in the yeshiva might initially cause family and friends to react negatively, such a reaction is eventually replaced by increased understanding and respect. Such support is characteristically absent for the *hozrim beshe'elah*. While some form of relationship is maintained with immediate family, it is both strained and awkward because they are now identified primarily as individuals that have strayed from the proper Jewish path. A *hozer beshe'elah* relates:

> There are good reasons why leaving is difficult. One is friends, good friends. There each person is connected to the other. Really, just like brothers. Each person speaks to others. People lend each other money and provide other kinds of help. . . . So everyone has friends. The moment one leaves, one is cut off from all one's friends.

Both in the case of the *baalei tshuvah* and *hozrim beshe'elah*, the newfound orientation—religion in the first instance and secular life-style in the other—results in a redefinition and reorientation in one's relationships with friends. As a *baal tshuvah* explains:

> I kept in touch with some of my closer friends, but we just stopped writing. They couldn't relate to my religious beliefs. They accepted where I was intellectually and seemed pleased that I was happy with myself, but they couldn't really relate. I really don't think I'd have much to say to them today.

The remarks of a former *haredi* are virtually identical. When asked whether he keeps in touch with at least one or two of his haredi friends, he replies: "No one. Simply because I haven't anything to talk with them about. We haven't anything in common. I'm not them and they're not me."

Although relinquishing ties with former friends is common both to newly observant Jews and former *haredim*, it impacts more strongly on the latter both because of the long-standing nature of the terminated relationship and especially because such friendships are not easily replaced by new ones. Of course, there is nothing to prevent the former haredim from forming new friendships; but that takes time, and even then, it is not easily achieved. The case of one *hozeret beshe'elah*, who shed the 'ultra' part of her ultra-Orthodox life-style, offers an interesting illustration. She had believed that it would be simple for her to become friendly with members of the Agudat Yisrael, a religious political party, but she was soon disabused. As she explained: "They believe that each person should follow in their parents' footsteps. As soon as a person changes from the ways of his parents, he's blemished." She then tried to become friendly with women who had been pupils in an ultra-Orthodox girls' school, but she said: "Well, they don't accept me because they know, they soon find out, that I left Toldos Aron [a *haredi* community]. This tells them that there's something wrong with me."

Obviously, the persons with whom the defectors share a great deal in common are other defectors from the *haredi* world. One *hozer beshe'elah*, while lamenting the painful loneliness of the defection experience, describes the importance of the shared experience:

> There are very few people who went through what they went through. So they [former *haredim*] can know a lot of people but they don't have a deep relationship with them, like somebody with whom you have a lot of interests... because, just very simply, they won't be able to tell them a Yiddish joke, a pornograhpic joke about Gemara. If you come from the same background, you love it; but if you don't it won't mean anything to you.

Much like the difficulties in establishing new friendships experienced by ex-Moonies (Beckford 1985), the new friendships cultivated by the *hozrim beshe'elah* are mainly superficial, hardly enabling them to engage in conversations about matters of a personal and meaningful nature. A *hozer beshe'elah* expresses this point tellingly:

> The friends you lose you can't replace. You meet a number of new people but they aren't anything more than acquaintances for the most part. There is a limit to how much you can share with them because you don't know them that well and they don't know you. So you might know a number of people but none on an intimate level. You can't imagine what it's like when you don't have people to share with, to turn to for advice, for help. You're alone, really, all alone.

For the ex-*haredim*, a wide gulf exists between the idealism and support that surrounds them in the *haredi* society and the necessity of fending for themselves in the secular world. Upon learning to cope with the demands and expectations of the secular society, the *hozrim beshe'elah* are compelled to accustom themselves to the materialism and open search for personal advantage of their secular compatriots, that is, to the attitudes and values that run counter to the principles that rule haredi society. This dramatic contrast is well captured by a *hozer beshe'elah* in his observations about the two different worlds. Reflecting upon the transition from *haredi* to secular society, he explains:

They [ex-*haredim*] come from a world where ideals are everything, the basis for everything, the beginning and end of everything. And they get to the secular world which is not idealistic at
all. Which is very mundane and materialistic. It's living your life
and caring about yourself and not caring about other people....

In analyzing the process of becoming a marijuana user, Becker
(1953) shows how the culture of users provides the novice not only
with the technical aspects of where to acquire "pot" and how to use it,
but with a value system as well. In becoming *baalei tshuvah*, novices
are provided with access to a particular symbol-moral universe that
assists them in defining the meaning of the religious experience; an
atmosphere and environment from which they derive social accept-
ability and suport against outside disapproval; and a vocabulary by
which they can justify, and meaningfully interpret, their experiences.
Such subcultural support is unavailable to the *hozrim beshe'elah* who
must negotiate the transition to the secular world alone. The following
section focuses on three specific components or properties of the
negotiated transition that are influenced by the collective versus the
solo nature of the transformation experience.

PROPERTIES OF THE CONVERSION EXPERIENCE

Learning the Cultural Script

In his analysis of the moral career of the ex-Moonie, Beckford (1985)
suggests that "there is little in the way of a cultural 'script' for the
passage of a person from being a member of an intense religious group
to being a non-member" (1985, 174). Because such a transition has
not figured prominently in the popular literature or drama, it involves,
in technical terms, 'transition to a non-scheduled status'. As the previous discussion has indicated, the opportunities for familiarization
with the newly adopted cultural script differ dramatically for ex-
haredim and newly observant Jews.

In contrast to the situation faced by ex-cult followers, the *haredi*
defectors encounter a double bind: in addition to unfamiliarity with
the process of departure from *haredi* society, they are also not at-
tuned to the norms and values of the secular world from which they
have been sheltered and with which they have become aligned. The
disillusioned cult followers, on the other hand, come from a secular
background and know the life-style to which they will revert. Moreover, there are usually caring persons who are eager to guide them

back—often, indeed, who would have used all available means to persuade them to return to the bosom of their families. For the defecting haredim, on the other hand, as one of them explained: "Outside, there's nothing. There's one big void. Whoever doesn't fill that void before he goes out is destined to great suffering." However, it is extremely difficult for them to prepare for the secular would while still pretending to observe ultra-Orthodox practices. Some of them do arrange to spend a period away and thereby learn something of the practices of nonobservant Jews before formally abandoning their allegiance the *haredi* code of behavior. For others who suddenly find themselves on the other side of the fence, the shock is often traumatic. After years of living in a community where the sexes are strictly separated, it is not easy to mix informally with women. For example, one individual claims to be confused and embarrassed when he began having girlfriends. Another recalls his reaction when, immediately after leaving his ultra-Orthodox yeshiva, he went to a department store to buy new clothes:

> The colors baffled me. I didn't know how to match them up. Generally speaking, I wasn't used to seeing so many bright colors. I finally bought a black suit. It seemed to stand out less and I didn't want to be noticed.... When I completed the black suit with a pair of sandals, I truly looked as if I came from another planet. After a year I burned the suit that reminded me of how ridiculous I must have looked. I used to sit on the porch outside my room watching people pass by as if they were in a fashion show, in order to decide what clothes to buy.

Yet another comments on the basic problems facing those who study in *haredi* institutions when they leave to join mainstream secular Jewish society in Israel:

> They don't have the basic education, basic knowledge of mathematics, of geography, of history. All the things that are taken for granted, they don't have. That means that they can't get into this new society.... They can't talk to people. Things people take for granted, they won't know. They don't know how many continents there are in the world, as an example,... so they can't talk to people.

Without exception, the ex-*haredim* make painstaking efforts to fill the gaps in their knowledge of the secular world, mainly through a voracious appetite for reading and by attending public lectures.

Under the circumstances, it is not surprising that they feel bewildered when they are suddenly thrown or, rather, when they deliberately throw themselves into the secular world.

By contrast, *baalei tshuvah* are not required to completely abandon the secular values and behavior that form the central guiding orientation in their lives. To be sure, aspects of such behavior eventually require modification, but such adaptions can be organized and comprehended within their established secular frame of reference. In fact, in its attempts to persuade students to remain in the yeshiva, the administration mainly appeals to their powers of logical reasoning, rooted in the secular culture, that it encourages them to utilize in understanding the demands of Torah Judaism. As one of the rabbis explained:

> Even though what we're asking of students is not that simple, I mean it's difficult to change, they can handle it gradually. No one insists that they change overnight. But more importantly, the changes we're interested in don't require that they adopt a fundamentally different approach to reasoning. Basically, we're asking them to reason and then, of course, to act on that reasoning.

And, as a student offers:

> Even though I'm introduced to a new world of meaning and material objects, like I didn't know about *tefillin* [phylacteries] and *tzitzes* [ritual fringes], I can assimilate that information within my own frame of reference. To put it differently, I haven't had to invert my way of thinking.

Thus, institutionalized supports offered by the yeshiva, coupled with the informal networking of peers, provide *baalei tshuvah* with a cultural script both for assessing as well as managing their progress into the Orthodox world. Stated otherwise, the convert requires and receives "an organized community within which they may regularly act out, in the company of others, the behavioral implications of the experience which he has undergone" (Cohen et al. 1987, 327).

Centrality of Time

While the pace at which the transition occurs is more regularlized for the *baalei tshuvah*, the process of change extends over a period of time for both groups. To the outsider, the observed changes in the individual's behavior usually signify strong measures of identification with the newly chosen life-style. Recruits themselves, however, observe that the changes, while appearing to be sudden, are more typically the culmination of a lengthy period of reflection. Both in the case of *baalei tshuvah* and *hozrim beshe'elah,* the element of time becomes the critical mediator in their identity transformation. Their resulting changes are best conceptualized as a temporal process involving sequences of steps that gradually alter their self-conception, thereby contributing to an increased identification with and commitment to a changed way of life.

The following comments reveal the centrality of time in the transformation experience of *baalei tshuvah:*

> When I first came [three years ago] I was hopelessly confused and didn't know what the hell I was doing there. At first I wasn't sure that I could trust the people here. I mean were they really sincere or just pretending? But because I gave this place a chance, the situation changed and I know that my decision to become a practicing Jew was right.

> In the beginning, for the first couple of months, the experience was simply overwhelming. There was so much happening that I couldn't assimilate it all.... But time makes such a big difference because it allows you to see things in perspective. I've gone through some incredible changes since I've come eight months ago. Everybody here, I would say, goes through stages. The rabbis talk about stages. Like at first there's the stage of feeling overwhelmed and confused. You just can't get a firm grip on things.... Then there's a stage of rebellion or challenge. You argue, you take issue with their [the rabbis'] arguments.... Eventually, if you're here long enough, and if you open yourself to the possibility for change, you accept not only the logic of the arguments, but you also become attached emotionally and spiritually. You can't predict how long these stages last, but you see it all over here.

The passage of time is instrumental in assisting the *baalei tshuvah* determine how best to express their connection with Orthodox Judaism. Although this necessarily involves the adoption of religious practices, both their pace and sequence varies with the individual's background and inclination to change. Two individuals remark:

> I started with tefillin immediately. That has been easy for me to

do, but I still have trouble wearing a *kippah* [skullcap] when I go into the city. You're expected to participate in prayer and that's becoming more meaningful as time goes on.

I don't put on telfillin, I just don't put them on. [You don't put them on at all?] Sometimes I do but usually I don't. It's a very heavy act for me. It's very complete and I'm not comfortable enough with it to say everything in Torah is true and I am going to do it. This is me.

In time, however, as individuals become committed to remaining in the yeshiva, alterations in their external behavior blend with the emergence of a new self-conception involving newly adopted priorities, values, and goals. The passage of time is significant for yet another reason as it enables the *baalei tshuvah* to persuade parents and friends to accept their new religious orientation, thereby assuaging their apprehension concerning an Orthodox Jewish life-style.

Whereas the *baalei tshuvah's* encounter with the yeshiva world and Orthodox Judaism are typically unplanned, the *hozer beshe'elah's* departure from the *haredi* fold is premediated. All of the respondents characterize their departure as preceded by considerable internal debate and distress. One, aged 25, who had defected only months before we met, seems to speak for all respondents when he says:

It must sound strange to you that despite my questions and criticisms, it took me years to leave. But you can't imagine how difficult it is. You're always debating with yourself whether you're making the right decision. You know that you want to leave, but you're just not sure. You can't imagine how much courage you need to make the break.

Departure is consistently portrayed as a process involving intense reflection. One individual, in his early forties, who left his *haredi* community in the 1960s to fight in the Six-Day War, describes his efforts at reaching a decision:

From an internal standpoint, it's a matter of process that takes years. But all the time, externally, I didn't change any of my customs, and I continued to follow the halakah up to the point where I decided that I'm sure that this isn't my way. Then, only then, did I change drastically. Now for outsiders it looked like it happened one bright day but internally it's a process of years.

However long the internal process, the adoption of behavior violating strict religious commandments or dressing in a manner offending the community's prescribed mode is conceptualized temporally. As one individual recalls:

> There's always a first time. And this first time is difficult. It's painful. It cuts. But the transition . . . can take a number of years. There's the first time I took of my *kippah*, there's the first time that I stopped putting on tefillin, there's the first time that I drove on the Sabbath, there's the first time that I didn't eat kosher, there's the first time that I ate on Yom Kippur, and so on. This doesn't occur over a period of a week; it doesn't all happen on the same day.

For many, the failure to observe the commandments is accompanied by fear of divine retribution. For instance, an individual speaks of the fear he experienced of incurring terrible consequences after driving on the Sabbath for the first time:

> I was very scared the first time. . . . I remember it well. I was scared. It was Shabbat, and I was nervous. I was on a kibbutz in the north and we went to the sea, the Kinneret, and we hitchhiked. Whenever a car didn't stop, I felt good. . . . In the end, some tourists stopped and we went down by the old road. . . . It was very emotional. There were a lot of curves in the road and I was afraid at each one of them. It wasn't a rational fear. It was Sabbath.

The realization that divine retribution is not immediately forthcoming enables these individuals to continue distancing themselves from their respective *haredi* communities. For instance, as a male who left his community seven months prior to our conversation recalls:

> Without question, the beginning is the most difficult. You're unsure of yourself, you've never done any of these things before, like not keeping kosher or violating the Sabbath. But over time you learn how to deal with the feelings you experience and become better at rationalizing your behavior.

As I have suggested, then, both for the *baalei tshuvah* and *hozrim beshe'elah*, the alteration of behavior proceeds gradually; time becomes the central element through which the experiences are distilled and incorporated into the person's new identity.

Redefining Family Relations

A separate, but related, feature affecting the individual's transformation centers around changing relations with family and friends. Because their behavioral changes are typically defined as radical by those close to them, a strained family relationship is common to both groups under investigation. In each case, the relationship is initially characterized by intense upheaval followed by gradual accommodation. Yet this situation also differs significantly for the two groups: in contrast to the usual reconciliation between *baalei tshuvah* and their parents, the ex-*haredim's* movement away from the ultra-Orthodox fold remains a festering sore causing deep anguish and emotional tension.

According to the baalei tshuvah, the initial reply from their parents, in response to a letter explaining that they wish to study in the yeshiva for an extended time, is typically negative. Although this reaction is expected, its intensity varies. For example:

> I wrote them a letter that I was at the yeshiva and that I was planning to stay for a couple of months. They were really opposed. My father wrote me this letter saying that I was copping out of my chances and he was going to send me $200 to get home and that was it. He said he couldn't force me to come home, but don't expect any more money. He said, "Personally, I think you're blowing it."

Another individual illustrates a more negative reaction:

> When my parents found out that I was here, they immediately enlisted the help of a Conservative rabbi to get me to leave. They called a few times each day to say that I was involved in a cult and to get out while I had the chance. They weren't prepared to listen. They were shocked and disappointed, but most of all frightened. I might as well have ended up with the Moonies as far as they were concerned.

While the deteriorating relationship between *baalei tshuvah* and their families intensifies for some, the more usual outcome, as time passes, involves a rapprochment between them. A successful resolution of the conflict involves the writing of carefully crafted letters, drafted with the advice of yeshiva personnel and seasoned senior students. This outcome is significant in enabling baalei tshuvah to adopt a favorable self-image with respect to their changed life-style. As one person remarks:

> Your parents really want you to be happy. When they found out I wasn't a Moonie and acting like a robot ... they were really happy for me. I just got a letter from them the other day.... My mother said, "I am really glad that you have found serenity and I wish that you could share it with me, and I am really looking forward to when you come home so that you can teach me the techniques that you learned in the yeshiva." This is so remarkable and it shows that I have a very open-minded family.... This kind of letter make such a difference in terms of my abilities to concentrate and apply myself here. I know they're behind me.... Apparently it takes all the parents a while and it isn't until they come here and see what we're doing that they're really happy for the kids.

While the gulf separating the ex-*haredim* and their family narrow slightly—both make efforts to maintain the tenuous relationship—the distance between them remains wide. Each of the defectors is very concerned about the effect that their departure would have on their family and close friends. As one of them says: "One of the most difficult things for me was the anguish I caused my mother. That, for me, was the most difficult. She knew I was leaving, but she didn't know the details—what I eat, don't eat—but she knew." Another leaves home but doesn't formally tell his parents that he has abandoned the ultra-Orthodox life-style. He explains that he did not announce, "I drive on the Sabbath" or that he is no longer observant; but his parents realize that he has changed, and his mother has been greatly saddened.

The case of yet another ex-*haredi*, in his early forties, helps illustrate the tension characterizing his relationship with his mother and relatives. He has moved away from his former home in B'nei Brak and is living in Tel Aviv with his secular second wife and their child. His first wife is a member of the haredi community and he divorced her within months of their marriage. He now wants his young daughter to get to know her grandmother and to have a loving relationship with her. His father died shortly after he had become reconciled to his son's defection, but his mother has continued to be resentful. He finally persuaded her to agree to receive her granddaughter, and about twice a month on a Saturday he brings the child to her. He explains:

> I observe the commandment of honoring one's parents. I don't really talk to my mother, I haven't much to say to her. I go into a

room and lie down, sleep, but don't involve myself with my mother.... Other relatives? I have an aunt who lives close by, but I have nothing to do with her. I have no connection with my uncles, with any of them.... About a month and a half ago I was sitting in a restaurant in Jerusalem and right behind me was my cousin.... So I said to my friend in a loud voice, "Do you see the *vantz* [Yiddish for bedbug] sitting behind me? That's my cousin." So my friend went and asked him and he said, "Yes, he was strange when he was a boy." And three years ago I met his brother and said, "Do you know who I am?" and he said, "You're my cousin. *Gay avek* [Get out of here]."

Another ex-*haredi* is also uneasy when he visits his family after he left the community. But he does his best not to offend them and he wears a skullcap when he comes to see them. But he is always under strain: "I can't be there for more than one quarter to half an hour. It's just too difficult. It's too intense, so I leave." By contrast, another claims that his relations with his parents and with his brothers and sisters are amicable now. His wife, however, is more realistically aware of the deep rift that his departure has created. When he is asked how frequently he visits his family, she says that he goes only about once a month and on the Sabbath, and he comments: "Yes, it disturbs them all very much."

Although not necessarily critical in terms of their integration into the secular world, the *hozrim beshe'elah's* stilted relationships with family influence their patterns of adjustment. It is, indeed, difficult for a person to regard himself as a worthwhile individual without receiving support from those that he loves and respects. Lacking support and understanding from family, coupled with the absence of a set of sympathetic peers, the hozrim beshe'elah's departure from the *haredi* world, and their integration into the larger society, is experienced is isolating, confusing, and painful, irreparably damaging the bonds that previously existed with parents, other family members, and friends.

CONCLUSION

Based upon research conducted in Israel, this chapter highlights and analyzes some of the comparisons and differences between newcomers to Orthodox Judaism and defectors from the ultra-Orthodox *haredi* fold. Further research along this line might focus on additional component of the status passage, namely, for example, whether it is reversible, the kinds of legitimation that might be required and sought from authorized agents, and the clarity of the signs marking the transformation.

In offering an overview of the transformation experience, I have not attended to all of the intricate dynamics underlying its management. In both cases, for instance, the manipulation of convincing presentations before various audiences signifies the individuals' progress along the chosen route. As well, just as there are various modes of *tshuvah* (Aviad 1983), so too might it be possible to delineate different trajectories by which *hozrim beshe'elah* negotiate their exit from haredi society. In a world where definitions are shaped by gender distinctions, further research might attend to how this dimension imposes itself upon the experienced transformation.

The art of coordinating a convincing self-presentation figures prominently in any conversion experience. While impression management is central both for newcomers to Orthodox Judaism and the religious defectors, the respective dynamics regarding the relationship between attitudes and behavior differ. In light of the institutionalized context within which the conversion experience is situated, hozrim betshuvah quickly adopt the appropriate behavioral trappings of Orthodox Judaism, including dress, language, study, and prayer, hoping to acquire eventually the requisite attitudes that correspond to their behavior. While outwardly displaying confidence in their behavioral commitment to Orthodox Judaism, they inwardly engage at realigning their understanding of life's meaning and purpose to fit the requirements of their new life-style. This sequence appears to be reversed for the *haredi* defectors. The decision to exit from the haredi community is accompanied by attitudinal and emotional changes concerning the authenticity of the haredi life-style and Orthodox Judaism in advance of the behavioral changes that eventually reflect their altered life-style. Presenting themselves to their peers and others in *haredi* society as suitably committed members of the community, they secretly violate the governing norms of their society and seek the appropriate opportunities to embark publicly upon a radically different way of life. The commonly used tactics for negotiating a new identity constitute a central component of the conversion experience.

REFERENCES

Albrecht, S. L., and H. M. Behr. 1983. Patterns of religious disaffiliations: A study of lifelong Mormons, Mormon converts, and former Mormons. *Journal for the Scientific Study of Relgionn* 22 (4): 366–79.

Aviad, J. 1983. *Return to Judaism: Religious renewal in Israel.* Chicago: University of Chicago Press.

Barker, E. 1984. *The making of a moonie: Choice of brainwashing:* New York: Basil Blackwell.

Becker, H. S. 1953. Becoming a marijuana user. *American Journal of Sociology 59* (November): 235-42.

Beckford, J. A. 1978. Through the looking-glass and out the other side: Withdrawal from Reverend Moon's unification church. *Archives de Sciences Sociales des Religions* 45 (1): 95-116.

Behr, H. M. 1986. *Cult controversies: The societal response to the new religious movements.* New York: Tavistock Publications.

Bittner, E. 1963. Radicalism and the organization of radical movements. *American Sociological Review 29 (6): 928–40.*

Brinkerhoff, M. B., and K. L. Burke. 1980. Disaffiliation: some notes on "Falling from the Faith." *Sociological Analysis* 41 (1): 41-54.

Catton, W. R. 1957. What kind of people does a religious cult attract? *American Sociological Review* 22 (5): 551-66.

Cohen, E., N. Ben-Yehuda, and J. Aviad. 1987. Recentering the world: The quest for 'elective' centers in a secularized universe. *The Sociological Review* 35 (2): 320-46.

Cromer, G. 1981. Repentent delinquents: A religious approach to rehabilitation. *The Jewish Journal of Sociology* 23 (2): 113-22.

Davis, R. and J. T. Richardson. 1976. The organization and functioning of the children of God. *Sociological Analysis* 37 (4): 321-39.

Friedman, M. 1986. Haredim confront the modern city. In *Studies in Contemporary Jewry* II, ed. P. Y. Medding, 74-96. Bloomington: Indiana University Press.

Glaser, B. G., and A. L. Strauss. 1971. *Status passage.* Chicago: Aldine Atherton.

Glock, C. Y., and R. N. Bellah, ed. 1976 *The new religious consciousness.* Berkeley: University of California Press.

Goffman, E. 1961. *Asylums.* New York: Doubleday.

Gordon, D. 1974. The Jesus people: An identity synthesis. *Urban Life and Culture* 3 (2): 159-78.

Harrison, M. I. 1974. Sources of recruitment to Catholic Pentacostalism. *Journal for Scientific Study of Religion* 13 (1): 49-64.

Jacobs, J. 1984. The economy of love in religious commitment: The deconversion of women from nontraditional religious movements. *Journal for the Scientific Study of Religion* 23 (2): 155–71.

Kanter, R. M. 1972. *Commitment and community: Communes and utopias in sociological perspective.* Cambridge, Mass.: Harvard University Press.

Kitsuse, J. 1970. Editor's preface. *American Behavioral Scientist* 14 (2): 163–65.

Kornhauser, W. 1962. Social bases of political commitment: A study of liberals and radicals. In *Human Behavior and Social Processes*, ed. A. Rose, 321–29. Boston: Houton Mifflin.

Lofland, J. 1986. *Doomsday cult: A study of conversion, proselytization and maintenance of faith.* Englewood Cliffs, N.J.: Prentice-Hall.

Mauss, A. 1969. Dimensions of religious defection. *Review of Religious Research* 10: 128–35.

Mills, C. W. 1940. Situated actions and vocabularies of motive. *American Sociological Review* 5 (October): 904–13.

Peter, K., E. D. Boldt, I. Whitaker, and L. W. Roberts. 1982. The dynamics of religious defection among Hutterities. *Journal for the Scientific Study of Religion* 25 (1): 327–37.

Shaffir, W. 1983. The recruitment of *baalei tshuvah* in a Jerusalem yeshiva. *The Jewish Journal of Sociology* 25 (1): 33–46.

Shaffir, W., and R. Rockaway. 1987. Leaving the ultraorthodox fold: *Haredi* Jews who defected. *The Jewish Journal of Sociology* 29 (2): 97–114.

Travisano, R. 1970. Alteration and conversion as qualitatively different transformations. In *Social Psychology Through Symbolic Interaction*, ed. G. P. Stone and H. Faberman, 594–606. Waltham, Mass.: Ginn-Blaisdell.

Wheeler, S. 1966. The structure of formally organized socialization settings. In *Socialization After Childhood: Two Essays*, ed. O. G. Brim, Jr. and S. Wheeler, 53–116. New York: John Wiley & Sons.

Zygmunt, J. F. 1967. Jehovah's Witnesses: A study of symbolic and structural elements in the development and institutionalization of a sectarian movement. Doctoral dissertation, University of Chicago.

8

Judaism and the New Religions in Israel: 1970–1990

BENJAMIN BEIT-HALLAHMI

The new religions that have appeared in Israel since the early 1970s, and have grown more forcefully after 1973, are the same ones that have appeared in the West since the 1950s. Their message, when they come to Israel, is the same as it is elsewhere. Only their audience is radically different, and so is the reception they are likely to get. New religions are belief minorities, in constant opposition to the world around them, which challenges the plausibility of their beliefs. The challenge, and the opposition, are going to be particularly fierce in the case of Israel.

In February 1982, an interdepartmental government commission was appointed by the Education Minister to investigate and report on "Eastern cults." The appointment of this commission is in itself an indication of the growth of the new religions in Israel. It was a result of pressure from parents' groups, orthodox religious groups, and the media. Active membership in all these groups was estimated at 3,000. The appearance and growth of new religious movements in Israel since 1973 has included not only well-known new religions that appeared in the West since 1950, but also older movements, such as Anthroposophy, Theosophy, and Jehovah's Witnesses, dating to the late nineteenth century.

New religions only partly fit the "ideal type" of religious sect, as formulated by Troeltsch (1961). Voluntariness, selectness, egalitarianism, cooperativeness, intimacy, and opposition to the world characterize this "ideal type." *Sectarian religion* means a total personal commitment, a frequent emotional expression of ecstacy, a total departure from the rest of society. Every religious sect, by definition, is in open rebellion against the ways of the world, and against the views of the majority. Every religious sect oversteps the boundaries of the area assigned to religion in secular society, and this is what is annoying and threatening. The sectarian rebellion against the majority is invisible in most cases because sects tend to withdraw from the wider society or keep to their original environment. A few sects are visible and annoying, and attract much attention when their members perform deviant acts, but the more remarkable fact is that most of the time sect membership leads to very conventional behavior. Still, sect membership itself, which involves a total commitment and a total personal involvement (living with other sect members, donating income), is deviant.

Glock and Stark (1965) define cults as "religious movements which draw their inspiration from other than the primary religion of the culture," whereas sects are "schismatic movements... whose concern is with preserving a purer form of the traditional faith" (p. 24). By this definition, all new religions in Israel are cults because they draw their inspiration from non-Jewish traditions. Within their own frame of reference, some of the new religions can be regarded as sects because they proclaim their own goal of preserving a purer form of Hinduism (ISKCON) or of Christianity (The Unification Church). One reason in favor of using the term new religions is its affective neutrality. Unlike "sects" or "cults," which are often used to derogate, "new religions" is neutral.

The concept of new religions can be traced back to Needleman (1970), who first made it popular. Following Needleman, we can define the new religions through three main characteristics:

1. They were founded after 1950.

2. They display modern, often businesslike methods of organization and recruitment.

3. They all have a conscious psychotherapeutic component in their belief systems and practices.

We are looking at groups whose formal organization, if not their belief system, is of relatively recent origin. Some of the groups promote beliefs and practices that seem beyond the traditional scope of religion, especially in two areas: occultism and self-improvement. This might be one of the characteristics of the new religions, as opposed to the old ones. Nevertheless, what the old and new religious movements always share is the *supernatural premise*, the belief in the invisible world, the world of spirits, or a "spiritual world," that believers must relate to (Wallace 1966). The existence and centrality of occult practices and beliefs and of various psychotherapy techniques indeed vary among the new religions, but what unites them are traditional religious beliefs about the immortal soul and about gods and other unseen cosmic forces.

There are organizational differences, related as well to the newness of the new religions. They are young in terms of organizational life cycle, and they are also very much belief minorities. Because the new religions do not enjoy the privileged status of the old ones and have to compete with them, their problem is the problem of every cultural innovation: how to create openness to new and different ideas? It is hard to gain plausibility for deviant beliefs, and the problem of new religions is gaining plausibility in the eyes of potential members and of the public.

In most new religions, the member is offered a system of psychological and sometimes physical exercises such as meditation, individual psychotherapy, and group therapy aimed at self-improvement and psychological well-being. This might be one of the differences between the old religions and the new ones, and it reflects the historical process of the psychologization of religion (compare Beit-Hallahmi 1985). The technology offered by the group, whether meditation, chanting, or psychotherapy, creates support for weak egos. This psychotherapeutic aid will naturally attract and help individuals with a range of personal problems, from mild neurosis to active psychosis. Some of the groups take a gnostic stance, claiming esoteric knowledge that is available only to group members. Sharing in this knowledge creates an understandable feeling of superiority. The insiders naturally feel superior to the unlightened majority, and this feeling might exert a powerful attraction.

The resocializing effects of membership in new religions, which often lead members to stop self-destructive behaviors and to reenter the owork world, have been widely recognized (Kiev 1969; Robbins 1969; Robbins and Anthony, 1972). Only rarely has the claim been made that membership in new religions can have negative consequences in terms of psychological functioning (Kiev 1964).

New religions, as opposed to old ones, are close to what Judah (1967) has called modern metaphysical movements in the content of their beliefs and practices. Especially prominent in these groups are two characteristics listed by Judah: first, the identification of religion and science as mutually supportive and continuous, and the psychotherapeutic approach to individual well-being. According to the classification offered by O'Dea (1968), the new religions in Israel can be classified as either *introversionist,* that is, seeking to withdraw from the world in order to cultivate inner "spirituality," or *gnostic,* that is, offering some special esoteric knowledge. The eschatology of the new religions covers two realms. First, there is the promise of radical change in the individual, in the direction of self-improvement, perfect health, longevity, and even immortality. Second, there is also, in some groups, the expectation of a cosmic catastrophe, which only the faithful will survive.

In attempting to assess the existence and growth of new religions in Israel since 1973, we are fortunate to have a survey published in 1972, done by two researchers at the Hebrew University (Cohen and Grunau 1972). This detailed survey of ethnic and religious minorities in Israel at the time included a section on cults. Using informants, official statistics, published research, and media reports, it gives us what we can call our baseline. It shows that the situation in Israel in 1972, as regards new religions, was strikingly different from that in Western Europe or the United States. The only groups listed were Theosophy, Anthroposophy, "Yoga according to Vente Kesananda," Transcendental Meditation, ISKCON, Subud, Zen, Kirshnamurti, Rosicrucians, and Spiritualists. The total number of members was at most 250. Most of the groups that became prominent later, such as Scientology and the Divine Light Mission, were simply unknown then. The number of Transcendental Meditation practitioners was estimated at less than ten.

In defining new religions in Israel we have an unexpected source of help. In Israel, where there is no constitution, no separation of religion and state, and a Ministry for Religious Affairs, there is a clear legal definition of new religions. These are all the religious communities not recognized by the state. According to Israeli law, all residents must belong to some religious community, whose rules they must then follow in regard to marriage, divorce, and burial. The Israeli system of religious divisions uses the *millet,* the religious community as a basic unit. This notion is taken from Turkish law (Cahnman, 1944). Under the millet system, the Israeli government recognizes certain established religious groups, whose leaders are accorded special status even when they represent tiny minorities. These religious communities are also entitled to government financial support for maintaining their churches or mosques, their separate legal systems, and their clergy. The only groups recognized by the state are Orthodox Judaism, Islam, Druze, and the historical Christian denominations. These groups have an official standing, their leaders are treated as dignitaries, and they are eligible for financial support and tax exemptions.

All other groups, ranging from Reform Jews to ISKCON, are not recognized.

Conversions from one millet to another are possible under the system, but have to be registered with the state to be legally valid. The British Mandate government recognized ten religious groups in 1922, namely Jews and nine Christian denominations, all recognized by the Israeli government after 1948. The Israeli government since then has recognized the Druze (1957), the Evangelical Episcopal Church in Israel (1970), and the Bahai faith (1971). The Moslems have not been officially recognized, but their religious courts have been empowered by two Israeli laws (1953 and 1961). Cases of conversion from one recognized group to another number fewer than 300 a year, most of them conversions from one Christian church to another. About five cases of Jews converting to Christianity are officially registered every year, and about 20 cases of Jews converting to Islam.

The boundaries of religious legitimacy and religious experimentation in Israel of the 1950s are faithfully described by Weiner (1961). The boundaries of religious legitimacy in Israel in the 1970s are delineated in Israel Pocket Library's *Religious Life and Communities* (1974), which contains material taken from the *Encyclopaedia Judaica*. The religious communities described as Jews, Muslims, Christians, Samaritans, Karaites, Druze, and Bahais.

REACTIONS TO THE NEW RELIGIONS:
THE ANTICULT LOBBY IN ISRAEL

The development and impact of new religions can be assessed by looking at the reactions they have brought about. We will look at reactions in the media, communities and community organizations, religious organizations, and government agencies, including the police. In response to the growth of new religions in Israel since the early 1970s, a counteraction has occurred in the form of the development of an anticult movement and an anticult lobby, similar to their parallels in the United States and modeled after them in some ways. We will survey the history of the movement by looking at its various components, including the Israeli government, the police, and nongovernmental organizations. New religions in Israel had to contend with the hostility of the religious establishment, the hostility of the public, the hostility of families of members, and the hostility of the media, which were guided by all the above. The threat and the deviance represented by the new religions in Israel inevitably caused a strong reaction. The opposition started, naturally, with Jewish religious groups, then came from parents, organizations, and then involved the media, the Israeli government, and the public.

Israeli society clearly exhibits a low tolerance for non-Jewish old religions and even for non-Orthodox branches of Judaism. New religions present a direct challenge to the religious establishment everywhere. In Israel this challenge is more serious because it is directed towards Jewish identity and Zionism, and thus touches the ideological base of the state itself. In a 1984 survey of Israeli youth, only 11 percent of respondents regarded joining new religions positively, while 85.6 percent regarded it negatively. On the other hand, the return to Judaism was viewed positively by 61.5 percent, while 32 percent viewed it negatively (Shem-Tov 1985). In a public opinion survey in 1984, Israelis were asked whether they considered certain actions damaging to Israeli society. Among the acts listed was "converting away from Judaism." Among those between the ages of 20 and 24, 52 percent considered it as damaging to society, while among those over the age of 24, the percentage was 66 percent (Hacohen 1984). Most new religions in Israel, as we have seen, have been imported. Not all of them have been treated in the same way by the Israeli establishment. Some have been singled out for harsher treatment—those that present a threat through their basic message and their mere existence.

Action has been taken against groups that challenged military service obligations (universal in Israel), loyalty to the state, or loyalty to Jewish identity. One can be a secular Jew but still preserve a nominal Jewish identity. Joining a new religion means, for an Israeli Jew, a rejection of Jewish identity. The positive step of joining ISKCON or Ananda Marga is a religious conversion, leaving behind the conventional Jewish identity and the attachment to the Jewish collective. Any ideology offering an alternative identity will by subject to vigorous attack and persecution. The touchstone is an alternative to the standard Jewish identity. Where there is no real claim of an alternative identity, reactions to new religions have been milder.

The attitude towards new religions can be compared to the attitude towards Neturei Karta (Marmorstein 1969), an Orthodox Jewish anti-Zionist group. Neturei Karta is opposed and denounced for its anti-Zionist stance, but it is nevertheless tolerated as part of the Jewish identity sphere. On the basis of that common identity it can be attacked and criticized, but certain basic rights of its members, such as the right to live in Israel, will not be challenged.

CONCERNED PARENTS AGAINST CULTS

Concerned Parents Against Cults, an organization modeled after similar groups in the United States, was founded in 1980 in Haifa and became formally incorporated as a nonprofit organization in 1982. In July 1981 it had fifteen members, but by late 1981 membership grew to sixty families. The organization has been active in lobbying the media and the government. Its chairman, N.B., has made numerous media appearances, including appearances on television in which his face and full identity were hidden.

Concerned Parents Against Cults has published its own leaflets containing information about various new religions, even referring to *est* as a cult. Their general level of accuracy and sophistication is rather low. N.B. has also been active in addressing letters to newspapers whenever any neutral or favorable mention was made of any of the new religions. The organization has been instrumental in bringing the film *Ticket to Heaven* to Israel, which drew much media attention, including television coverage. There can be little doubt that effective lobbying by Concerned Parents was instrumental in the creation of the government commission of inquiry in February 1982, and members of the organization appeared several times before the commission and kept in informal contact with its staff. Concerned Parents was effective in creating contacts with other government agencies, such as the Health Ministry.

On 12 May 1983 a daylong symposium was held in Tel Aviv, entitled "The problems and treatment of cult adepts." It was organized jointly by Concerned Parents Against Cults and by the mental health division of the Health Ministry. It was addressed, among others, by the director of mental health division and the legal counsel for the Health Ministry. Other participants included psychologists, psychiatrists, and former cult members. "Cult exit counseling" and "deprogramming" were introduced by individuals who wanted them imported into Israel. The individuals presenting and advocating "deprogramming" were Americans, who were ready to discuss their own experiences and offered their services. It should be emphasized that strong doubts were expressed about the legality of such procedures in Israel.

Materials distributed to the audience at the symposium consisted of articles published in the United States, such as the article by Singer (1979), and an annotated bibliography of books on cults, again published in the United States, well known to anybody studying the new religions. The overall solution offered at the symposium was the medicalization and psychologization of the new religions phenomenon.

"ANTI-MISSIONARY" GROUPS AND THE NEW RELIGIONS

Yad La'Ahim (Help to Our Brothers) is a nonprofit organization, with eight branches in Israel. Its members fight against abortions, The drafting of women into military service, autopsies, and other issues of concern to the Orthodox community. According to Avneri (1982), they also fight against mixed marriages between Jewish women and Arabs. *Yad La'Ahim* constitutes an "antimissionary" lobby in Israel, active since the 1950s. The ideology of the organization is clear: it represents Orthodox Judaism, and anything incompatible with that should be eliminated from the state of Israel. Any group that presents a challenge to the loyalty of Jews to Orthodox Judaism (including other Jewish traditions) should be confronted and thwarted. There is no differentiation, in the ideology of *Yad La'Ahim*, between old and new religions. Their struggle against the new religions in the 1970s and 1980s is a continuation of their struggle since the 1950s against Christian missionary groups, which culminated in the passing of an antimissionary law by the Knesset in 1977. The only way in which the new religions might be different, and more dangerous for *Yad La'Ahim*, is in that they do not carry the cultural stigma attached to old religions and their competition with Judaism. Thus, they are not as easily recognized for what they are and might be able to attract Israelis. This is exactly what has happened.

    Yad La'Ahim activities include media relations, publications, and actual harrassment of new religions. The most obvious and noticeable activity is initiating newspaper articles about new religions. According to an official statement by *Yad La-Ahim* in 1987, between 1982 and 1987, the organization succeeded in getting 286 Israelis to leave new religious groups. Some of the articles sound like press releases and include wild claims about the success of new religions. Thus, Fisher (1979) claims that "Hundreds of young people in the Haifa area have fallen prey to mysterious cults from the East." Lior (1981) claims that there were 100 cults operating in Israel, with more than 50,000 members.

    Yad La'Ahim publishes a monthly bulletin of activities against "missions and cults," which includes information about alleged Christian missionaries, Messianic Jews, and new religions. It also publishes special reports and reprints articles appearing in the press. In 1982, a booklet containing testimonies of former members of new religions, who were now Orthodox Jews, was published. It contained seven personal stories. A special report listing 17 "cults" operating in Israel was also published in 1982. *Yad La'Ahim* submitted a memorandum to the commission of inquiry investigating cults. The memorandum included 12 recommendations for action against new religions, from close police surveillance to declaring Scientology's E-Meter illegal. The organization also arranged for witnesses to appear before the commission.

MEDIA COVERAGE OF THE NEW RELIGIONS

As we survey the Israeli press, it will be hard to find references to specific new religions, or "cults" in general, before 1973. The only new religions whose existence in Israel can be gathered from the Israeli written media before the 1973 War were ISKCON and Transcendental Meditation (TM). The first wave of media attention to the groups follows the 1973 War. Press attention to TM was positive or neutral, and the first press campaign against new religions in the spring of 1974 singled out the Divine Light Mission. No similar campaign is to be found in the Israeli press until 1982–83, when no group is singled out, and the topic is "cults" in general. This second wave of media coverage, totally negative in tone, coincides with the creation of the government commission of inquiry on cults and the increased activity by Yad La'Ahim, the Orthodox antimissionary organization. It also coincides with the formation of the Concerned Parents Against Cults organization, active since 1980. In many of the articles, the hand of Yad La'Ahim can be immediately recognized. In a few cases it is the parents' organization that initiates such articles.

The electronic media, which in Israel are owned and controlled by the government, have also entered the fray. Radio and television programs have discussed "cults" with illustrations taken from the activities of specific new religions. ISKCON, TM, and Emin have been singled out on these programs.

The articles range from news reports covering the new religions and their relations with the community and government authorities, to interviews with professionals and academics, and reports on lectures by professionals with different orientations. Most major Israeli newspapers have carried not just major articles on "cults," but also a series or two on "cults in Israel." *Al Hamishmar* carried an eight-part series in March 1982, and *Davar* had two major articles in December. 1983 was a banner year for newspaper articles about cults. In addition to hundreds of articles about specific groups, there was an eight-part series in *Haaretz*, Israel's leading daily. The confidential National Police Intelligence Report on Cults (Soffrin and Yodfat 1982) was leaked to the press as soon as it was ready, and excerpts were duly published (for example, Frenkel 1982).

The tenor of all newspaper articles was negative, and some of them were purely sensational, The only exceptions to the moral crusade in the newspapers were those articles in which the new religions were defended on the basis of general democratic principles (for example, Geffen 1982) and on the basis of their similarity to the Judaization movement (Tumarkin, 1983). While Zaretsky and Leone (1974) suggest that the American media have given new religious movements an apearance of legitimacy, in Israel, for cultural and historical reasons, the situation is totally different. The media present new religions as definitely illegitimate and deviant.

AMERICAN JEWISH GROUPS AND NEW RELIGIONS IN ISRAEL

Jewish communities and Jewish organizations in the United States have been engaged in anticult activities since the early 1970s. News of new religions in Isreal, and of anticult moves in Israel, reached the United States in the early 1980s, and patterns of collaboration emerged between the old and the new cult-busters. According to *Jewish Times*, of Baltimore (1981), the Israeli government and, specifically, the Interior Minister, Yossef Burg, of the National Religious Party, had been in touch with the Jewish Community Relations Council's Task Form on Missionaries and Cults. Dr. Seymour P. Lachman, Chairman of the Task Force, is quoted as saying that the Task Force compiled a special report for Dr. Burg as it became clear that the same new religions were operating in both the United States and Israel. Rabbi Rubin R. Dobin, an American anticult activist, appeared on Israeli state television in 1982 to warn about cult activities in Israel. In an interview with Amdur (1982), Dobin is quoted: "Not only have I approached the Education, Interior, Religious Affairs, Health, Defense and Foreign Ministries, but the Prime Minister himself has shown an interest in the problem. I now intend to go to see Mr. Begin . . . to prove to him just how severe the problem is and to push for some kind of government legislation." Rabbi Yehuda Fein, who is described as an exit counselor and director of Choices for the Jewish Family, a New York organization, is also reported to have contacts with Israeli anticult groups (Guberman 1982).

THE KIBBUTZIM AND NEW RELIGIONS

The kibbutzim, collective settlements that invest much energy and concern in the education of their young people (Rabin and Beit-

Hallahmi 1982) make up less than 3 percent of the Israeli population. Nevertheless, they are much more visible in Israel society—and in the world of the new religions—than their numbers indicate. It is hard to determine the exact representation of individuals born and raised in the kibbutz, in the new religions, but they are clearly more than 3 percent. They are perhaps 10 percent in some groups and thus are clearly overrepresented. Joining a new religion means usually leaving the kibbutz, and the kibbutzim, justifiably concerned about desertions, have reacted to this threat.

One large kibbutz reached an important policy decision in 1983 (*Davar* 1983). Because kibbutz members usually do not have private funds, the kibbutz used to cover membership dues in any external organization. In the case of new religions, members who had joined them while still in the kibbutz applied to the kibbutz education committee, claiming that membership in TM or the Emin Society was an educational activity. Concern was shown by education committees when the training courses never ended, and when more became known about new religions. The kibbutz in question decided to stop any such payments, and thus force the member to choose between the kibbutz and the outside group.

The kibbutzim have their own centralized educational organizations and their own psychotherapy clinics. The policy in regard to new religions has been formulated by educators, psychiatrists, and social workers. Most of the 260 kibbutzim in Israel belong to two large federations. As of 1984, there was an anticult task force in each federation, staffed by educators and mental health professionals. The task force has been active in organizing symposia and lectures to kibbutz educators and to kibbutz members (Tene 1982). In addition, there are treatment groups for families whose children have joined new religions and lectures to high school students in the kibbutzim (Tene 1983). Training courses for professionals have also been organized by the Kibbutz Child and Family Clinic in Tel Aviv, under the heading "Mystical cults—how to prevent and treat."

THE INTERMINISTERIAL COMMISSION OF INQUIRY ON CULTS

The Interministerial Commission of Inquiry on Cults was appointed by Education and Culture Minister Zebulun Hammer on 5 February 1982. Miriam Glazer-Ta'asa, Deputy Minister for Education and Culture, was appointed to head the commission. The commission was assigned to investigate "Eastern cults," and its mandate was formulated as follows:

Determining the extent of cult growth in Israel, their locations and dimensions.

Locating the causes for this growth.

Obtaining information on the nature of the cults: modus operandi, significance of effects, actions, and aims.

Consequences of cult activities for the individual and for society.

Determining ways for coping, through the educational system, with the cults.

Recommending treatment modes (legal, public, educational etc.) (Hammer 1982).

The appointment of the commission of inquiry was the result of lobbying by Concerned Parents Against Cults, by individual parents whose children had joined the new religions, and Yad La'Ahim. This showed that the new religions had become a pressing reality for the Israeli establishment. It is possible that in view of media attacks on the new religions, and public sentiment in some communities, the creation of the commission was seen by some members of the government, and by its chairperson, Mrs. Glazer-Ta'asa, as an opportunity for gaining popularity. Mrs. Glazer-Ta'asa indeed had, since her appointment as Deputy Minister for Education and Culture in July 1981, been in the public eye. She had become the spokesperson for reactionary and nationalist views, and had gained the enmity of intellectuals and liberals in Israel. She expressed views critical of nudity in the theatre, explicit sexual references in poetry, and the lack of nationalist spirit in Israeli culture. Before becoming a Knesset member affiliated with the Herut right-wing party, she was a schoolteacher and a principal.

The first indication of an interest by the Ministry of Education and Culture in new religions came on 29 October 1981 when newspapers (for example, *Haaretz* 1981) reported a meeting at Mrs. Glazer-Ta'asa's office to discuss the "Guru Maharishi cult." The meeting was held following requests from Yad La'Ahim and Concerned Parents Against Cults. On 14 January 1982, the Director-General of the Ministry issued a special memorandum to all high schools in Israel, titled "Educational measures in view of the trend, of some youth to turn to various cults" (Shmueli 1982). The memorandum, clearly inspired by the October 1981 meeting, alerts teachers to the existence of cults and recommends general measures of "reinforcing value education" and helping the institution of the family to prevent cult involvements. It should be pointed out that most new religions in Israel do not recruit high school students.

The first session of the commission took place on 22 February 1982 in Jerusalem, and about 30 sessions of the full commission were held. Representatives of Concerned Parents, Yad La'Ahim, the kibbutz task forces on new religions, ex-members of new religions, and parents of members and ex-members were heard. In addition, the leadership of two new religions, Transcendental Meditation and Emin, volunteered to appear before the commission in order to persuade its members of the nonreligious nature of their activities. The commission was not convinced. The commission received written reports and memoranda from the police, Yad La'Ahim, Concerned Parents Against Cults, and several of its own members. Detailed reports submitted by members dealt with various religions and with legal aspects of their activities.

The commission worked for five years without publishing a report, and this has aroused curiosity. Normally, such a commission is expected to release a report within a few months following its appointment. The "final draft" of the commission report was published in December 1982 by an eager journalist (Be'er 1982), but a final report was still in the making for four more years. Another "final report" was published in February 1983 (Shapira 1983a, 1983b). Lior (1984) announced again the impending release of the commission report, which would lead to police action against new religions because of fraud and misrepresentation. When the Commission Report was finally released in February 1987, it was a long and cumbersome document of 503 pages, including a 74-page bibliography. It contained detailed background surveys on Scientology, Emin, est, Transcendental Meditation, Rajneesh, Ananda Marga, the Unification Church, ISKCON, Divine Light Mission, and Divine Intervention. The Commission treats est as a religious cult, despite the fact that there is nothing religious in its teachings or practices. The Commission recommended more energetic enforcement of consumer protection laws, the laws governing nonprofit organizations, tax laws, and immigration laws in Israel, as ways of limiting the activities and influence of new religions. In addition, the Commission recommended government activity in collecting and circulating information about new religions, educational activities, and help to former members, families of members, and "vulnerable populations." Following the publications of thge Commission report, the two groups that cooperated with the Commission, Emin and Transcendental Meditation, published lengthy rebuttals. The Emin document contained 63 pages, and the TM report, "The Truth about TM versus the Commission Report," about 100 pages of documents, including a list of 355 "scientific studies" of TM.

OTHER GOVERNMENT AGENCIES

The Israeli police has not acted against any of the new religions, with one exception where illegal drug use was involved. As mentioned elsewhere, there were two confidential police intelligence reports, one in 1974 on the Divine Light Mission, and one in 1982 on various groups. Both reports emphasize that no criminal activity on the part of new religions in Israel is suspected. The liberal treatment by the police is matched by the behavior of the Interior Ministry. The Minister of the Interior in Israel, who is in charge of immigration, has the absolute authority to deport aliens or bar their admission, without legal proceedings, if they are judged undersirable. This authority has been often used against Black Hebrews, Messianic Jews, and others. It has rarely been used against foreign representatives of new religions, though scores of such individuals have visited Israel and stayed for long periods since the early 1970s. The Department for Special Services in the Ministry of Religious Affairs engages in the "prevention of conversion by Jews" (Israel, Ministry of Religious Affairs 1975). It has worked with *Yad La'Ahim* rather closely and has had an active interest in new religions as a potential locus of conversions.

LOOKING BACK: NEW RELIGIONS AND
THE BOUNDARIES OF RELIGIOUS LEGITIMACY IN ISRAEL

Members of new religions are still a minority within Israeli society. Activities of new religions in Israel can in no way be compared to the richness of similar phenomena in the United States, where thousands of new religious movements have operated. Many strands of new religious groupings, such as spiritualism, UFO beliefs, or Buddhism, are totally absent from the Israeli scene.

Looking back at the development of new religions in Israel, we can reach the following conclusions:

1. There is a inverse relationship, not too surprising, between the degree to which a group deviates from majority norms and its success in recruiting members in israel. There is also a positive relationship, again not too surprising, between the degree of deviance and the degree of opposition to the group, regardless of its size. Thus, ISKCON, the Divine Light Mission, and Ananda Marga have achieved only limited success but have aroused much opposition.

2. The successful religions are those that combine a medium degree of deviation from the majority in regard to beliefs and life-style, and a medium degree of separation from the member's previous social attachments. Such groups are Transcendental Meditation, Scientology, and Emin.

The appearance of new religions in Israel can be described as a cultural innovation. It is an innovation because it represents behaviors previously unknown in the culture, which within a relatively short time have become established as the norm for a significant minority. This innovation has appeared together with several others (for example, return to Orthodox Judaism) and this should be analyzed within a broader context. The appearance of new religions in Israel in a major way is much more radical in its implications than the growth of new religions in the United States.

New religions in Israel are based on imported beliefs, that is, their belief systems were created abroad and then introduced to Israelis who have accepted them. The necessary condition for the acceptance of those believers is an openness to religious ideas as an answer to one's distress. Without this openness, this basic legitimacy of the religious viewpoint, the new religions cannot recruit any members. Those who become members are ready to experiment with new beliefs or are engaged in an active search for meaning.

We can speculate that the style of activity of these groups, in both management and recruitment, gives rise to opposition and antipathy. In some of these groups, members remind outsiders of aggressive salesmen, especially when their membership is growing rapidly. Other "new religions," such as Anthroposohy and Jehova's Witnesses, do not arouse these reactions because of their gentle manners. Christian missionary groups, active in Israel for a long time, are often referred to in the Israeli media as "cults," but the way they are treated in practice is totally different. New religions have been clearly more successful than old-style Christian missions in recruiting young Israelis. One reason is that the new religions do not suffer from the cultural stigma attached to Christianity. Their lack of history, and lack of historical contact and conflict with Judaism, works in their favor.

In most Western societies today, new religions are perceived as a threat, first by relatives (usually parents) of members and then by various government authorities and professional groups. Parents' organizations, commissions of inquiry, and legal actions are indications of that. In Israel, the new religions have been regarded as threatening cultural uniformity and, more seriously, because of the nature of Israeli identity, as threatening basic loyalties to the state.

Concern about losing Jews to other religions is as old as Judaism itself. Old Testament prophets thundered against pagan practices and Diaspora Jews, living in the midst of the majority culture, and always lost in the battle against it. In modern Israel, there was always concern about Christian missionaries, and the term "mission" (pronounced mee-ssee-yon) has become part of the spoken language in Israel since the 1950s. Any Christian coming to live in Israel and Christian organization active in Israel has been suspect. The lessons of Jewish history have not been forgotten, and for Orthodox and non-Orthodox alike, this became a battle cry. When Billy Graham visited Israel in the late 1950s, he was denied the use of a city auditorium in Tel Aviv and was only allowed an appearance in Nazareth before an audience of Christian Arabs.

The concept of "Jewish unity" is used by both religious and secular Jews in Israel as the basis for overall cultural and political unity. Jewish identity, and specifically religious symbols and actions, unify Jews from all ethnic origins and cultures and also differentiates Jews from Arabs. The new religions are seen as a threat to the solidarity and uniformity of Israel society. They present the prospect of an alternative loyalty, or at least a divided loyalty. Something which is an important part of Jewish tradition, and long precedes the state of Israel, is the sentiment of community loyalty, beyond and above the wide spectrum of differences in beliefs and individual behavior.

For some Israelis, giving up Jewish identity means undermining completely the Zionist claims to exclusive rights in Palestine and to privileges over the local Arabs, and giving up the tie with Jews in the Diaspora, who are Israel's main support in the world in many tangible ways. The reaction to new religions in Israel is indeed in accordance with the threat they present to the Jewish identity of most Israelis. When we observe reactions to various new religions, it becomes clear that what creates an opposition is not the size of a group, but its ideology. ISKCON, with a score of members that rejects the Israeli identity, is more of a threat than Emin, with hundreds of members who still keep the Israeli identity, and the reaction develops accordingly.

The largest new religions, Emin, Scientology, and Transcendental Meditation, have been treated more leniently by surrounding Israeli society, and thus have grown most, because they are more ambiguous in the challenge they pose to the traditional Israeli identity. These groups do not offer the members an exclusive new identity, and still allow them to claim loyalty to the state of Israel. Other new religions promote an explicit rejection of Israeli identity.

Members of new religions feel under a real threat from the establishment. This perception is realistic, in view of the lack of constitutional guarantees to the freedom of religion. Unlike many other countries, Israel does not have a constitution or a bill of rights for citizens. In response to public condemnation, a new religion in Israel can claim that its members can still preserve their Jewish identity. Thus it can remain within the pale, but not all new religions can or will make this claim.

Many groups function as resocializing agencies and provide a positive environment for a population of individuals who were maladjusted and deviant before joining them. Usually, these individuals were in a state of crisis. After joining, they live in a milieu that is warm, accepting, and meaningful. They finally have a home, or a community they can relate to. They are valued for their contribution and are reeducated to work hard and consume little. Members of new religions demonstrate, for the whole world to see, many of the virtues of the Protestant Ethic. They are hardworking, devoted, and frugal. They do not use illegal drugs, and they obey the law scrupulously because they want to appear respectable. As others have observed, the new religions offer their adherents a community, a feeling of belonging, a meaning system, and sometimes even individual psychotherapy.

If we ask members of the new religions, they are eager to tell us how good they feel and how well they function. They all report being calm, happy, and saved. The life-style of members in most new religions is extremely active. Moreover, many of the members work extremely long hours for the group. Their energy level is amazing, given their objective difficulties and the external reactions. This is of course, exactly how these groups manage to survive.

Eister (1974) suggested that cults are likely to flourish in modern societies that are undergoing culture crises in the form of "Dislocations in the communicational and orientational institutions" (p. 612). The historical period of the deepening crisis of Zionism gives rise to both the success of new religions in Israel and the crusade against them. The new religions can be regarded as breaking up the old monolitic ideology, and pushing Israeli culture towards pluralism. The other part of the process has been the resistance to such a push.

The analysis of these new religions has to be informed by the nature of Israeli society, the Israeli-Jewish identity and its problems, and by the crisis of Zionism. What is remarkable about the new religions in Israel is their phenomenal growth during a very short period, in what had been earlier regarded as a monolithic culture.

The boundaries of religious experimentation in Israel before 1973 can be assessed by relying on the evidence provided by Weiner

(1961) and Cohen and Grunau (1970). These boundaries were fairly narrow, and were tied to the unchallenged centrality of Orthodox Judaism. The new religions are a symptom of the breakdown of cultural consensus in Israel, and the breakdown of monolithic Israel ideology. It is a symptom of social stress and personal distress. New religions have not taken over the country because by their very nature they cannot reach more than a small segment of the population, but they have definitely become a permanent part of the cultural scene.

Table 8-1   The development of the anticult movement in Israel

1974	(spring) First Hostile media campaign. The main target: Divine Light Mission.
1874	Confidential police report on the Divine Light Mission.
1980	Concerned Parents Against Cults—first informal organization
1981	Concerned Parents Against Cults—formal incorporation
1982	(February) Commission of Inquiry appointed by Education Minister
1982	Report by *Yad La'Ahim* on "Cults in Israel"
1982	Confidential National Police report on "Cults in Israel"
1982	Anticult task forces created by kibbutz federations
1982–83	Second media campaign against new religions. Targets: all groups.
1987	(January) Commission of Inquiry report is released to the public.

REFERENCES

Amdur, M. 1982. Campaigning against cults. *Newsview*, 2 February.

Avneri, A. 1982. Uri Zohar against the Guru Maharaj Ji and Hare Krishna. *Yediot Aharonot*, 12 March (Hebrew).

Beit-Hallahmi, B. 1989. *Prolegomena to the psychological study of religion.* Lewisburg, PA: Bucknell University Press.

Cahnman, W. J. 1944. Religion and nationalism. *American Journal of Sociology* 49:524–29.

Cohen, E., and H. Grunau. 1972. *Minorities in Israel.* The Hebrew University, The Institute for Asian and African Studies. p. 116 (Hebrew).

Davar. 1983. Membership in the cult—or in the kibbutz. 29 June (Hebrew).

Eister, A. W. 1974. Culture crises and new religious movements: A paradigmatic statement of a theory of cults. In *Religious Movements in Contemporary America*, ed. I. I. Zaretsky and M. P. Leone. Princeton, N.J.: Princeton University Press.

Fisher, R. 1979. Hundreds of young people in Haifa fall prey to mysterious cults from the East. *Kol Haifa* 30 November (Hebrew).

Frenkel, S. 1982. Cults are the target. *Haolam Hazeh*, 20 September (Hebrew).

Geffen, Y. 1982. Ticket to heaven (first class). *Maariv*, 21 October (Hebrew).

Glock, C., and R. Stark, 1965. *Religion and Society in Tension.* Chicago: Rand McNally.

Guberman, J. 1982. Cults in Israel. *The Advisor*, August/September.

Haaretz. 1981. Ways to stop youth from joining Guru Cult discussed. 28 October (Hebrew).

Hacohen, E. 1982. The young are more "lenient." *Al Hamishmar*, 24 October (Hebrew).

Hammer, Z. 1982. Letter to Miriam Glazer Ta'asa. 5 February.

Judah, J. S. 1967. *The history and the philosophy of the metaphysical movements in America.* Philadelphia: Westminster Press.

Kiev, A. 1964. Subud and mental illness. *American Journal of Psychotherapy* 8:66–70.

Kiev, A. 1969. Primitive religious rites and behavior: Clinical considerations. *International Psychiatry Clinics* 5:119–31.

Lior, G. 1981. Come dance with us at the cemetery. *Yediot Aharonot*, 22 April (Hebrew).

Marmorstein E. 1969.*Heaven at Bay*. London: Oxford University Press.

Israel, Ministry of Religious Affairs. 1975. Report on the Activities of the Ministry. Jerusalem.

Needleman, J. 1970. *The New Religions*. Garden City, New York: Doubleday.

O'Dea, T. F. 1968. Sects and cults. In *International Encyclopedia of the Social Sciences*, ed. D. L. Sils, vol. 14, New York: Macmillan.

Rabin, A. I. and B. Beit-Hallahmi. 1982. *Twenty years later: Kibbutz children grown up*. New York: Springer.

Robbins, T. and D. Anthony. 1972. Getting straight with Meher Baba. *Journal for the Scientific Study of Religion* 11:122-40.

Robbins, T. an D. Anthony. 1972. Getting straight with Meher Baba. *Journal for the Scientific Study of Religion* 11:122-40.

Shapira, B. 1983a. From "Divine Intervention" to "Amanda Marga" I. *Yediot Aharonot*, 21 February (Hebrew).

Shapira, B. 1983b. From "Divine Intervention" to "Amanda Marga" II. *Yediot Aharonot*, 28 February (Hebrew).

Shem-Tov, S. 1985. Hamtza survey: Cults or return to Judaism. *Hamtzan*, 31 January (Hebrew).

Shmueli, D. 1982. Special memorandum. Ministry of Education and Culture. State of Israel, 14 January.

Singer, M. T. 1979. Coming out of the cults. *Psychology Today*, January.

Soffrin, G., and H. Yodfat. 1982. *Cults in Israel*. Confidential Intelligence Report, Intelligence Department, Israel National Police Headquarters, 22 August.

Tene, S. 1982. When the kibbutz member is searching for meaning. *Yediot Aharonot*, 15 June (Hebrew).

Tene, S. 1983. Parents and children fight the temptation of the cults. *Yediot Aharonot*, 27 March (Hebrew).

Troeltsch, E. Church and sect. In *Theories of Society*, ed. T. Parsons et al. New York: The Free Press, p. 961.

Tumarkin, T. 1983. Who is more frightening, Uri Zohar or Hare Krishana? *Davar*, 1 July (Hebrew).

Wallace, A. F. C. 1956. *Tornado in Wocester: An explanatory study of individual and community behavior in an extreme situation.* Washington, D.C.: National Academy of Sciences.

Weiner, J. 1961. *The Wild Goats of Ein Gedi.* New York: Meridian.

Zaretsky, I.I. and M.P. Leone. 1974. Introduction to *Religious movements in contemporary America,* ed. I.I. Zaretsky and M.P. Leone. Princeton University Press.

Part III

The Religiosity Factor

9

Effects of Religiosity on Attitudes and Behavior

LEONARD WELLER

In this chapter we examine how religiosity affects behavior and attitudes in Israel by reviewing all the studies we could locate. In many instances, the sole concern of a given research was the effect of religiosity on a specific variable, while in other instances (especially the later studies) religiosity was one factor among others, such as sex, social class, and ethnicity, in attempting a particular attitude or behavior.

FAMILY

There were six studies relating to family attitudes and behavior. Two dealt with fertility behavior (M. Hartman 1984; Neuman and Zeiderman 1986); one with breast feeding behavior (Zuriel and Weller 1986); one with sexual functioning and dysfunctioning (Hoch, Safir, Peres, and Shepher 1981); one with attitudes towards sex (Notzer, Levran, Mashiach, and Soffer 1984); one with marriage, pregnancy, and birth (Fishman 1979); and one dealt with women's roles (H. Hartman 1984).

The greater fertility of the Eastern family is clearly associated with greater religious observance. Matras and Auerbach (1962) showed that the desired number of children and the practice of contraception were influenced by religious observance: the less religious the couple, the greater the likelihood that they had considered family planning. In the Jerusalem sample, 72 percent of the nonobservant women, 40 percent of the partially observant women, and 8 percent of the observant women reported previous contraceptive practice. Similarly, 59 percent of the nonobservant women, 37 percent of the partially observant women, and 5 percent of the observant women reported having considered family planning. Because a large proportion of women practicing contraception are daughters of mothers who did not practice contraception, it might have been expected that the partially observant or nonobservant daughter of a partially observant mother would more readily resort to contraceptive devices than would such a daughter whose mother had been religious. This was studied and found not to be the case.

M. Hartman (1984) examined the effect of religiosity on fertility behavior and related pronatalistic tendencies of Jewish women in Israel. Hartman pointed out that while Judaism has elements that encourage high fertility, Jews also have been noted to be most efficient contraceptive users and family planners. The study is based on data collected in 1975 from a sample of 1,755 married women up to the age of 55. Religiosity was measured by the extent of reported performances of various religious rituals, scaled according to the Guttman Scale. The results are presented in terms of a seven-point breakdown of this scale. Religiosity was found to affect the women's pronatalistic tendencies strongly. This includes number of children born, expected family size, age at marriage, and labor force participation. However, contraceptive use was not affected by religiosity except among the extremely religious women. The effects of religiosity were found to be comparable with the effects of education, social status, and ethnic origin.

Neuman and Zeiderman (1986) also examined the effect of religiosity on fertility. Their data consisted of a representative sample of male and female salaried workers in Israel in June 1986. Two measures of religiosity were employed—self-definition and the amount of time devoted to religious observances. The results showed that the more religious have a higher fertility rate and a lower rate of contraceptive use. Their findings are similar to Hartman's with regard to fertility, but differ regarding the relationship between religiosity and contraceptive use.

Zuriel and Weller (1986) examined the psychological and sociological factors of mothers who breast-feed and mothers who bottle-feed. Most of the data came from 124 Israeli mothers who had given birth to their first child, but selective data were also collected on three additional samples. The two psychological measures, the Bar-Ilan Sex Role Inventory and body image (as measured by the drawing of a dressed and a naked woman), did not distinguish between the two groups of women. However, social factors, including degree of religiosity (the Orthodox and traditional were grouped into one category), did affect breast-feeding behavior. Religious mothers were more likely to breast-feed than were nonreligious mothers. The discriminant function analysis—which predicted 73 percent of the cases—showed that religiosity, mother's education, and her perceived support of friends and relatives were the most important factors in determining whether or not the mother breast-fed her baby.

Fishman (1979) studied attitudes to marriage, pregnancy, and birth of ultra-Orthodox and secular girls. One hundred and thirty girls between the ages of 17 to 22, 65 ultra-Orthodox and 65 secular, completed a questionnaire measuring attitudes in these areas. The criteria for ultra-Orthodox was either self-definition or the institution in which the girl was either studying or working. The results showed differences between the two samples in all the domains. Giving birth and taking care of children was seen as the primary purpose of marriage by a considerably larger percentage of Orthodox than secular women.

Harriet Hartman (1984) was concerned with married women's roles in Israel. The data are based on interviews with 1,754 married Jewish women living in urban parts of Israel. Labor force participation was defined as part-time or full-time work for wages or unpaid work in a family business. The average number of weekly hours determined the extent of the woman's labor force participation. The division of labor in the family was measured by responses to the question, "Who usually does the household tasks?" Attitudes toward women's and family roles were also measured. Multiple regression was used to analyze the relative importance of a number of factors on these dependent variables.

The degree of religiosity was found to be related to attitudes but not to actual behavior. Religiosity had no effect on labor force participation. Nor did it have an effect on family roles. It was, however, significantly associated with attitude toward women working and desired division of labor in the family; less religious women were more favorable to women working and more desirous of a more equitable division of labor at home. The religiosity beta coefficient was one of the highest among the significant beta coefficients for the dependent variable, "attitudes toward married women working," but the lowest of the three significant coefficients for the dependent variable, "desired division of labor in the family."

Notzer et al., (1984) studied the effect of religiosity on sex attitudes, experience, and contraception among university students. The student population consisted of 483 Tel Aviv University freshmen who completed an anonymous questionnaire on sexual activity. Students defined their religiosity according to the following scale: 1) Orthodox, ional, 3) secular but slightly observant, 4) secular, 5) opposed ᴛᴏ ᵣₑₗᵢ ᴏn. As the Orthodox students did not answer the question pertaining to sexual activity, this group was excluded from the results. For the other groups, there was a strong impact of religiosity on the dependent variables. Sex was the only variable that was controlled.

Hoch et al. (1981) identified correlates of sexual inadequacy by comparing sexually dysfunctioning and adequately functioning couples. The sample consisted of 120 married couples who applied during a one-year period to a sexual counseling and therapy clinic. The control group was chosen from couples living in the same area as the patient population. Traditional and Orthodox couples were grouped together. Among the factors seemingly associated with sexual dysfunction were traditional/religious upbringing and current religiosity of the male but not the female patient. In the analyses, sex was the only variable that was statistically controlled.

Summary. The results are consistent. There is a definite influence of religiosity on attitudes and family behavior. In each of the six studies, the religious differed from the nonreligious. Moreover, in only two of the studies were the findings on the effect of religiosity only partial: Hoch et al. (1981) found religiosity related to sexual dysfunction only for the male patients, while Harriet Hartman (1984) found religiosity to be related to attitudes but not to behavior.

Four of the six studies limited their samples to women. The more religious women have different expectations regarding marriage, including the number of children desired. They view the primary purpose of marriage as childbearing and child care, are more likely to breast-feed, are less favorable to women working, and are less desirous of a more equitable division of labor at home, the more religious students, both men and women, are more conservative in their attitudes towards sex and contraception. Finally, sexual dysfunction is associated with religiosity among male but not female patients.

ATTITUDES ON CIVIL RIGHTS, EASTERN JEWS, ARABS, AND THE HANDICAPPED

Zuckerman-Bareli (1975, 1975) studied the effects of religiosity on a host of attitudes; and Scher, Nevo, and Beit-Hallahmi (1979) studied beliefs about equal rights; Schwartzwald (1980) examined religious and ethnic stereotypes; and Rofé and Weller (1981) were interested in seeing whether Orthodox Jews were more negative to Arabs than secular Jews. We also include a study that investigated the mutual perceptions of religious and nonreligious students (Barnea and Amir 1981). Florian (1977) examined attitudes toward the physically disabled; and Weller and Aminadav (1988a, 1988b), in two studies based on the same sample, studied attitudes toward the mentally retarded.

In two papers, Zuckerman-Bareli (1975, 1975) examined whether the religious factor influenced the opinions of Israeli youth. The sample consisted of 387 eleventh grade pupils (17 years old) who attended religious and secular high schools. The degree of religiousness was established by subjective self-evaluation: Orthodox (N = 81), traditional (n = 136), not religious (N = 170). The questionnaire, composed mostly of closed-ended questions, covered the following: education and work, democracy and social equality, Israeli and national identity, leisure activity, political ideology and preferences, individualism and collectivism. In addition to the chi-square analyses, the data were analyzed by multiple stepwise regression to determine which of the three factors—religiosity, country of origin or sex—is the most important factor affecting students' attitudes.

For a large number of questions, (17 our ot 45) dealing with education, occupation, democracy, welfare, and the social gap, there were two differences between the religious and nonreligious groups. In 14 questions, concerning national and cultural identification, there were large religious differences, often tending to polarization. In another 14 questions, on such topics as the relations with the Diaspora, the image of the state, and the treatment of Arabs, there were statistically significant differences, although these differences were not as large as in the former group of 14 questions. With regard to the middle group of traditional youth, in some questions such as national unity, they supported the religious, but in other issues, such as cultural isolationalism, they were closer to the nonreligious. In the multiple-regression analyses, it seems that the religion, sex, and country of origin are of equivalent importance.

Scher, Nevo, and Beit-Hallahmi (1979) had 246 applicants from the University of Haifa respond to a Hebrew version of the Beliefs About Equal Rights Scale. The ranges of ages was between 18 to 38 with an average age of 23.2. The independent variables were: sex, religious belief (nonreligious, traditional, Orthodox—we are not told the criteria of religiosity), age (18-22, 23-38), and residence (city, small town, village, kibbutz). According to the results of the analysis of variance, only two independent variables were statistically significant: sex and degree of religious belief. Females (x = 20.45) believed in greater equality than males (x = 18.16). Those who observed Jewish law more strictly were least liberal, while those who reported not observing a religious code were more liberal. The mean score for the nonreligious sample was 19.79 (N = 184); for the traditional sample, the mean score was 17.54 (N = 49); and the Orthodox group, it was 16.77 (N = 13), F = 6.208 < .002.

Schwartzwald (1980) examined stereotypes held by junior high school students. To this end, 1,055 junior high school students from religious and nonreligious schools were asked to describe four types of Israelis by means of the Semantic Differential Scale. These types were: a) a nonreligious Oriental-Israeli; b) a religious Oriental-Israeli; c) a nonreligious Western-Israeli; d) religious Western-Israeli. On some descriptions, but not on all, the stereotypes of the religious students were different from that of the nonreligious students.

Rofé and Weller (1981) hypothesized that Orthodox Jews would be more negative to the Arabs than secular Jews. Their subjects were 430 high school students, aged 15-17, of both sexes. They were categorized as Orthodox, traditional, and secular, according to their self-definitions. The students evaluated three types of Arabs—enemy Arabs, territory Arabs, and Israeli Arabs—on a six-point scale consisting of 15 bipolar characteristics (for example, good-bad, warm-cold) taken from the semantic Differential Scale. They also responded to a social distance scale. On the Semantic Social Differential Scale, the Orthodox were less positive toward the Arabs (x = 4.4) than the secular (c = 4.0) and the traditional (x = 4.1), F = 4.75, p < .05. On the Social Distance Scale, likewise, Orthodox Jews were more negative toward Arabs than were secular Jews (p < .001).

Barnea and Amir (1981) investigated the mutual perception and attitudes of religious and nonreligious students, as well as whether there is a change in attitude as a result of contact between the two groups. Four hundred and eighteen religious and nonreligious students, male and female undergraduates, responded to a multidimensional questionnaire inquiring about their preferences and attitudes to the respective outgroup. For both groups, there was a clear ingroup preference and an almost total rejection of the outgroup when activities of a more intimate nature were involved.

Florian (1977) compared Jewish and Arab high school students in terms of their attitudes toward the physically disabled. Those students—both Jewish and Arab—who viewed themselves as being less or not at all religious had more positive attitudes than students who considered themselves religious. Florian's finding is comparable to those of E. Feldman (1976), who compared attitudes of Arab and Jewish community leaders toward disability and rehabilitation. In both Jewish and Arab villages, those who defined themselves as less religious held more positive attitudes than did the more religious leaders.

Weller and Aminadav (1988, 1988) hypothesized that people would hold more negative attitudes to the severely retarded than to the mildly retarded. They were also interested in the effects of religiosity, class, and sex on attitudes toward the mentally retarded. A random sample of 338 adults completed a multidimensional questionnaire (Weller and Aminidav, 1988) and a projective test (Weller and Aminidav, 1988) aimed at measuring their attitudes to mental retardation. While the respondents did evince more positive attitudes to the mildly retarded, neither religiosity, class, or sex was found to affect attitudes toward the mentally retarded. Multidimensional analyses were employed.

Summary. Religious differences were found in five of the six studies: because the two papers on mental retardation are based on the same sample, we will consider them as one study. In the one study where religiosity had no effect, namely, attitudes toward mental retardation, neither did any of the other background variables—sex and social class. In one study (Schwartzwald 1980) on stereotyping, religious differences were not always found. In the other four studies, the differences were clear and consistent. The picture that emerges is that the more Orthodox are more likely to be more nationalistic, more negative to Arabs, less liberal, and more negative to the physically handicapped. Both Orthodox and non-Orthodox students prefer to maintain friendships within their own group.

MORALITY

In this section, we present studies whose common theme is whether the religious differ from the nonreligious in questions of morality and deviant behavior. These studies cover a wide spectrum of topics. Schindler (1983) inquired whether the degree of religiosity of the physician affects his willingness to reveal to the patient his state of illness. Baum and Loewenberg (1988) raised the question whether religiosity affects the practice of social workers.

Yinon and Sharon (1984) hypothesized that religious persons would exhibit more prosocial behavior than nonreligious persons. Guttman (1984) examined the effects of religious beliefs on social morality. Javetz and Shuval (1984) inquired into which groups are more vulnerable to drug use. Kandel and Sudit (1982) studied drinking practices among urban adults in Israel.

Shuval (1964) inquired into the occupational interests of a sample of 1,266 students in the last two years of high school. Her hypothesis that religious girls would be more interested in nursing than nonreligious girls was partly supported. The very religious girls were the most interested in nursing, but there were no significant differences between the nonreligious and partially observant girls. When ethnicity was cross-classified with religiosity and family tension, a very high interest in nursing was found among religious immigrant girls who had been experiencing strain in their family relationships. The interpretation offered is that the nursing role, because it is consistent with traditional family patterns, offers a legitimate avenue of escape for the girl who does not wish to sever relationship with her family.

Shuval found the more religious girls to be interested in teaching, another feminine profession. Twenty-five percent of the nonreligious girls, 32 percent of the partially religious girls, and 37 percent of the very religious girls professed an interest in teaching.

Weller and Tabory (1972) raised the question of whether religious nurses relate to patients differently than do nonreligious nurses. Specifically, it was predicted that nurses who were not religious should be more likely to manifest a "scientific-technical orientation," which implies the perception of the patient as a "case" to be cured, coupled with an understanding that the nurses' tasks are to assist the doctor. On the other hand, nurses who were religious were expected to manifest an "affective orientation," which implies a desire to be with the patient, to consider him as a whole person, and to assume responsibility and act independently.

One hundred and fourteen students from two hospitals served as subjects. One of them is a religious hospital, recruiting mostly religious nurses. The other is a secular hospital. The student nurses filled out a questionnaire on their religiosity and their orientation towards nursing. On the basis of their responses the nurses were categorized as to whether they were religious, traditional, or secular. After unsuccessful attempts to construct a unidimensional scale of patient orientation, each question was analyzed separately.

Four of the six items were statistically significant and consistent with the hypothesis that religious nurses would be more person-oriented than nonreligious ones. One statement was not statistically significant but pointed in the direction predicted. In only one item was there no difference between the religious and nonreligious nurses. No trend, however, was found for the middle group, the traditionally oriented. Depending on the specific question, the patient orientation of the traditionally oriented either resembled the religious nurses, resembled the nonreligious nurses, fell between the two groups, or bore no resemblance to either the religious or nonreligious nurses.

Schindler (1983) inquired whether the degree of religiosity of the physician affects his willingness to reveal to the patient the state of his illness. Thirty-two doctors practicing in a large general hospital responded to a questionnaire on telling the truth. The sample was broken down into Orthodox, conservative, and nonreligious doctors. Physicians who were Orthodox were less likely to inform patients of their illness in contrast to doctors whose religious orientation was conservative or nonreligious. In terms of sharing information with the patient, for example, 40 percent of the Orthodox, 25 percent of the conservative, and 8 percent of the nonreligious said that they never share information with their patents.

Baum and Loewenberg (1988) raised the question of whether religiosity will affect the practice of the social worker. To this end, 67 second-year students were given an instrument that described critical incidents of social work practice in dealing with abortion requests, euthanasia, birth control, homosexuality, premartial sexual relations, and fatal illness. Religiosity was determined by responses to a religious values test especially designed for the study. The population was divided into three religious groups, but the middle group was omitted from the analysis. The data provides partial support for the hypothesis that religious values affect practitioner behaviro: the responses of the more religious students (N = 25) on four of the eight critical incidents.

Adar and Adler (1965) sampled over five hundred children from various kinds of communities that included children going to the state religious schools and state secular schools. The authors expected that the values of religious students would be closer to the values of a traditional culture than would be the values of students attending secular schools. Pupils of religious schools, it was argued, would be less prone to accept universalistic, democratic values, the appreciation of the intrinsic value of work, and equality between the sexes. They also anticipated that religious children would be less tolerant of other religious and ethnic groups.

As expected, the children of religious schools registered higher scores on a religiosity scale composed of nine questions. The findings showed that religious students of Eastern origin were the most amenable to the idea of religious imposition. The students in religious schools proved to be more ethnocentric. In one specific case, the statement was offered that "The Jewish people are more important than other people." Approximately 75 percent of the students attending religious schools answered affirmatively, in contrast to 25 percent of the students attending secular schools. However, no significant differences concerning attitudes towards Arabs were found. Attitudes towards citizenship were also examined (such as preferences for a democracy and rights of the citizens). They showed that religious students had less citizenship orientation than their nonreligious counterparts.

Another question examined the reasons for pursuing education. Children of Eastern descent, regardless of whether they attended a religious or secular school, showed the same attitude to education. However, the kind of school one attended had an effect on children of Western descent. Pupils of religious schools valued education more than did children of nonreligious schools. This finding is, of course, consistent with the importance attached to learning in Orthodox circles, although it is not clear why such differences were not found among Eastern children.

To sum up, a number of significant differences were found between religious and nonreligious students in areas concerning religious values and in areas not concerned with religious values, although these differences were greater in the group composed of those of lower socioeconomic status.

Yinon and Sharon (1985) hypothesized that people who consider themselves to be more religious will exhibit more prosocial behavior than those who consider themselves secular. In an experiment designed to test this, 107 religious and secular men and women were requested by a religious/secular solicitor to donate money to a needy family. All subjects lived in apartment houses in an upper middle class, religiously mixed neighborhood. The religious subjects donated more money than the nonobservant subjects (p < .002).

Guttman (1984) was concerned whether religious belief affects one's social morality. Sixth grade pupils from public schools, secular and religious, replied to the Morality Test for Children, a measure of cognitive morality, and a Maze Test that measured moral behavior. The results on cognitive morality show that religious subjects resisted temptation significantly more than the secular subjects (p < .001). They also scored significantly higher than the secular group on the Moral Reasoning Test (p < .005). However, on a test of actual cheating behavior, the secular group cheated significantly less than the religious group (p < .05). The study did not employ the middle category, "traditional."

Javetz and Shuval (1984) had 5,914 students, aged 12 to 18, complete a questionnaire on involvement in petty delinquency, delinquency, exposure to illicit drugs, and various aspects of drug behavior. Among the subgroups more vulnerable to using drugs were students whose families did not observe any religious traditions.

Kandel and Sudit (1982) studied drinking practices among

urban adults in Israel. The sample consisted of a representative sample of 464 adults, 20 years or older. The degree to which respondents observed religious customs was the criteria of religiosity. Respondents answered whether they: (1) observed all religious customs, (2) observed customs to a great extent, (3) observed customs somewhat, and (4) were secular. The largest difference was between those who observed all customs and all other respondents. A positive relationship was found between Orthodoxy and drinking experience, and an inverse relationship with frequency of drinking. Thus, 53 percent of the observant as compared to 33 percent, 38 percent, and 32 percent of the other religious categories claimed to have drunk in the last 30 days. However, in terms of how many drank 11 or more times within the last 30 days, the results were: 0 percent for the observant, 16 percent for the observant to a great extent, 14 percent for the somewhat observant, and 17 percent for the secular. Other variables were examined, such as country of origin, but multidimensional analyses were not employed.

Summary. The results are clear and consistent. The religious differ from the nonreligious. The less religious doctors are more willing to reveal to the patient his state of illness. Religious social workers will deal differently with their clients than nonreligious social workers. The religious are more likely to exhibit prosocial behavior and score higher on a questionnaire measuring moral behavior. They are less vulnerable to drug use and are less likely to be heavy drinkers. The only exception is one of the findings of Guttman (1984) that showed that on a test of actual cheating behavior, the secular group cheated significantly less than the religious group.

FEAR, ANXIETY, EMOTIONAL STRESS, AND FEAR OF DEATH

Fear, Anxiety, and Emotional Stress

There are several reasons for expecting that religious people would be more authoritarian. First, being Orthodox might imply a general submissiveness. Second, religious people might be less tolerant of other groups, which is itself related to authoritarianism. It might also be that religious families, in their desire to train their children to be religious, resort to punishment more often than do nonreligious families. Then again, it is just as reasonable to expect a high degree of association between authoritarianism and religiosity as it is between authoritarianism and political ideology, a much-studied relationship.

Weller and several of his associates (1975) felt that such would be the case. Two independent samples were used. The first consisted of 176 high school students who were given a translated version of a modified F Scale. On the basis of their reported religious behavior the students were classified as religious, traditional, or secular. They also answered whether they considered themselves as being religious, traditional, or nonobservant. On both the objective and subjective measures of religiosity, the more religious were significantly more authoritarian (p. $<$ .001).

In another sample, this time with 125 college students between the ages of 21 and 29, the differences were again highly significant. The religious were more authoritarian than the traditional or nonreligious. In the amount of authoritarianism, the traditional students were closer to religious students than they were to secular students. Thus, among the college students, the mean authoritarian score for the religious students was 5.02 as compared to 1.08 for the traditional student and -6.79 for the secular students. (The higher the score, the greater the authoritarianism.)

In the sample of college students, the respondents were further divided into four groups: (a) both student and father religious, (b) son more religious than father, (c) son less religious than father, and (d) both son and father not religious. It was hypothesized that authoritarianism would be highest in group a, next to highest in group b, next to lowest in group c, and least in group d. The results confirmed the hypothesis at or better than the .001 level of confidence. The means for the respective groups were 9.06, 6.83,-4.29 and -8.07.

Rim and Kurzweil (1965) thought that religious Jews would be more likely to risk a material loss than would secular Jews. To test his hypothesis, a group of seven individuals was given a problem, along with instructions to arrive at a unanimous recommendation. Each recommendation involved a different degree of suggested risk. After the discussion and the group decision, as a rule unanimous, the subject stated his individual opinion, which often differed from the one he expressed in the group. One hundred and fifty subjects from diverse backgrounds participated in the study. Significant differences on risk taking between Orthodox and non-Orthodox Jews were not found.

Four studies examined the effects of religiosity on fear, anxiety, and emotional stress, with three studies dealing specifically with tear (Levy and Guttman 1976, Klingman and Wiesner 1983, Rofé and Lewin 1980).

Klingman and Wiesner (1983) examined differences in responses between religious and secular school populations to the

Israeli Fear Survey Schedule for Children. The subjects were 479 children, 283 from secular schools and 196 from religious schools, drawn from various areas of Israel, of a similar middle-calss background, and of the same age group (school grades 6-8). Religiosity was defined on the basis of school attendance. Of the 99 items, 18 were significantly different on the basis of religious/secular school attendance. In 15 of these 18 items, the religious students were more fearful than the nonreligious, while an opposite trend was found for the other three significant items. Sex was the only variable controlled for.

Levy and Guttman (1976) studied the interrelations among feelings of worry, fear, concern, and coping a half year after the Yom Kippur War. The sample consisted of 1,726 adult respondents. The effects of five background factors—sex, education, age, family income, and religious observance—were examined by means of a multiple regression analysis. Worries and fears were operationalized as the responses to eight specific questions. Religious observance was defined in terms of the respondents' replies from "very observant" to "not observant at all." The correlations of religious observance to fear and worry were small and in most instances close to zero, as were the correlations of the other background variables. However, some of the topics, sex and education were relatively highly correlated with feelings of fear and worry.

Rofé and Lewin (1980) examined the relationship between daydreaming and a war environment and the personality dimension, repression-sensitization, strength of religious conviction, and sex. The subjects were 426 high school students from a border town in Israel. The students stated whether they were Orthodox, traditional, or secular. The Fear Questionnaire consisted of four factors. On only one of these was there a significant difference by religiosity. Religiosity was not significant on any of the three factors constituting the daydreaming scale.

Levav and Abramson (1984) conducted a multipurpose community health survey in a Jewish neighborhood in western Jerusalem. Ten key questions, adopted from the Cornell Medical Index, served as the instrument for measuring emotional stress. Among the factors examined as possibly affecting emotional distress was religiosity. The respondents stated whether they were religious, traditional, or not religious. For the men, there were no significant differences among the religious (N = 260), traditional (N = 903), and the nonreligious (N = 907). Among the women, the religious women (N = 383) were the least emotionally depressed (X = 46.6), the traditional women (N = 104) were in between (X = 52.7), and the nonreligious were the most depressed (54.6) (p < .05).

Summary. The results are weak. Klingman and Wiesner (1983) found significant differences for only 18 of the 99 items. Levy and Guttman (1976) found essentially no differences, and Rofé and Lewin (1980) reported significance for only one of four factors measuring fear. Levav and Abramson (1984) forund the religious to be least depressed, but this only for women. The conclusion, then, is a weak relationship at best between religiosity and fear and anxiety.

Fear of Death

There are several studies on fear of death, three by Florian and his associates (Florian and Har-Even 1983; Florian and Kravetz 1983; Florian, Kravetz, and Frankel 1984) and one by Rosenheim and Muchnik (1984).

Rosenheim and Muchnik (1984) examined whether religious Jews would be less fearful and anxious of death than nonreligious Jews in each of three different levels of awareness: conscious, preconscious, and unconscious. This hypothesis was based on the traditional Jewish approach to death. On one hand, Judaism accepts the gory, defeating, and repulsive nature of death. On the other hand, Jewish theology holds that physical existence is only one stage of the human life cycle and that there is a transcendental existence, called the Olam Hab'a. Sixty-four Israeli students, aged 19 to 27 both sexes, completed a questionnaire measuring the three levels of awareness of death. There was no significant difference between the religious and nonreligious on "conscious fear of death," and on "preconscious death anxiety." On the third measure, "unconscious death anxiety," the nonreligious group expressed stronger anxiety ($X = 49.05$) ($p < .001$). The sample was divided into religious (N = 25) and nonreligious (N = 41), with no middle group. Religiosity was measured by Ben-Meir and Kedem's index of religiosity.

Florian and Har-Even (1983) examined the effects of sex and religiosity on fear of personal death. The sample consisted of 225 high school students, studying in the state religious and nonreligious schools, who completed a questionnaire on fear of personal death. Religiosity was determined by a combination of two factors: type of school and self-report of religious belief. The intermediate religious group was not included. In only two factors, "anticipated punishment in the hereafter" and "consequences to family and friends," did the religious group show greater fear of death than the nonreligious group. No differences were found for the other four factors.

Florian, Kravetz, and Frankel (1984) employed direct and indirect multidimensional measures of fear of personal death. Four TAT cards, known to elicit a relatively high frequency of death themes, and an index of Jewish religious commitment were administered to 178 males. The sample consisted of an approximately equal number of university students, yeshiva students, and military cadets. The ages of the total sample ranged from 18 to 30 years, with a mean age of 21.5 years. The religious group was more threatened by death than either the moderately religious or the nonreligious groups. The religious group's responses reflected higher levels of centrality of death, guilt, and anxiety than did the moderate and nonreligious groups' responses.

Florian and Kravetz (1983) examined individuals' fears of their own death. A multidimension measure of fear of personal death was conducted and administered, together with a index of religious belief and practice, to 178 males. Six factors emerged from the principal component factor analyses of the response to the Fear of Personal Death Scale. The religious group disclosed significantly more fear of punishment in the hereafter and significantly less fear of self-annihilation than the less religious group. However, the finding that the moderately religious group expressed significantly more fear of death's consequences to family and friends than the other groups is not readily understandable.

Summary.   The findings are inconsistent with any trend for the religious to be more fearful of death than the nonreligious. Rosenheim and Muchnik (1984-1985) reported no significant differences on two of the three measures; on the third, the nonreligious expressed stronger anxiety than the religious. Florian and Har-Even (1983) reported that the religious group showed greater fear of death—but in only two of the four factors. In two studies that might be on the same sample, (Florian and Kravetz 1983; Florian, Kravetz, and Frankel 1984), the religious group was more threatened by death than the nonreligious group.

LEISURE TIME ACTIVITIES

A book entitled, *The Secularization of Leisure: Culture and Communication in Israel* by Katz and Gurevitch (1976) examined leisure activities of Israelis, with religiosity being one of the major explanatory variables. A religious person was defined as one who did not turn on the radio on the Sabbath; a nonreligious person as one who did.

There was no intermediate religious category.

Over 2,000 people responded to the survey. Such activities as social life, television watching, club and organizational participation, sport, hobbies, and newspaper and periodical reading were examined.

In general, there were large differences between the religious and nonreligious groups in their leisure time activities. On attitudes toward a five-day week, religious people were more favorable than their nonreligious neighbors of comparable education. Religious people participated less in public activities than nonreligious people. But even comparing persons of equivalent educational level, the non-religious were more active in cultural pursuits like theatre- and movie-going. It seems to have affected daytime activities less than nighttime activities. The more religious the person, education remaining constant, the more he was concerned that Israel should be foremost in the cultural and educational spheres. However, neither religiosity nor ethnicity, age, or sex affected the rate of reading. Not surprisingly, at each level of education, religious persons were more likely to be engaged in study than nonreligious persons. The religious asserted that Israel should be more moral than other nations. At each educational level, the more observant persons were more likely to aver that the traditional attributes, beliefs, study, ascetic living, and sense of mission, characterize the Jewish people today. Religious observance was found to be negatively associated with almost all aspects of the consumption of culture.

Schneller (1980) studied religious differences in television viewing among 14 to 17-year-olds. His four sources of data included a national survey. Unlike other studies, he differentiated three categories of religiosity: regular religious school, yeshiva high school, and yeshiva college. And, of course, there was a nonreligious group. Among his many findings: religious and nonreligious youth watched about the same amount of television, although the former group watched about 10 percent less than the latter group. There are a number of programs with religious content, which the religious youth watched more than the nonreligious youth. There were some, but not substantial, differences in the type of programs watched by the religious and the non-religious. One difference, though, concerned entertainment programs that were watched and enjoyed more by the religious group, although this group was less satisfied with news and informative programs.

Summary. Even though Schneller's (1980) study does not point to major differences in television-viewing by religious and non-religious youth, both studies taken together demonstrate large differences in the leisure time activities of the religious and nonreligious population.

MISCELLANEOUS

Three studies unrelated to one another are presented. The first concerns the self-image and professional orientation of religious and non-religious student nurses (Weller, Harrison, and Katz 1988). Another one deals with sex role typing and ego identity among high school students (Zuriel 1984). The last study presents data on the relationship between religiosity and children with Down's Syndrome (Sharav 1985).

Weller, Harrison, and Katz (1988) tested hypotheses concerning the development of self-image and professional orientations among students in two nurses' training schools, one of which was religiously affiliated and the other secular. The study involved a longitudinal comparison of attitudes at the beginning of the program and after three months, and a cross-sectional comparison of the attitudes of the attitudes of students in each of the three years of the nurses' training program. No support was found for the hypothesis predicting that religious students would show greater change in their image of the professional nurse and their own self-image. However, it was found that the gap between the religious students' professional image and that held by their instructors was greater than it was for secular students. Moreover, the supervisors in the religious schools had a different image of their profession than their secular counterparts.

Zuriel (1984) examined sex role typing and ego identity among 1,207 eleventh and twelfth grade students who came from religious and secular schools. The students rated their religiousness on a three-point scale ranging from religious to secular with traditional as the middle category. Each student completed the Adolescent Ego Identity Scale and the Bar-Ilan Sex Role Inventory, the latter being similar to Bem's Androgny Scale. On two of the three subscales of the Adolescent Ego Identity Scale, religious adolescents were higher than secular adolescents. But in the regression analyses, religiousness predicted total ego identity among the girls, but not among the boys.

Sharav (1985) analyzed data from 55 Jewish children with Down's Syndrome. The children were born between the years 1968 and 1982. A considerably larger proportion came from Orthodox families than from non-Orthodox families. There were no differences between the Orthodox and non-Orthodox groups in mean age of the parents, sex of the child, and ethnic origin. No good explanation is offered.

Summary.   In these three diverse studies, religious differences were found, at least up to a point. While religiosity did not affect the change of the nursing student's self-image or her professional image, it did influence the relationship between the student's professional image and that held by her instructors. Moreover, the supervisors in the religious schools were shown to hold different images of the profession than the supervisors in the nonreligious schools. Religiosity seems to affect adolescent ego identity, at least among girls. Finally, it was shown that a larger proportion of Down's Syndrome children from Orthodox families.

CONCLUSION

The results of the research on the effects of religiosity are consistent with large differences between religious and nonreligious. In such areas as family planning, occupational preference (that is, teaching and nursing), patient orientation, authoritarianism, and general values, the religious and nonreligious differ. Several studies demonstrate that the observed religious differences are not specious influences of social class or ethnicity. Nevertheless, the religious factor would seem to warrant further study, for when one examines the findings carefully, the internal pattern is not as consistent as it first appears. Thus Matras and Auerbach (1962) demonstrated a strong relationship between religious observance and contraceptive practice: the more religious the woman, the less likely that she had considered family planning. This finding was clearly according to expectation. However, the authors also anticipated that a partially observant or nonobservant daughter of a nonobservant mother would more likely use contraceptive devices than such a daughter of a religious mother—a plausible but unconfirmed hypothesis.

Shuval (1964) found that religious high school students were more interested in nursing than were nonreligious high school girls, but she did not find statistically significant differences in interest in nursing between the nonreligious and partially religious students. Matras and Auerbach (1962) showed marked differences between the partially religious and nonreligious in contraceptive behavior, albeit Weller and Tabory's (1972) findings are interesting both for what they did and did not reveal. The general hypothesis was again confirmed: religious nurses showed an affective orientation to their patients in contrast to nonreligious nurses who displayed a scientific-technical orientation. However, the traditional nurses did not show a middle pattern as predicted: in fact, they revealed no consistent pattern at all. While there was no ambiguity about the finding that the more religious were more authoritarian, no relationship was found between taking risky decisions and degree of religiosity.

The middle group, called the traditional group, would seem to be deserving of more study. We also feel that the studies have been rather simplistic in their breakdown of the population into religious and nonreligious. It would be fruitful to employ a more refined criteria of religiosity, as for example whether one is intrinsically or extrinsically religious. Finally, none of the studies examined the cause of these religious differences. We do not know if they reflect values of two subcultures, the religious and nonreligious, or if they arise out of differential socialization practices. This is the kind of question we might assume will be asked in future research on the religious factor in Israeli society.

Many different kinds of attitudes and behavior were studied, depending on the individual interest of the investigator: attitudes toward civil rights, Eastern Jews, the handicapped, morality, drinking behavior, drug use, leisure time activities, orientation of nurses, attitudes to marriage and family including breast-feeding, general fears and anxieties, and fear of death. The only exception in which consistent findings were not found was in the last category cited—general and specific fears. And even here, there was a trend.

The religiosity factor is so strong and consistent that future research in Israel should control for it. Until now, it has been fashionable to control for country of origin and not for religiosity. Unfortunately, there were only a few cases in which religiosity, ethnicity, and education were examined together. In these studies, religiosity is at least as strong a factor, if not stronger, than the others. Thus, Zuriel and Weller (1986) found in their study of breast-feeding behavior that in the discriminant function analysis, religiosity—but not ethnicity—was one of the few factors determining whether or not a woman breast-feeds.

The failure of most of the research to control simultaneously for education, ethnicity, and maybe sex raises the question as to whether the reported effect of religiosity is not spurious. Due to the consistent findings on religiosity and the results of the few researches that employed multivariate analyses, we feel confident that this is not the case. Still, we are not certain if many of the reported findings on the effects of religiosity would hold up were the data subjected to multivariate analyses. We hope that the period is over when research on the effects of religiosity is limited to univariate analyses. Because religiosity is related to country or origin, education, and probably sex, analysis should include these variables.

One question raised above remains unanswered—the pattern of the traditional category. Very often results are presented according to two categories only: religious and nonreligious. What happens to the middle traditional group? Sometimes it is included with the religious group, sometimes with the nonreligious group. Seemingly, the criteria is the investigator's convenience; a small religious or nonreligious sample encourages the investigator to attach the in-between group to the smaller one.

Two studies based on the same sample found no effect of religiosity at all. These are the works of Weller and Aminadav (1988a, 1988b) on attitudes toward retardation. Not only was religiosity not significant, but neither were the other sociological factors—education, ethnicity, and sex. It seems that when all other sociovariables fail to predict, neither does religiosity.

Finally, a caveat. Virtually all published studies found large significant differences. We all know the difficulty, if not the near impossibility, of publishing results that find no differences. Is it not possible that for every study reported here, there is at least one more that did not find a significant effect and was not published, either because the researcher did not even bother to submit the article or because the editor refused to accept it? Of course, this remark has pertinence for research in other areas.

REFERENCES

Adar, L., and C. Adler. 1965. *Education for values in schools for immigrant children in Israel.* Jerusalem: School of Education of the Hebrew University (Hebrew).

Barnea, M., and Y. Amir. 1981. Attitudes and attitude change following intergroup contact of religious and nonreligious students in Israel. *Journal of Social Psychology* 115:65–71.

Baum, N. C., and F. Loewenberg. 1988. *Are religious social workers different?* Unpublished manuscript. Ramat-Gan, Israel. Department of Social Work, Bar-Han University.

Feldman, E. 1976. *Attitudes of Jewish and Arab village leaders toward rehabilitation of the disabled.* Unpublished master's thesis. Jerusalem: Hebrew University.

Fishman, B. 1979. Attitudes of ultraorthodox and secular girls in marriage, pregnancy and birth. *Society and Welfare* 2:64–71 (Hebrew).

Florian, V. 1977. A comparison of attitudes toward the physically disabled between Jewish and Arab high school students. *Megamot* 2:184-92 (Hebrew).

Florian, V. and D. Har-Even. 1983. Fear of personal death: The effects of sex and religious belief. *Omega—Journal of Death and Dying* 14:83-91.

Florian, V. and S. Kravetz. 1983. Fear of personal death: Attribution, structure, and relation to religious belief. *Journal of Personality and Social Psychology* 44:600-607.

Florian V., S. Kravetz and J. Frankel. 1984. Aspects of fear of personal death. levels of awareness, and religious commitment. *Journal of Research in Personality* 18:289-304.

Guttman, J. 1984. Cognitive morality and cheating behavior in religious and secular school children. *Journal of Educational Research* 77: 249-54.

Hartman, H. 1984. Economic and familial roles of women in Israel. *Israel Social Science Research* 2: 26-37.

Hartman, M. 1984. Pronatalistic tendencies and religiosity in Israel. *Sociology and Social Research* 68: 247-58.

Hoch, Z., M. Safir, Y. Peres and J. Shepher. 1981. An evaluation of sexual performance—comparison between sexually dysfunctional and functional couples. *Journal of Sex and Marital Therapy* 7: 195-206.

Javetz, R. and J. Shuval. 1984. Drug use among high school students in Israel: A syndrome of social vulnerability. *Youth and Society* 16: 171-94.

Kandel, D., and M. Sudit. 1982. Drinking practices among urban adults in Israel. *Journal of Studies on Alcohol* 43: 1-16.

Katz, E., and M. Gurevitch. 1976. *The secularization of leisure: Culture and communication in Israel.* Cambridge: Harvard University Press.

Klingman, A., and E. Wiesner. 1983. Analysis of Israeli children's fears: A comparison of religious and secular communities. *International Journal of Social Psychiatry* 29: 269-74.

Levav, I., and J. H. Abramson. 1984. A community study of emotional distress in Jerusalem. *Israel Journal of Psychiatry and Related Sciences* 21: 19-35.

Levy, S., and L. Guttman. 1976. Worry, fear and concern differentiated. *Israel Annals of Psychiatry and Related Disciplines* 14: 211-28.

Matras, J., and C. Auerbach. 1862. On rationalization of family in Israel. *Milbank Memorial Fund Quarterly* 40: 453-480.

Neuman, S., and A. Zeiderman. 1986. How does fertility relate to religiosity?: Survey evidence from Israel. *Sociology and Social Research, 70:* 178–80.

Notzer, N., D. Levran, S. Mashiach, and S. Soffer. 1984. Effect of religiosity on sex attitudes, experience and contraception among university students. *Journal of Sex and Martial Therapy 10:* 57–62.

Rim, Y., and Z. E. Kurzweil. 1965. A note on attitudes to risk-taking of observant and nonobservant Jews. *Jewish Journal of Sociology 7:* 238–45.

Rofé, Y., and I. Lewin. 1980. Daydreaming in a war environment. *Journal of Mental Imagery 4:* 59–75.

Rofé, Y. and L. Weller. 1981. Attitudes toward the enemy as a function of level of threat. *British Journal of Social Psychology 20:* 217–18.

Rosenheim, E., and B. Muchnik. 1984–85. Death concerns in differential levels of consciousness as functions of defense strategy and religious belief. *Omega—Journal of Death and Dying 15:* 15–24.

Scher, D., B. Nevo, and B. Beit-Hallahmi. 1979. Beliefs about equal rights for men and women among Israeli and American students. *Journal of Social Psychology 109:* 11–15.

Schindler, R. 1983. Reaction to truth-telling among Israeli physicians. *Omega—Journal of Death and Dying 13:* 277–86.

Schneller, R. 1980. Religious youth watching Israeli television. *Israeli Journal of Psychology and Counseling in Education 13:* 23–36 (Hebrew).

Schwartzwald, J. 1980. Relatedness of ethnic origin and religiosity to the stereotype of the Israeli as seen by junior high school students. *Megamot 25:* 322–41 (Hebrew).

Sharav, T. 1985. High risk population for Down's Syndrome: Orthodox Jews in Jerusalem. *American Journal of Mental Deficiency 89:* 599–61.

Shuval, J. 1964. Parental pressure and career commitments. *Megamot 13:* 33–39 (Hebrew).

Weller. L. 1974. *Sociology in Israel.* Westport, Conn: Greenwood Press.

Weller, L., and C. Aminadav. 1988. *Attitudes toward mild and severe mental retardation.* Unpublished manuscript. Ramat-Gan, Israel: Department of Sociology, Bar-Ilan University.

Weller, L. and C. Aminadav. 1988. *A projective method of measuring attitudes toward the mentally retarded.* Unpublished manuscript. Ramat-Gan, Israel: Department of Sociology, Bar-Ilan University.

Weller, L., M. Harrison, and Z. Katz. 1988. Changes in the self and professional images of student nurses. *Journal of Advanced Nursing* 1988.

Weller, L. and D. Tabory. 1972. Religiosity of nurses and their orientations to patients. In *Memorial to H. M. Shapiro*, ed. H. Hirschberg, E. Don-Yehiya, and L. Weller, 97–110. Ramat-Gan, Israeli: Bar-Ilan University.

Weller, L., S. Levinbok, R. Maimon and H. Shoham. 1975. Religiosity and authoritarianism. *Journal of Social Psychology, 95:* 11–18.

Yinon, Y., and E. Sharon. 1985. Similarity in religiousness of the solicitor, the potential helper, and the recipient as determinants of donating behavior. *Journal of Applied Social Psychology 15:* 726–34.

Zuckerman-Bareli, C. 1975. Religion and its connection to consensus and polarization of opinions among Israeli youth. *Megamot 22:* 62–81 (Hebrew).

Zuckerman-Bareli, C. 1975. The religious factor in opinion formation among Israeli youth. In *On Ethnic and Religious Diversity in Israel*, ed. S. Poll and E. Krausz. Ramat-Gan, Israel: Bar-Ilan University Press.

Zuriel, D. 1984. Sex role typing and ego identity in Israel: Oriental and Western adolescents. *Journal of Personality and Social Psychology 44:* 440–57.

Zuriel, D. and L. Weller. 1986. Social and psychological determinants of breast-feeding and bottle-feeding mothers. *Basic and Applied Social Psychology 7:* 85–100.

10

Dimensions of Jewish Religiosity in Israel

PERI KEDEM

Surveys carried out between 1962 and 1985 (Antonovsky 1963; Ben-Meir and Kedem 1979; Liebman and Don-Yehiya 1983) found that about 15 to 25 percent of the population define themselves as Orthodox (*dati*), 40 to 45 percent as traditional (*mesorti*), and another 35 to 45 percent as non-Orthodox (*lo dati*). But what do people mean when they thus define themselves?

How many Jews in Israel are religious?
Who are they?
How does this religiosity express itself?
What role does religion play in the lives of Israelis?

It is with these questions that this chapter is concerned. The approach here is that religion is a multifaceted concept. Four of the five dimensions presented by Glock and Stark (1965) in their model of religion will be separately analyzed in an attempt to answer the questions posed.

*The author wishes to thank the many people who collaborated with her in the various aspects of her studies: Dr. Yehuda Ben-Meir for his initiative in conducting the first survey and for supervising her Ph.D. dissertation; Dr. Mordechai Bar-Lev for his consent to publish the findings of two of our shared studies; by students Naomi Brontvain and Isaac Prilleltensky for their cooperation in the attempt to study religious experience; and Grace Hollander for her assiduous editing.

1. *The ritualistic dimension* deals with religious practices. The Jewish religion has an established ritual that covers every aspect of social and private behavior. These rituals are codified in many books, the *Shulhan Aruch* being the one most referred to.

2. *The ideological dimension* deals with specific religious beliefs. In comparison to the ritual dimension, this dimension is much less defined. Jewish theology stresses actions, including rites, above theoretical belief—quoting *The Encyclopedia of the Jewish Religion* (Werblowsky and Wigoder 1960):

> The absence of a supreme ecclesiastical body authorized to formulate a creed is not the sole reason for the virtual absence of creeds in Judaism, and it was often felt that the very idea of such formulation ran counter to certain fundamental tendencies in Jewish theology, which is concerned not only with beliefs but very largely with commandments. (101–102)

3. *The experiential dimension* deals with emotions related in some way to God or to religion. This has had a strong impact on psychology since the nineteenth century, as seen in William James' classic *The Varieties of Religious Experience* (1902).

In the Bible one is commanded to "love God" and to be in "awe" toward God. There is also a commandment to rejoice in the holidays. The manner of expressing such emotions obviously cannot be codified. Over generations, various schools of thought have emphasized different emotions, the most famous being the Hassidim who emphasize rejoicing, while the *Mitnagdim* emphasize rational thinking and the feeling of awe.

4. *The consequential dimension* deals with attitudes and values that stem from the individual's approach to religion. In Israel, the most direct consequence of a religious stance is the approach to the issue of state and religion. There is a difference of opinion about how much public observance should/must be enforced in order to maintain the Jewish character of the state, without arousing open hostility. This chapter will try to integrate the findings of six studies that the author and coauthors conducted over the years in order to understand how complex religiosity is in Israel.

THE RITUALISTIC DIMENSION

Judaism has a codified law of 613 commandments. In actual practice there is a very specific gradation in the percentage of people observing each commandment: some commandments are observed by almost everyone, while others are kept by hardly anyone.

The Ben-Meir and Kedem Commandments Scale (Table 10-1) shows the gradations of observance (The Guttman Reproducibility coefficient was 0.93 and the scalability, 0.69) as found in a survey of a representative sample of the adult Jewish population of Israel. (See Appendix, Study I)

Table 10-1 Ben-Meir and Kedem's Commandments Scale

	PERCENT OBSERVING THE COMMANDMENT
Participates in a seder	99
Has a mezuzah at the entrance to the house	89
Participates in the ligthing of Hanukah candles	88
Does not eat bread on Passover	82
Buys only kosher meat	79
Fasts on Yom Kippur	74
Koshers the meat (in water and salt)	61
Lights Shabbat candles with a blessing	53
Uses special Passover dishes	54
Separates meat and milk dishes	44
Makes kiddush on Friday night	38
Attends synagogue on Shabbat	23
Does not travel on Shabbat	22
Hears havdalah Saturday night	21

Table 10-1 (Continued)

	PERCENT OBSERVING THE COMMANDMENT
Goes regularly to the ritual bath (wives)	14
Covers hair (wives)	11
Wears skullcap regularly (men)	11
Goes to synagogue every day (men)	6
Does not use any electricity on Shabbat	1

Are these findings still valid today, 20 years later?

An indication of the similarity of ritual behavior over the hears can be found in surveys carried out by the Israel Institute for Applied Social Research. Table 10-2 demonstrates the similarity of responses of representative samples over a 26-year span.

Table 10-2 IIASR Observance of the religious tradition

RESEARCHER YEAR OF SURVEY	ANTONOVSKY 1962	ARIAN 1969	SHYE 1982	LEVINSON* 1988
Complete observance	15%	12%	14%	10%
Observance to a large extent	15%	14%	20%	18%
Some observance	48%	48%	41%	40%
No observance at all	22%	26%	25%	32%

*The survey found that 75% fast on Yom Kippur, and 25% do not travel on Shabbat; this is almost an exact replica of the 74% and 22% found two years before.

In studies on different samples of university students in 1977, 1978, 1980 (see Appendix, Studies II, IV, V), the same hierarchical order of observed commandments was found as in the Ben-Meir and Kedem scale. A similar Guttman scale was created by Laslau and Schwarzwald (1985) to study observance among 710 parents of kindergarten children. The results are given in Table 10-3.

Table 10-3 Laslau and Schwarzwald's Commandments Scale

| | PERCENT THAT OBSERVE COMMANDMENTS | |
	Sepharadim	Ashkenazim
Eats kosher meat	95	83
Lights Shabbat candles	85	66
Separates dishes	77	53
Goes to synagogue on Shabbath	59	44
Doesn't travel on Shabbat	39	29
Doesn't watch TV on Shabbat	28	25
Prays daily wearing phylacteries	26	23
Goes to synagogue daily	16	8

Considering the many differences between the Ben-Meir and Kedem study and the Laslau and Schwarzwald study (the 17-year interval between them, the different sample composition, the dissimilar wording of the questions), the similarity in the results is astounding. The results of these studies demonstrate a continuum ranging from the extremely observant, through various degrees of religious and traditional behavior, to the almost completely nonobservant.

Although the continuum indicates that the ritual behavior is unidimensional, the varying degrees of observance and the finding that many of the observant do not define themselves as religious (*dati*), led to an attempt to categorize the commandments into clusters according to their "popularity" among the three types of people. A factor analysis of the ritual behaviors measured in the Ben-Meir and Kedem study yielded three rotated factors that mirrored the theoretical division of different levels of commandments. The first factor included all those behaviors that can be defined as Orthodox: not using electricity on Shabbat, synagogue attendance, wearing a skullcap, women covering their hair, ritual bath, havdalah, not traveling on Shabbat. The second factor can be defined as traditional: praying on Shabbat, kiddush, separate dishes, Passover dishes, blessing candles, koshering meat, and fasting on Yom Kippur. The third, secular factor consisted of those three rituals in the scale that over 88 percent of the population kept: Passover seder, mezuzah, and Hanukah candles. This last factor was found to be correlated with practices not included in the scale, such as setting the table in a festive manner and cooking special food for the Sabbath meals, which also were observed by the vast majority of the sample.

The fact that people who call themselves nonreligious observe quite a few commandments led a few researchers (Liebman and Don-Yehiya 1983; Shelah 1975) to differentiate between Orthodox and secular, or civil religion, the assumption being that the commandments kept by the nonreligious are different conceptually than those kept only by the Orthodox.

As stated above, the belief code is far from a defined dogma. Yet, though there is no official set of beliefs, rabbis through the ages have formulated principles of faith. Closest to a creed are the "Thirteen Principles of Faith" of Maimonides, which served as the basis for the Ben-Meir and Kedem belief scale. As a result, the belief scale in the Ben-Meir/Kedem study (Appendix, Study I) was more limited than the ritual scale. Only 6 items were found to fulfill the demands of a Guttman scale, with a narrower range of answers. Within these constraints it was found that the belief scale is unidimensional, discriminating between people as to their "amount" of belief. The reproducibility coeffieient of the belief scale was found to be 0.92, and the scalability was 0.80 (Table 10-4).

Table 10-4   The Traditional Belief Scale

	PERCENTAGES		
Do you believe...	Believe	Don't Know	Don't Believe
In God?	64	6	31

Table 10-4 (Continued)

Do you believe...	PERCENTAGES		
	Believe	Don't Know	Don't Believe
That the Jews are the chosen people?	57	6	37
That God gave Moses the Torah on Mt. Sinai?	56	14	30
That there is a transcendental power who directs the history of the Jewish people?	47	15	38
In the coming of the Messiah?	36	12	52
That the soul continues to exist after death?	29	20	51

The percentage of "don't know" concerning belief "in God" and "that the Jews are the chosen people," is quite small in comparison to the percent of those that don't know what they believe regarding existence after death.

All other studies (Appendix, Studies III, IV, and VI) led to the same conslusion. Beliefs about God and the Jewish people are the most accepted, while beliefs about life after death are the most doubted. This finding might be a reflection of the lesser emphasis in the Jewish religion on the afterlife (hell and heaven) than in the Christian tradition.

Beliefs appearing in certain theological writings are regarded by some as part of traditional Jewish belief and by others as superstition, or as mysticism. One such question was asked in the Ben-Meir and Kedem study: Do you believe in the evil eye? It was found that 64 percent of the population did not believe, 4 percent didn't know, and 32 percent believed.

In a most recent study (Bar-Lev and Kedem 1988) (Appendix, Study VI), students attending religious high schools answered questions about six such beliefs (Table 10-5).

Table 10-5   Mystical Beliefs Scale

| | PERCENTAGES | | |
Do you believe...	Believe	Don't Know	Don't Believe
That the blessings of a rabbi can help a sick or needy person?	74	14	12
That the righteous men have caused and are still causing miracles	51	30	19
That prayer at the grave of a zaddik has power to help men?	50	29	21
Reincarnation (the soul will be reborn in another Jew's body)?	51	32	17
That amulets can bring luck and prevent injury?	19	28	54
That devils and spirits exist and even interfere in the life of man?	9	20	70

The students' responses to the Traditional Belief Scale is very different than their responses to the Mystical Belief Scale. Factor analysis of the items from the combined belief scales yielded two separate factors, following the theoretical division. The students, on the whole, believed much more in the traditional than the mystical beliefs: 89 percent held traditional beliefs versus only 46 percent who held to the mystical beliefs, the "don't knows" 7 percent versus 22 percent and the "nonbelievers" 4 percent versus 32 percent.

The differences between students of Sepharadi and Ashkenazi origins as far as traditional beliefs were concerned were minimal; when it came to mystical beliefs, there were significantly more Sephardi than Ashkenazi believers.

THE EXPERIENTIAL DIMENSION

In the last few years, interest in the experiential dimension has increased due in part to the large number of conversions to conventional religions or to cults (Lofland and Skonovd 1981; Stark and Bainbridge 1981).

In Israel, research on the experiential aspect of religion has been almost completely neglected. A few studies dealing with converts or penitents investigated this experiential dimension (Glanz and Harrison 1978; Aviad 1980; Kedem et al. 1985), but we limited to a qualitative analysis of yeshiva students "returning" to religious living from their former secular life, which represented a specific group and not the general population.

The lack of quantitative analysis of religious feeling might stem from the absence of emphasis on epiphany in the Jewish religion, which stresses the theological legalistic system and intellectual comprehension rather than emotional experience. However, it might well be that the paucity of work on the experiential dimension is due merely to methodological difficulties, emotion being more subjective and elusive than behavior or attitudes, making its measurement more complex and more problematic.

To conceptualize religion, a consideration and an evaluation of emotional involvement must be made. In this chapter, despite the methodological flaws in the studies under analysis, an attempt will be made to interpret some of the findings in this dimension. The Ben-Meir and Kedem study (Study I) is the most informative because it is based on a representative sample. But the question format was somewhat limited. The Bar-Ilan survey (Study II) is almost a replication of the former study, and it is based on an observant sample. The Brontvain and Prilleltensky study (Study V) delved into the subject in much greater depth than the former studies, but this study suffers from an unrepresentative sample.

The Ben-Meir and Kedem study (Study I) asked the question "Was there ever any incident in your life which led you to feel close to God?" Forty-six percent of the representative sample confirmed that indeed they had such experiences. They were then asked "What was the event that promoted this feeling?" Ten percent claimed that they felt close to God when an event of *national importance* occurred (such as winning the Six-Day War). Twenty-nine percent mentioned that they experienced a feeling of "closeness to God" during a *personal event:* 21 percent referred to personal survival in war, the Holocaust, sickness, and accidents; family events, 2 percent; personal success, 1 percent; and sundry intimate personal happenings 5 percent. Only 1 percent mentioned prayer as an instigator of such feelings. A marginal 1 percent were unable to pinpoint any particular incident, moment, or event because they "always feel close to God."

The question, "In which of the following events do you feel religious emotion?", though similar in spirit to the former question ("Which events led you to feel close to God?"), did not evoke the same reaction. To the question on *religious* emotion, 39 percent answered that they had never had a religious emotion and 18 percent said they always have such a feeling. Eighteen percent have such a feeling when they pray, 15 percent claimed that they feel religious when "something important happens to the state or the nation"; 7 percent mentioned having the feeling when they "do a good or just deed," and 3 percent when there is "happiness in the family." No one revealed a religious feeling about "Shabbat and the holidays," "when alone," "when afraid or worried or when very happy."

In another attempt to study religious emotion, a representative sample of Bar-Ilan students (Study III) were asked a question, similar to the previous one, about events arousing religious feelings. Instead of being required to choose only one situation from a list of situations, they were required to respond to each situation independently. With this changed format, all the events seemed to have equal arousal potential. All events mentioned triggered religious feeling in about to to 70 percent of the students.

In the study specifically dealing with religious experience (Study V), the students were given a list of 20 situations, and they were required to check those situations that arouse spiritual experiences. The situation that aroused the greatest emotion was "watching national events" (70 percent). "Listening to music" was second with 50 percent. Other situations were mentioned by a third of the respondents: prayer; birth, marriage, and death; disaster, fear, and war. Religious feelings provoked by works of art, poetry, or literature were scarcely mentioned.

To a list of 50 emotions that could be felt during a religious-spiritual experience, the division was as following: words used to express the religious-spiritual experience were "a feeling of well-being, pleasure," 56 percent; "calm", 54 percent; "security," 40 percent; "love," 39 percent; "close to God," 28 percent. The feelings mentioned by James (1902) and others (Hood 1975, Margolis 1979) as part of the religious experience and especially during conversion—that is, "transcednance of body," "voices heard," "bodily change," etc.—were not mentioned at all.

To summarize: emotions are varied and it is not possible to create stable factors, or scales. There does, however, seem to be on one hand a strong emphasis on personal or individualized religious feeling and, on the other hand, a feeling of religious emotion stemming from national events.

The consequence of a religious attitude that most strongly affects daily life in Israel is the incorporation of religious law into civil law. Sociologists (Tabory 1981a,b; Smooha 1978) stress the tensions arising from these problems. The Ben-Meir and Kedem (Study I) measured what people thought about the dilemma. The State and Religion Scale (Table 10-6) was a Guttman scale of 17 items (reproducibility 0.89 and scalability 0.67).

Table 10-6   State and Religion Attitude Scale

	PERCENTAGES	
	for	against
Are you for or against a law:		
Prohibiting all traffic on Shabbat	13	87
Prohibiting taxis on Shabbat	18	82
Closing gasoline stations on Shabbat	24	76
Closing cafes and restaurants on Shabbat	31	69
Prohibiting entertainment programs on Shabbat	32	68
Closing the cinemas on Shabbat	44	55
Prohibiting the sale of nonkosher meat	41	59
Obliging pupils in secular schools to wear skullcaps during Bible lessons.	41	59
Prohibiting buses from travelling on Shabbat	43	57
Prohibiting civil marriage?	47	53
Prohibiting the raising of pigs?	54	46
Prohibiting intermarriage with non-Jews?	59	41

Table 10-6 (Continued)

	PERCENTAGES for	against
Closing the streets to traffic on Shabbat in religious neighborhoods	70	30
Closing shops on Shabbat	79	21
That the government supply religious needs like synagogues and ritual baths for interested citizens	80	20
That the government guarantee separate religious education to all who desire it?	83	17
That the general school curriculum should include lessons in Jewish tradition?	86	4

This scale, like the Commandments Scale, is wide-ranging, hierarchical in nature, and consistent over time. Studies on students some years later (Appendix, Studies II, III, IV) showed high correlations with the original scale.

Although the attitudes can be constructed into a unidimensional scale, a factor analysis revealed a subdivision into four factors. The first factor included all the attitudes about Shabbat laws except for the closing of shops. Only a minority of the sample endorsed the items in this factor. The second factor included laws dealing with the selling of nonkosher food, raising pigs, civil marriages and intermarriages, and the ruling about wearing skullcaps. About 50 percent of the population endorsed those laws.

The third factor included items that showed tolerance towards religious people's needs. The vast majority endorse those laws that commit the government to supply synagogues or education for the religious and the right to close a street in a religious neighborhood on Shabbat. The fourth factor included those civil religious laws that the vast majority endorsed for everyone: closing stores on Shabbat, and teaching Jewish tradition in the elementary school. The endorsement of the last two factors by the majority shows that the concept of separation of state and religion is understood differently in Israel than it is in the United States. People see no contradiction in the endorsement of these laws even while many (47 percent) claim to support the separation of state and religion.

THE CONNECTION BETWEEN RELIGIOUS DEFINITION AND THE RELIGIOUS DIMENSIONS

The Relationship between the Dimension and Self-definition

What do people mean when they define themselves as Orthodox, traditional, and non-Orthodox? An answer might be found by relating to the other religious dimensions. In Table 10-7, the correlations of the six studies are presented. (Because the studies varied in the number of dimensions measured, each study includes different correlations).

Table 10-7   Correlations between religious self-definition and ritual, belief, attitude to the state-religion issue and emotion

	STUDY I	STUDY II	STUDY III	STUDY IV	STUDY V	STUDY VI
Ritual	.72	.89	.84	.82	.71	.61
Belief	.65	.77	.71	.67	.45	
State & Religion	.80	.70	.73	.78	.40	
Religious Emotion	.43	.43				

The correlations indicate that all the dimensions are significantly correlated to religious self-definition, the ritual dimension being the most related. In other words, in Israel people define themselves as Orthodox, traditional, or nonreligious on the basis of the observance of religious commandments. The lower correlations in study VI result from the limited range of answers because the sample consisted only of students from religious high schools.

The correlation between self-definition and the attitude toward the state-religion connection attitude was almost as high as that with ritual. The more people define themselves as religious, the more they want the country to have a religious civil code. Belief is less related to definition, and indices of religious experience show the least relationship.

These results lead us back to Jewish tradition in which carrying out the commandments takes the predominant role, while belief and feeling are secondary. This explains the high significant correlation between ritual and self-definition. It would be virtually impossible to find anyone considering himself religious who does not keep the rituals.

Another way of analyzing the results is to compare the three groups of people—religious, traditional, and nonreligious—as to the amount of religiosity professed on the various scales. The Ben-Meir and Kedem study (Study I), as the most representative and the broadest in scope, has been chosen for presentation. As described above, we found that ritual can be subdivided into three factors and the state-religion attitude into four factors. Belief was a single factor, and emotions did not yield stable factors, but we saw that the situations arousing religious feeling can be clustered into national and personal situations. Table 8 will show how the different self-defined groups respond to these various indices of religiosity.

Table 10-8   Religiosity of the three self-defined groups

| | RELIGIOUS SELF-DEFINITION | | |
	Dati Religious	*Mesorti* Traditional	*Lo Dati* Not religious
Religiosity index	n = 258	n = 619	n = 641
Ritual	72.16	> 45.46	> 27.66
orthodox ritual	48.06	> 7.67	> .82
traditional ritual	84.88	> 66.41	> 33.64
secular ritual	99.22	> 93.86	> 86.88
Belief	88.43	> 45.46	> 27.66
State and religion	79.75	> 51.75	> 30.49
orthodox attitude	68.93	> 26.84	> 7.49
traditional attitude	84.88	> 53.50	> 20.44
secular attitude	92.44	= 88.21	> 76.99
tolerance attitude	85.53	> 73.77	> 65.63

Table 10-8   (Continued)

| | RELIGIOUS SELF-DEFINITION | | | | |
| | *Dati* | | *Mesorti* | | *Lo Dati* |
	Religious		Traditional		Not religious
Experience					
close to God	81.39	>	54.60	>	23.56
national	12.40	=	13.57	>	.06
personal	33.72	>	25.69	>	10.92
religious feeling	72.16	>	45.46	>	27.66
always	41.86	>	11.15	>	.02
never	.78	<	9.85	<	53.51

Note: (a) In order to compare the various indices, all scores were transformed to be expressed 0 to 100 giving the scores a meaning similar to percentage. (b) Significance of $p < .0001$ is marked by >.

Table 10–8 shows how the amount of religiosity of the three self-defined groups accord with their position on the various religious dimensions. As can be expected, religious people, on the average, observe more ritual than the traditional, and they in turn observe more than the nonreligious. By dividing the observances themselves into factors, we find that the more extreme ones we named Orthodox observances were not observed at all by those that defined themselves as nonreligious. The traditional group also hardly kept those strict rules, and only about 50 percent of the religious group held to all of the Orthodox observances. The traditional rituals were observed not only by the majority of religious people, but also by a majority of those who define themselves as simply traditional. Even those who defined themselves as nonreligious kept about 33 percent of the traditional rituals. The secular rituals were kept by a vast majority of the population no matter how they defined themselves.

The religious group endorsed about 88 percent of the beliefs in the scale, the traditional group about 50 percent, and even the nonreligious people held to about a third of the beliefs. In the study of the religious high school students (Study IV), mystic beliefs were held by 69 percent of those who defined themselves as religious, 66 percent of the traditional group, and 52 percent of the nonreligious students. It is interesting to compare these figures with the beliefs of the same high school students on the Traditional Belief Scale. On that scale, the religious students scored 96 percent, the traditional 91 percent, and the nonreligious 69 percent. The nonreligious students (by self-definition) believed less than the other two groups, but the gap was much greater for the traditional beliefs than for the mystical ones.

The state and religion category shows the same trend as the ritual scale. The majority of the nonreligious group favor enforcing the religious laws affecting the general public. They are also tolerant of the needs of religious people.

The experience category shows, as would be expected, that the less religious by self-definition have less feeling of closeness to God and less religious feeling. Even among the nonreligious, however 47 percent claim that they have had religious feelings at one time or another.

DISCUSSION

Can we explain the descending hierarchy or ritual, belief, and attitude and particularly the religiosity of nonreligious people who define themselves as traditional or nonreligious?

Neuman (1982) tried to theorize that the amount of ritual observed is determined by the amount of effort required to observe the ritual. By applying ingenious mathematical formulas to Ben-Meir and Kedem's data (Study I), she "proved" her hypothesis. Obviously it takes more time and effort to pray daily than to pray once a year. It also has an appeal because it can serve as an explanation for Jews abroad as well as for Israeli Jews. The theory, however, is in error. The amount of effort many nonreligious women put into housecleaning before Passover is cogent disproof. Moreover, the theory does not explain the descending order of attitudes connected with the subject of the state and religion or the belief scale: Neither more nor less effort is required for any given belief than for an alternative one.

Two other theories are more helpful. Shelah(1975) did a study called "Indications towards secular religion in Israel." On the basis of theoretical writings and on an empirical study of women who defined themselves as traditional or secular, she concluded that secular religion is separate from traditional religion. Her indication of secular religion is that rituals observed are based upon free personal choice, while according to her, traditional religion is dictated.

The secular-traditional Jew, according to Shelah, observes the rituals not because of faith in supernatural factors, but from faith in social values derived from Jewish tradition, while others maintain a faith in universal social values such as human life, the family, and the home. She emphasized the dominant role the family has in the secular religion. She considers it to be "a substitute for religion, constituting a focus for ritual activity."

Liebman and Don-Yehiya (1983) developed and documented a theory of civil religion. Their theory is based mainly on writings of politicians, authors, philosophers, and the media and is backed by a small number of surveys.

The theory states that civil religion went through three stages. From 1919–1945 Zionist socialism was predominant and claimed that "there is no inherent relationship between religion and Judaism." They tried to create the "new Jew" and rebelled against their own religious background in the Diaspora. The second stage, "statism" (1948–1956), repeated the "no inherent relationship" theme. At that time, ritual was either discarded or subjected to change, both in interpretation and in behavior. The Shavuot holiday serves as a good example. The new Shavuot emphasised only the agricultural aspect of the holiday, disregarding the religious significance of the day the Torah was given to the Jewish people. The third stage, from 1956 until today is the period of the "new civil religion." In this stage there is a complete reversal: Israel as a Jewish state must recognize the relationship between religion and Judaism. "Some measure of religious observance, of knowledge about and respect for the Jewish tradition are important attributes of the good Israeli. The state itself should incorporate traditional Jewish symbols." Liebman and Don-Yehiva, (p. 219).

Before attempting to integrate the findings of the six studies within a theoretical framework, something must be said about Jewish religious identity of non-Israelis and Jewish identification of Israelis. Studies in the United States on religiosity found a similar descending order of ritual and belief (Lazerwitz 1973, 1978; Liebman 1973; Polasky 1958; Sklare 1958). Percentages are different, as are ways of building samples and representation within the samples, but the trend is similar to what happens in Israel.

As far as Jewish identity of Israelis are concerned, findings of research (Herman 1977, Levy and Guttman 1975, Levy 1986, Etzyoni-Halevy 1969, Bar-Lev and Kedem 1986) at different times, on different types of samples, with differently worded questionnaires, all disclosed some similar trends. In Study IV a representative sample of students were presented with a list of 30 components of Jewish identity. They were required to state how much each component contributed to their identity as a Jew. The 30 components led to six factors.

The most important factor in the students' Jewish identity was Israeli identity: about 90 to 100 percent mentioned living in Israel, being in the army, and speaking Hebrew as important components.

The second most important factor was religious tradition. In this connection about 85 ot 90 percent mentioned marriage to a Jew, marriage in a religious ceremony, circumcision, celebrating a bar mitzvah, religious burial, celebrating Jewish holidays like Passover. Belief in one God belonged to this factor as well, although a smaller percent of students (75 percent) mentioned it as contributing to Jewish identity. Jewish solidarity, Jewish history, and reaction to anti-semitism are important components for about 75 percent of the sample.

The factor that the vast majority of students saw as having no relevance to their Jewish identity was the Jewish ethics factor. They did not perceive that values—honesty, honoring parents, not stealing, good family relations, study, and care for the needy—as part of their specifically Jewish identity, but only as the universal identity.

Integration of the various findings on Jewish religiosity in Israel requires one to accept that much religious behavior can be explained by individual emotions tied to childhood memories and the desire to instill similar memories in children.

Secular religious behavior is related especially to special occasions that have child-centered elements. Much of the seder night ritual is carried out to appeal to the child's interest. Yom Kippur and Rosh Hashanah are filled with symbolic behavior to distinguish those Days of Awe from all others. In Israel, the synagogues are filled with children when it is time for the blowing of the shofar. Certain Shabbat behaviors—lighting candles, saying kiddush, a festive table, and traditional food—all can be related to a holiday atmosphere that children respond to from generation to generation.

On the other hand, the same people might observe the same behaviors out of identification with the Jewish nation as well. The rituals serve as symbols expressing attachment to the Jewish people. All Israeli Jews circumcise their sons as part of the Jewish covenant. The bar mitzvah is also a religious act expressing national identity. All these rituals have existed for generations among Jews all over the world and hence link the Jews in Israel and those in the Diaspora. As the Israelis see it, being Israeli is an integral part of being Jewish. These symbols are perceived as part of their Jewish-Israeli identification.

The state and religion attitudes are another expression of the collectivistic approach of most Jews in Israel. All the population want the state to have a Jewish identity. The difference lies in the amount of laws considered necessary. There is also a difference of opinion on the degree of coercion that can be applied tactically or diplomatically. As we saw, the most accepted civil law related to religion is the one stating that children should be taught something about their Jewish religious tradition. In the political context, too, religious laws are acceptable in relation to children.

Beliefs are also affected by national feeling. Many people believe in Jewish destiny. Mystic beliefs seem related to ethnic group. Those youngsters who grew up in a culture that believes, accept them. But as these beliefs are not universal among Jews, they are not accepted even by all those who define themselves as Orthodox.

Religious experience has a personal-individual aspect and a Jewish-Israeli aspect. In the main survey, 22 percent of the respondents mentioned a personal event, while 10 percent mentioned a national event as causing a religious experience. University and high school students both mentioned personal and national situations that aroused religious feeling.

Another question is whether there is a dictated "religious" religion and a freely chosen "secular" religion, as postulated by Shelah (1975) and previously mentioned. The Orthodox also seem to be making a choice. In the six studies where the religious group was compared to the traditional or even to the nonreligious, we saw that all groups had personal motivation and national associations, and the difference was more in degree than in kind. Religious people, however, see religion as more encompassing, more part of their whole being, and more as emanating from a divine source.

REFERENCES

Antonovsky, A. 1963. Israeli political-social attitudes. *Amot 6:* 11–12 (Hebrew).

Arian, A. 1973. *The choosing people: Voting behavior in Israel.* Cleveland: The Press of Case Western Reserve University.

Aviad, J. 1980. From protest to return: Contemporary teshuva. *The Jerusalem Quarterly, 16:* 71–82.

Bar-Lev, M. 1977. *The graduates of the Yeshiva high-school in Ertz-Yisrael: Between tradition and innovation.* Docroral dissertation, Bar-Ilan University, Ramat Gan, Israel (Hebrew).

Bar-Lev, M., A. Har-Even, and P. Kedem. 1981. *The Jewish world of the Israeli student: His social, national, religious and cultural values.* Ramat Gan & Jerusalem, Bar-Ilan University in cooperation with Van-Leer Institute in Jerusalem (Hebrew).

Bar-Lev, M., and P. Kedem. 1986. Unity and compartmentalization in Israeli students' perceptions of their Jewish-Zionist identity and identification. *Hebetim Bechinuch 1:* 155–77 (Hebrew).

Bar-Lev, M., and P. Kedem. 1988. *Youth Aliya students of Yishivot and Ulpanas.* Ramat Gan: Bar Ilan University. Research report submitted to Youth Aliya.

Ben-Meir, Y., and P. Kedem. 1979. A measure of religiosity for the Jewish population of Israel. *Megamot 24:* 353–62 (Hebrew).

Brontvain, N., and I. Prilleltenski. 1980. *Religious experience: An empirical and conceptual analysis.* Internal report. Bar-Ilan University, Ramat Gan, Israel (Hebrew).

Etzyoni-Halevy, H. 1969. Jewish Identity of Tel-Aviv University students. M.A. Thesis, Tel-Aviv University: Tel-Aviv Israel (Hebrew).

Glanz, D., and M. Harrison. 1978. Varieties of identity transformation: The case study of newly Orthodox Jews. *Jewish Journal of Sociology 20:* 129–41.

Glock, C., and R. Stark. 1965. *Religion and society in tension.* Chicago: Rand McNally.

Herman, S. N. 1977. *Jewish identity a social psychological perspective,* Beverly Hills: Sage.

Hood, R. 1975. The construction and validation of a measure of reported mystical experience. *Journal for the Scientific Study of Religion 14:* 29–41.

James, W. 1902. *The varieties of religious experience: A study of human nature.* New-York: The Modern Library.

Kedem, P. 1979. *Centrality, salience, and ego involvement as measures of the importance of the religious attitude.* Doctoral dissertation, Bar-Ilan University, Ramat Gan, Israel.

Kedem, P., and M. Bar-Lev. 1983. Is giving up traditional religious culture part of the price to be paid for acquiring higher education? *Higher Education 12:* 373–88.

Kedem, P., and I. Birinbaum, I. Kopiz, and R. Siboni. 1985. *The relationship between ego-identity and attraction towards new religious groups.* Abstract Israel Psychological Association. The 20th conference.

Kedem, P., and J. Lewin. 1978. *Change in attitudes on Judaism during studies at Bar-Ilan University.* Ramat Gan: Research Authority of Bar-Ilan University, Ramat Gan, Israel.

Laslau, A., and J. Schwarzwald. 1985. *Parents' considerations in applying for state religious schools for their children.* Jerusalem: Ministry of Education and Culture.

Lazerwitz, B. 1973. Religious identification and its ethnic correlates: A multivariate model *Social Forces 52:* 204-20.

Lazerwitz, B. 1978. An approach to the components and consequences of Jewish identification. *Contemporary Jewry 23:* 57-69.

Levinson, H. 1988. Attitudes and Evaluations of the public on religious and Jewish issues, and towards the institutes responsible for the religious services. Jerusalem: The Israel Institute of Applied Social Research (Hebrew).

Levy, S. 1986. *The structure of social values.* Jerusalem: The Israel Institute of Applied Social Research.

Levy, S. and L. Guttman. 1976. Jewish identity of Israelis in the midst of the war. In M. Davis (Ed.). The identity of the nation with the state following the Yom-Kippur war. Jerusalem: The Zionist Library (Hebrew).

Levy, S., and L. Guttman. 1976b. *Values and attitudes of Israel high school youth.* Jerusalem: The israel Institute of Applied Research (Hebrew).

Liebman, C. 1973. *The ambivalent American Jew: Politics, religion and family in American Jewish life.* Philadelphia: Jewish Publication Society.

Liebman, C. S., and E. Don-Yehiya. 1983. *Civil Religion in Israel. Traditional Judaism and political culture in the Jewish state.* Berkely: University of California Press.

Lofland, J., and N. Skonovd. 1981. Conversion motives. *Journal for the Scientific Study of Religion 20(4):* 373-85.

Margolis, R. D. 1979. A typology of religious experience, *Journal for the Scientific Study of Religion 18(1):* 61-72.

Maslow, A. 1964. *Religions, values and peak experience.* Columbus, OH: Ohio State University Press.

Neuman, S. 1982. Cost of time devoted to religious activities. Doctoral dissertation, Bar-Ilan University, Ramat Gan, Israel (Hebrew).

Polasky H. E. 1958. A study of Orthodoxy in Milwaukee: Social characteristics, beliefs and observances. In *The Jews,* ed. M. Sklare. New York, NY: The Free Press.

Samet, M. 1979. *Religion and state in Israel*, Jerusalem: Hebrew University (Hebrew).

Shapiro, J. 1977. *Democracy in Israel*. Ramat Gan: Massada Press.

Shelah, I. 1975. *Indications towards secular religion in Israel* Jerusalem: The Hebrew University Press (Hebrew).

Shye, S. 1983. *Public attitude towards religious literature and religious institutions*. Jerusalem: The Israel Institute of Applied Social Research.

Sklare, M. 1958. *The Jews*. New York, NY: The Free Press.

Smooha, S. 1978. *Israel: Pluralism and conflict*, London: Routledge & Kegan Paul.

Stark, R. and W. Bainbridge. 1981. Secularization and cult formation in the jazz age. *Journal for the Scientific Study of Religion 20*: 360-73.

Tabory, E. 1981a. State and religion: Religious conflict among Jews in Israel. *Church and State 23*: 275-83.

Tabory, E. 1981b. Religious rights as a social problem in Israel. In *Yearbook on Human Rights*. Tel Aviv: Tel Aviv University, Israel, 256-71.

Werblowsky, Z. R. J., and G. Wigoder. 1985. *The Encyclopedia of the Jewish Religion. NY: Holt, Rinehart & Winston, Inc.*

APPENDIX

STUDY I:
INDEX OF RELIGIOSITY OF THE JEWISH POPULATION OF ISRAEL

BEN-MEIR AND KEDEM

The sample consisted of 1,530 subjects chosen by area sampling design from the adutl urban Jewish population. The sampling procedure was done in two stages: the first stage consisted of a stratified random sample of 400 statistically divided areas from the whole of Israel. From this sample, 161 areas were chosen at random. In the second stage, 10 dwellings were chosen at random to represent each of the 161 areas. In each, one subject was interviewed, in the evening, by a female interviewer from the regular pool of a large opinion survey institute. All interviews were based on a standard questionnaire.

The questionnaire consisted of 150 questions, covering many different topics, directly and indirectly relating to religion. The analyses of the questions related to ritual, consequential, and ideological dimensions will be reported here. The choice of the questions was based on the following three conditions:

1. Derivation from established Jewish religious creeds.

2. The questions on ritual were linked to halacha.

3. The attitudes on state and religion were based on proposals for new laws or existing legislation.

Beliefs were taken mostly from Maimonides' "Thirteen Articles of Faith." In order to be readily understood, the questions were simply worded, short and concrete.

All the items stemmed from traditions common to all Jews.

Reference

Ben-Meir, Y., and P. Kedem. 1979. A measure of religiosity for the Jewish population of Israel. *Megamot 24:* 353–62 (Hebrew).

STUDY II:
CENTRALITY, SALIENCE AND EGO-INVOLVEMENT
AS MEASURES OF THE IMPORTANCE OF THE RELIGIOUS ATTITUDE

PERI KEDEM

Four hundred and forty-one students from five universities answered a questionnaire designed specifically to measure intensity of feelings toward keeping commandments and the issue of state and religion.

The sample was constructed so as to have a wide dispersion of positions along the state and religion continuum. About 60 percent the sample were graduates of a nonreligious high school, while the other 40 percent graduated from religious ones.

Reference

Kedem, P. 1979. *Centrality, salience, and ego involvement as measures of the importance of the religious attitude.* Doctoral dissertation, Bar-Ilan University, Ramat Gan, Israel.

STUDY III:
BAR-ILAN STUDENTS' ATTITUDES TOWARD JUDAISM

PERI KEDEM AND ISAAC LEWIN

A questionnaire was mailed to a representative sample of Bar-Ilan students, relating to all six dimensions of religiosity: ritual, belief, experiential, knowledge, and attitude relating the state and religion issue. Questions as to religious and Jewish identification as well as questions about the Jewish studies offered at the university were also put to them.

Bar-Ilan, unique in that it is a religious university, requires some basic Jewish studies for its degree. The student body is divided almost equally between religious and nonreligious students, very differently from other universities in Israel.

This study was executed in 1977, repeated in 1978, and again in 1980. Each study covered a representative sample as verified by comparison with university statistics: sex, percentage in various departments, age, and martial status.

Reference

Kedem, P., and J. Lewin. 1978. *Change in attitudes on Judaism during studies at Bar-Ilan University.* Ramat Gan: Research Authority of Bar-Ilan University, Ramat Gan, Israel.

STUDY IV:
THE JEWISH WORLD OF THE ISRAELI STUDENT

PERI KEDEM AND MORDECAI BAR-LEV

Sample A random sample (N = 1250) was a representative sample of all the Jewish undergraduates studying for their B.A. degrees in the academic year 1979-1980 at the six Israeli universities. The students received a closed questionnaire delivered by the secretary of the university. The questionnaire form bore only the heading of the Van-Leer Institute (a cosponsor of this research project) to disengage the research from the universities where the students studied.

MEASURES

1. *Ritual Dimension:* The questions were based on the Ben-Meir and Kedem Scale and on a scale designed for graduates of yeshiva high schools (Bar-Lev, 1979) dealing with more extreme Orthodox practices.

2. *Belief Dimension:* Five items were taken from the Ben-Meir and Kedem Scale with expanded answer categories. The three original "believe," "don't know," "don't believe" were increased to five with the addition of provision for degrees of doubt.

3. *Consequential Dimension:* The State and Religion Scale was based mainly on the Ben-Meir and Kedem Scale with new questions added to include current issues, that is, legalizing prostitution and abortion.

4. *Jewish Identity and Identification.* A chapter devoted to the question, "What are the components of Jewish identity, and how much does the student feel thus identified? (See Bar-Lev and Kedem 1986)

References

Kedem, P., and M. Bar-Lev. 1983. Is giving up tradition religious culture part of the price to be paid for acquiring higher education? *Higher Education* 12: 373–88.

Bar-Lev, M., A. Hareven, and P. Kedem. 1981. *The Jewish world of the Israeli student: His social, national, religious and cultural values*. Ramat Gan & Jerusalem, Bar-Ilan University in cooperation with Van-Leer Institute in Jerusalem (Hebrew).

Bar-Lev, M., and P. Kedem. 1986. Unity and compartmentalization in Israeli students' perceptions of their Jewish-Zionist identity and identification. *Hebetim Bchinuch 1:* 155–77 (Hebrew).

STUDY V:
RELIGIOUS EXPERIENCE

KEDEM, BRONTVAIN AND PRILLELTENSKY

Subject and Procedure. The sample consisted of 113 adolescents (16–18 years old), 56 were students in a religious high school and 57 in a nonreligious high school. The structured questionnaire was administered during a regular class session.

In order to measure feelings relating to religious-spiritual experience. The questionnaire was worded not in terms of "religious" experience but in terms of spiritual experience, so that the nonreligious student could feel comfortable with the questionnaire.

The items were derived from Glock and Stark's (1965) measurement of the experiential dimension; Margolis' (1979) typology of religious experience; Hood's (1975) work on mystical experience; Kedem and Lewin's (1978) study on students' religious attitudes; and items based on the theoretical works of James (1902) and Maslow (1964).

After a pilot test on a few students in the university, and a pretest on a class in a nonreligious high school, the items that were misunderstood or caused antagonism were deleted.

Reference

Brontvain, N., and I. Prilleltenski. 1980. *Religious experience: An empirical and conceptual analysis.* (Internal Report) Bar-Ilan University, Ramat Gan, Israel (Hebrew)

STUDY VI:
DIMENSIONS OF RELIGIOSITY OF HIGH SCHOOL STUDENTS

MORDECAI BAR LEV AND PERI KEDEM

In 1984, 2,580 students in religious high schools answered a questionnaire on various aspects of their lives. One chapter was dedicated to religiosity and contained many detailed questions not asked in the aforementioned studies about ritual. The belief questions included six from the Ben-Meir and Kedem scale as well as questions pertaining to mystical belief. Attitude and Jewish identity was measured similarly to Study V.

Reference

Bar-Lev, M., and P. Kedem. 1988. *Youth Aliya students of Yeshivot and Ulpanas*. Ramat Gan: Bar Ilan University. Research report submitted to Youth Aliya.

11

Religious, Ethnic, and Class Divisions in Israel:
Convergent or Cross Cutting?*

HANNA AYALON, ELIEZER BEN-RAFAEL,
AND STEPHEN SHAROT

Within the Jewish populations of Israel, the focus of public attention appears to have moved in recent years from the ethnic division between Jews of European and African or Asian origins to the division between religious and secular Jews. The mass media has reported numerous conflicts, some involving violent confrontations, between religious and secular Jews over such issues as public transportation on the Sabbath, opening cinemas on the Sabbath eve, burning bus stations displaying advertisements featuring women in swimming costumes or underwear, free movement of private transportation in areas close to religious neighborhoods on the Sabbath, the freedom of archaeologists to excavate ancient sites that might have included Jewish cemeteries, the legitimacy of conversion to Judaism under non-Orthodox auspices, and the question of who is a Jew. *Haredim* (ultra-Orthodox) rather than modern Orthodox Jews have been involved in these conflicts, but observers have argued that there is a trend within the the religious population toward *haredization*, a tendency to ultra-Orthodoxy, and that the Jewish population is becoming increasingly polarized with respect to religion.

A sociological analysis of the religious-secular division or conflict

*We wish to thank the Ford Foundation for funding, received through the Israel Foundations Trustees. Authors are in alphabetical order to denote equal contributions.

in Israel should not only examine its extent but also its relationship with other divisions, particularly those of ethnic group and class. Sociological discussions of conflict have emphasized that, whereas convergent or overlapping conflicts might lead to acute disruptions of society, crosscutting conflicts might serve to stablize or integrate society (Simmel 1955; Coser, 1956). The religious-secular division might be especially important in Israeli society, but if it crosscuts other significant divisions, there might be little danger that it will prove disruptive. A discussion of this question should focus on the relationships between the religious-secular division and ethnic and class divisions. Other divisions or aspects of stratification, such as gender and age, are less interesting in this respect because unlike religion, ethnicity, and class, whose basic unit of classification is generally the family, gender and age cut through the family unit.

The relationship of religious divisions to ethnic and class divisions has rarely been investigated within a single theoretical framework in Israel. The pluralist approach (Smooha 1978) has tended to deal with the division between religious and secular Jews as a separate dimension from the ethnic divisions of Arabs and Jews and of Ashkenazim (Jews of mainly European origin) and *edot ha 'Mizrah* ('communities of the East', referring to Jews from Asia and North Africa). The class or dependency model of ethnicity has emphasized the convergence of ethnic and class divisions in Israel but has paid very little attention to religion (Swirski 1981). Religion has been an important focus of the cultural perspective on ethnicity (Deshen and Shokeid 1974, Shokeid and Deshen, 1982, Ben-Rafael 1982), but there has been little probing of the relationship between class and religion (see, however, Ayalon, Ben-Rafael, and Sharot 1986; and Ben-Rafael and Sharot 1987).

An examination of the relationships among religious, ethnic, and class divisions should follow a number of guidelines. Firstly, objective and subjective dimensions of the divisions should be distinguished. Objective measures of the religious division or divisions include membership of different religiosity within a single religion. Ethnic classification might be made simply according to country or area of origin. An appropriate objective measure of class is, of course, the subject of an extensive literature, but most empirical analyses have used such measures as wealth, occupation, and education. The categories derived from each of these classifications (religious, ethnic, and class) can then be plotted in terms of their cultural distinctions, social distance (such as residential patterns and social networks), and conflicts. Subjective dimensions include levels of self-identification with the religious, ethnic, and class units; perceptions of cultural distinctions, social distances, and conflict among religious groups, ethnic groups, or classes; feelings of relative deprivation regarding the position of one's membership groups in the society; and support for the need to organize politically in order to advance the interests of one's membership groups.

Secondly, the investigation should look at the relative importance of the religious, ethnic, and class allegiances, divisions, and conflicts. At the objective level, it might be possible to compare, for example, the residential segregation of religious and secular groups with that of ethnic groups and classes. At the subjective level, questions can probe the relative importance of various identifications, which divisions are seen to be most salient and conflict ridden, which comparisons induce the most relative deprivation, and on what basis respondents are more likely to support political organization.

Finally, the extent to which divisions converge or crosscut each other should be investigated. At the objective level, one might ask, for example, if different religious groups (or groups within a single religion with different levels of religiosity) have different origins and occupy different positions in the class structure. At the subjective level, it is possible to discover whether people have coverging identifications; whether they perceive an overlapping of religious, ethnic, and class groups in their cultural differences, social distances, and conflicts; whether deprivations reinforce each other; and whether political support will focus on the basis of one affiliation or a combination of affiliations.

The argument here is that to assess the overall importance of the divisions relating to religion in Israeli society, it is necessary not only to compare them with ethnic and class divisions but also to examine their convergence or crosscutting with the other divisions. The various combinations of the relative importance of divisions and the ways in which they might converge or crosscut are numerous. For example, ethnic differences might crosscut the religious population more than they crosscut the secular population, but this might be of less significance for the religious population because, in comparison with the secular population, their allegiance to their position on religion outweighs their ethnic allegiance.

DIVISIONS IN ISRAELI SOCIETY

The most crucial division in Israel society is that between Arabs and Jews, and this is, to a large extent, a division between Moslems and Jews. The Arab population includes Christian groups, but these make up a small proportion, and there is considerable convergence of nationality (or nation) with religion in the Arab-Jewish division. Moreover, this is reinforced by considerable differences in class distribution with a very heavy concentration of Arabs in the working or lower class. The bare outlines of these convergences are clear, although the relative importance of national and religious allegiances among the Arab population and the interlinkage of these with class position are by no means obvious and appear to be in a state of flux. However, the subject of this study is the Jewish rather than the Arab population.

The major differentiation with respect to religion is according to levels of religious practice and identifications. These correspond to levels of religiosity: *dati* (religious), *mesorti* (traditional), and *hiloni* (secular). Although surveys of religiosity show that there is a continuum ranging from the most observant to the nonobservant with no breaks between clearly identifiable levels of observance (Ben-Meir and Kedem 1979; Ayalon, Ben-Rafael, and Sharot 1986), it is common for people to categorize themselves and others into two (religious and secular), three (adding traditional), or sometimes four (adding haredim) categories.

If the religious-secular division within the Israeli Jewish population is considered more important than ethnic or subethnic divisions, this is in part because religious Jews, unlike particular Jewish groups based on country or area origin, have successfully established separate institutions and organizations, such as schools and political parties (Smooha 1978, 220). With respect to ethnic or subethnic divisions within the Israeli Jewish population, there has been some dispute over the relative significance of community of origin or *eda* compared with the broad division between *edot ha'Mizrah* and Ashkenazim (Ayalon, Ben-Rafael, and Sharot 1985). Class dimensions have rarely been considered separately from ethnic ones in Israel, but overall patterns of inequality are similar to those of other capitalist industrial societies, and when asked, Israelis readily identify themselves with particular classes (Ayalon, Ben-Rafael, and Sharot 1988).

Some aspects of the convergence or crosscutting relationships of religious, ethnic, and class dimensions are well documented, although their significance is often in dispute. Many studies have focused on the overlap of ethnic origins and class. In broad terms, most Jewish manual workers are from *edot ha'Mizrah*, the lower white-collar ranks include roughly equal proportions of *edot ha'Mizrah* and Ashkenazim, and the higher white-collar ranks are predominantly Ashkenazim. There are important differences according to country of origin within the two broad categories, but generally the distinction between working class and middle class cuts across *edot ha'Mizrah* more than the

Ashkenazim, and the distinction between *edot ha'Mizrah* and Ashkenazim cuts across the middle class more than the working class.

The generally higher level of religious observance among *edot ha'Mizrah* has been demonstrated in a few studies (Goldscheider and Friedlander 1983; Ayalon, Ben-Rafael, and Sharot 1986). It would appear that religious-secular differences crosscut the Ashkenazi population more than *edot ha'Mizrah*, but this might be changing as there are signs of *haredization* among some religious sectors of *edot ha'Mizrah*.

There is little data on the relationship between religiosity and class, and almost nothing is known with respect to any of the dimensions of its subjective measures. Questions indicating the relative importance and interrelationships of the religious, ethnic, and class identifications, perceptions, and evaluations have rarely been asked. The study reported below is intended to clarify these aspects, especially the subjective ones.

SAMPLE

Interviews were conducted in 1982–83 with a disproportionate stratified sample of 826 male residents of Beersheba, the largest town in southern Israel. The majority of respondents migrated to Israel in their childhood or youth (a minority were born in Israel) and are between the ages of 30 and 50. The sample was composed of about equal proportions of four *edot* or communities of origin—Morocco, Iraq, Rumania, and Poland. The sample was further stratified to obtain a similar distribution of blue-collar and white-collar workers in each group of origin. Lists of appropriate respondents were made up from the records of primary and secondary schools, both secular and religious, supplemented in some schools by questionnaires administered to children. These gave the country of origin, years of education, and occupation of parents. Thus, a further parameter of the sample was that all respondents were fathers of school-age children. If the parents were born in Israel, inquiries were made to discover the countries of origins of their parents. All the background details of respondents, including origins, education, and occupation, were checked when the questionnaires were administered by our interviewers.

The four origin categories were chosen because they are the largest in Israel, and they cover the range of ethnic status in Israeli society. European groups are generally ranked higher than Middle Eastern groups, but within the broad categories, Poles are ranked higher than Rumanians and Iraqis higher than Moroccans (Kraus

1983, 1984). Ethnic status reflects, in part, the class distribution of the groups of origin: European Israelis are disproportionately concentrated in upper middle and upper white-collar ranks, and Middle Eastern Israelis are disproportionately concentrated in blue-collar occupations (Nahon 1984). The overlap between geographical origins and socioeconomic location is far from complete. Our sample allows for categories that have been largely ignored in Israeli sociological studies: middle class Israelis from Asia and Africa, and working class Israelis from European origins. This enabled us to examine the extent to which the religious factor converges with or crosscuts ethnicity and class.

The questionnaire included questions that indicate relationships both at the objective and subjective levels of religious, ethnic, and class divisions. The following discussion of findings begins with the objective level. The focus here is on the relationships between level of religious observance, country of origin, and socioeconomic status.

RELIGIOSITY, ETHNIC ORIGIN, AND SOCIOECONOMIC STATUS

In order to compare levels of religiosity, respondents were asked if they practice five specific mitzvot: donning tefillin (phylacteries) every day; not traveling on the Sabbath; using separate utensils for milk and meat; kiddush, the prayer recited over wine before the Sabbath meal; and fasting on Yom Kippur. These were chosen to range from an observance (donning tefillin) that is kept by only a minority who practice all or most Jewish observances to an observance (fasting on Yom Kippur) that is practiced by most Jews including those who practice few others.

In deciding which mitzvot to include in our questionnaire, we have had the benefit of the findings of the study in which Israelis were questioned regarding their performance of twenty mitzvot (Ben-Meir and Kedem 1979). No clear divisions in levels of religiosity were found; there was a continuum of religiosity ranging from the strictly religious, the population who performed fourteen or more of the twenty miztvot, to the nonreligious, 39 percent who performed six or fewer of the mitzvot. Observance of the individual mitzvot ranged from 1 percent who did not use electricity on the Sabbath to 99 percent who participated in the yearly seder meal at Passover. The five mitzvot were found to meet the requirements of a Guttman scale: the coefficient of reproducibility was .93 and the coefficient of scalability .77. Levels of observance were computed according to the number of mitzvot practiced, ranging from five to zero.

Table 11-1   Religiosity according to country of origin and socioeconomic status: averages (x), standard deviations (o), and coefficients of variability (v)

	x	o	v	N*
Moroccans				
High SES	2.90	1.30	.44	71
Low SES	3.45	1.42	.41	131
Iraqis				
High SES	1.64	1.01	.62	69
Low SES	2.44	1.21	.50	135
Poles				
High SES	.96	1.21	1.26	117
Low SES	1.45	1.43	.99	60
Rumanians				
High SES	1.61	1.39	.86	131
Low SES	1.86	1.18	.63	72
Total				
High SES	1.65	1.42	.86	388
Low SES	2.62	1.42	.56	398

*Reduction of N is due to missing data

Table 11-1 shows the levels of religiosity of respondents by country of origin and socioeconomic status. For purposes of this analysis, each group was divided into lower and higher categories of socioeconomic status (SES). The weighted SES index was constructed from three variables: years of schooling, occupational prestige (coded by Hartman's 1975 Israeli occupational prestige scale), and housing density (number of rooms in a house divided by number of household members).

The SES was based on the sum of the standardized scores of the three components. Each component was weighted by its factor loadings using the method of principal factor. A single factor accounted for 55.8 percent of the variance among the items. The loading of the items was: .42 for years of schooling, .83 for occupational prestige, and –.47 for housing density. SES scores lower than the average of the distribution were defined as lower status; scores higher than the average or equal to it were defined as higher status.

    Level of religiosity varies by both country of origin and SES. The Moroccans have the highest level of religiosity, followed by the Iraqis, Rumanians, and Poles. In each group of origin, higher socioeconomic status is associated with a lower level of religiosity, but SES divisions do not alter the placement of the most religious and least religious origin groups: the most religious of the eight categories is the low SES Moroccans, followed by the high SES Morrocans; the least religious is the high SES Poles, followed by the low SES Poles. The SES divisions do, however, cut across the differences between Iraqi and Rumanian origins; the third most religious group is the low SES Iraqis, followed by the low SES Rumanians; the high SES Iraqis and the high SES Rumanians have almost identical levels of religiosity. The coefficients of variability show that there is greater religious heterogeneity within the European groups of origin, especially in their higher socioeconomic stratum.

Table 11-2 Religious identities and respective levels of religiosity according to country of origin

	RELIGIOUS		TRADITIONAL		NON-RELIGIOUS		
	%	Level	%	Level	%	Level	N*
Moroccans	12	4.28	61	3.23	27	2.58	177
Iraqis	8	3.14	53	2.53	39	1.61	188
Poles	5	1.83	21	2.38	75	.71	155
Rumanians	3	2.00	24	2.67	73	1.16	169
Total	7	3.39	41	2.80	52	1.29	689

*Reduction of N is due to missing data

    Respondents were asked to divide up the Jewish population in Israel according to position toward religion and to identify themselves with one of the positions. The great majority of respondents distinguished either two (religious, or nonreligious or secular) or three (religious, traditional, secular) groups and identified themselves with one of these. Table 11-2 shows the distribution of the identification of respondents, and the average levels of religiosity of each identification by country of origin in Table 11-1. Whereas the dominant identification among Moroccans and Iraqis is traditional, that of the Poles and Rumanians is nonreligious or secular.

When we compare respondents from countries of origin with the same identification, the average level of religiosity of the Moroccan group is higher than that of the other groups. The average level of religiosity of the Moroccans who identified themselves as nonreligious is either higher or nearly the same as the average religiosity of respondents in the other three groups who identified themselves as traditional.

The differences in identification between the higher and lower SES categories in each group of origin (not shown in Table 11-2) were in the same direction, but not as substantial as the average differences in religiosity shown in Table 11-1. Only among the Iraqis was there a clear difference: 34 religious of the lower SES Iraqis and 52 religious of the higher SES Iraqis defined themselves as nonreligious Jews. In nearly all cases, for each identification, the lower SES had a higher average level of religiosity than the higher SES.

We have shown that Jewish religious-secular differences, in terms of both religious observance and identification, converge significantly, although far from absolutely with both ethnic and class divisions. The class religious differences crosscut the ethnic religious differences of Iraqis and Rumanians, but it should be remembered that our sample is disproportionately stratified and that in the country as a whole there is a considerable overlap of ethnic origin and class. The contrast between Moroccans and Ashkenazim in terms of both socioeconomic composition and religiosity is particularly clear. However, the implications of these convergences for divisiveness within the Israeli Jewish population will depend on people's perceptions and evaluations.

SUBJECTIVE DIMENSIONS

The subjective dimensions of our study can be divided into three broad components: cognitive, affective, and evaluative. The cognitive component is subdivided into three aspects: the extent to which respondents perceive cultural differences or similarities, social distance or amalgamation, and conflict or harmonious relations among ethnic, class, and religious-secular groups. Respondents were asked to indicate their positions in six-point scales ranging, for exanple, from no conflict to acute conflict. The affective component is indicated by the extent to which respondents take pride in their various identifications (as Jews, Israelis, their community of origin or eda, as part of edot ha'Mizrah or Ashkenazim, their class, and their position regarding religion). Respondents were asked to indicate their positions in six-point scales ranging from no pride whatsoever to very proud. The evaluative component is subdivided into two aspects. Firstly, in order to tap evaluations of justice or feelings of deprivation, respondents were asked whether their and other edot, classes, and religious positions had received what they deserved in economic rewards, social prestige, and in the political area. Respondents could choose one of three options: the group had received what it deserved, more than it deserved, or less than it deserved. Secondly, respondents were asked whether they believed that there was a need for their groups (ethnic, class, or religious) to organize politically.

Table 11-3 Cognitive dimensions.
Percentages of those who report high levels of cultural differences, social distance, and conflict, according to country of origin (the two highest options on a six-point scale).

	MOROCCANS %	IRAQIS %	POLES %	RUMANIANS %	TOTAL %
Cultural differences					
Own *eda* and other *edot* within broad category	32	26	12	17	22
Own *eda* and *edot* from other broad category	67	57	53	53	58
Edot ha'Mizrah and Ashkenazim	66	61	53	59	60
Own class and other classes	61	66	62	69	65
Religious from own *eda* and from other broad category	61	42	34	38	42
Religious from own *eda* and other *edot* within broad category	26	23	12	14	19

Table 11-3 (Continued)

	MOROCCANS %	IRAQIS %	POLES %	RUMANIANS %	TOTAL %
Social distance					
Among *edot* ha'Mizrah	17	21	25	22	21
Among *edot* Ashkenaz	14	8	6	12	10
Edot ha'Mizrah and Ashkenazim	35	28	20	30	28
Own *eda* and other broad category	35	29	26	31	30
Workers and owners	56	50	50	44	50
Religious and nonreligious	43	51	64	48	51
Conflict					
Ashkenazim and edot ha'Mizrah	34	35	29	36	33
Affluent and economically weak	38	39	30	31	35
Own class and other classes	25	19	20	16	18
Religious and nonreligious	50	56	59	58	56
Own *eda* and other broad category	31	21	17	24	21
Own *eda* and other *edot* within broad category	7	5	2	6	5

Table 11-3 summarizes the findings for the cognitive components. We focus here on the extent to which respondents perceived cultural differences, social distance, and conflict between religious and secular Jews, between classes, between their eda and othe edot, and between edot ha'Mizrah and Ashkenazim. For example, about equal proportions of respondents perceived a high level of cultural difference (5 and 6 on the six-point scales) between religious and secular Jews (65 percent) and between edot ha'Mizrah and Ashkenazim (60 percent). In comparison, only 33 respondents perceived a high level of cultural differences between their class and other classes in society. However, differences were perceived among edot within each of the two broad ethnic categories. Comparisons of religious groups from different ethnic categories show that cultural differences within each of the two broad ethnic categories were perceived to be much less than the difference between religious Ashkenazim and religious edot ha'Mizrah.

The data on the cognitive aspects indicate that the majority of Israelis perceive considerable cultural differences, social distance, and conflict between religious and secular Jews in Israel. Regarding social distance, the religious-secular division is perceived as great as a sharply divided class division between property owners and workers. Regarding conflict, the religious-secular conflict is perceived as considerably more acute than that between ethnic groups or classes. These patterns were the same for all groups of origin and for both higher and lower SES categories. Thus, most Israelis, whatever their origin or socioeconomic status tend to see the religious-secular division as more sharp and divisive than ethnic and class divisions.

Table 11-4   Affective and evaluative dimensions.
Percentages of those reporting high pride in identifications (the two highest options on a six-point scale), feelings of deprivation in political power, and support for political organization of groups, according to country of origin.

	MOROCCANS %	IRAQIS %	POLES %	RUMANIANS %	TOTAL %
High Pride					
Jew	93	82	68	73	79
Israeli	94	91	87	88	90
Broad ethnic category	75	67	28	28	50
Eda	76	68	20	32	50
Class	62	56	45	49	53
Religious position	63	42	38	34	44
Political deprivation					
Eda	57	38	3	20	31
Broad ethnic category	58	54	4	8	32
Class	24	27	20	22	24
Religious position	20	17	20	20	19

Table 11-4   (Continued)

	MOROCCANS %	IRAQIS %	POLES %	RUMANIANS %	TOTAL %
Support political organization					
Eda	16	3	0	1	5
Broad ethnic category	26	15	1	1	11
Class	27	17	14	17	19
Religious position	22	13	17	18	18

The dominant position of the religious-secular division at the cognitive level is not paralleled, among most Israelis, at the affective and evaluative levels. Table 11-4 summarizes the data for the affective or identificational component and the evaluative components. The patterns of the Moroccans and Iraqis differ significantly from those of Poles and Rumanians in these components. We have shown that the Moroccans and Iraqis have higher levels of religiosity than Poles and Rumanians, but the pride of Moroccans and Iraqis in their religious position is lower than all their other identifications. The pride of Poles and Rumanians in their religious position is lower than their class pride but higher than their pride in theri communities of origin and as Ashkenazim. These differences are mainly the consequence of the far greater ethnic pride of Moroccans and Iraqis, both as separate *edot* and as part of *edot ha'Mizrah.*

In the evaluative component, far more Moroccans and Iraqis feel deprived as members of edot ha'Mizrah than as members of their classes or in their religious positions. (Only the figures of those who believe in their group's political deprivation are included in the table, but the same pattern holds for economic and status deprivation.) Very few Poles and Rumanians feel deprived as Ashkenazim, and about the same proportions as among Moroccans and Iraqis feel deprived as members of a class or in terms of the religious or secular allegiance.

Within the Moroccan and Iraqi groups, about the same proportions support the need for political organization as edot ha'Mizrah, as members of their class, or for their religious position, but the proportions are relatively small in all cases. Almost no Poles or Rumanians support political organization on an ethnic basis, and similar small proportions support political organization on a class or religious basis. However, in contrast with the other components, support for political organization on a religious basis differs significantly according to level of religiosity. Of the least religious, who practice none of the five mitzvot in our index of religiosity, 17 percent support this kind of presumably secularist political organization. The proportion declines until it reaches its lowest level (9 percent) among those who practice three mitzvot. The proportion then increases among the more religious and reaches ts peak among the most religious who practice all five mitzvot. Almost 5 percent of the most religious, who are disproportionately of Moroccan origin, support political organization on a religious basis. This finding is in line with actual political support for the religious political parties in Israel: it has been estimated that about half of the religious sector of the population vote for the religious parties (Smooha 1978 221.)

In summary, a comparison of the subjective components of religious, ethnic, and class divisions within the Israeli Jewish population does not support the frequently made observation that a religious-secular division has come to exceed or will soon exceed the divisiveness of ethnic and class differences. It is true that the public perceive the religious-secular division as being the most acute, but with regard to the affective investments and proposed action of the majority, ethnicity and class prove to be more important than religious or secular positions.

A further question, however, is whether the religious, ethnic, and class divisions overlap or crosscut at the subjective level. We have used factor analysis in order to tap the connections within the cognitive, affective, and evaluative components with regard to religious, ethnic, and class differences. Factor analysis is based on the assumption that some underlying factors are responsible for the covariation among the ovserved variables. The question here is whether there is a common factor or a number of common factors that might be considered the cause or causes behind the formation of the subjective dimensions.

The term *factor analysis* refers to several statistical techniques with one common denominator. They allow the presentation of a set of variables by a smaller number of hypothetical variables usually named factors. Hence, factor analysis is based on the assumption that some underlying factors are responsible for the covariation among the observed variables. In the present analysis, the transformation of the given sets of observed variables into other sets of variables is based on principal factor solutions. The rotation does not improve the quality of the solution, and it is used only to obtain simpler and more readily interpretable results. We use the various methods of rotation that assumes orthogonality among the various factors. It simplifies the structure of each factor by maximizing the variance of its squared loadings. In our tables we present: (a) factor loadings that are equivalent to correlations between factors and variables; (b) eigenvalues that give an indication of the relative importance of the different factors; (c) percent of variance. We base our interpretation of the substantive meaning of the various factors on the assumption that loadings below the value of .40 indicate relative marginality of the variables. For detailed discussion on factor analysis see, for example, Kim and Mueller 1982a, b. In the following, factor analyses are performed separately for Moroccans and Iraqis (hereafter M + I), on the one hand, and Poles and Rumanians (hereafter P + R) on the other. Although the data for the groups constituting each pair are by no means identical, they are relatively close to each other. We have made this kind of analysis rather than a separate analysis for each group of origin because it is relatively economical.

Table 11-5 Perceptions of cultural differences among categories. Factor loadings (based on principal factor with varimax rotation)

SOCIAL CATEGORIES	MOROCCANS + IRAQIS		POLES + RUMANIANS		
	Factor 1	Factor 2	Factor 1	Factor 2	Factor 3
R's country of origin vs. his broad ethnic category	.23	.33	.20	.54	-.04
Specific ethnic category vs. the apposite broad category	.84	.15	.86	.05	-.02
Edot ha'Mizrah vs. Ashkenazim	.69	.23	.72	.25	.22
R's socioeconomic class vs. other classes	.28	.22	.18	.25	.18

Table 11-5   (Continued)

SOCIAL CATEGORIES	MOROCCANS + IRAQIS		POLES + RUMANIANS		
	Factor 1	Factor 2	Factor 1	Factor 2	Factor 3
Religious vs. nonreligious	.17	.37	.07	.03	.6
Religious people of R's country of origin vs. religious P. of R's broad ethnic category	.04	.71	.01	.68	
Religious people of R's country of origin vs. religious P. of the opposite broad ethnic category	.33	.47	.36	.31	
Eigenvalue	2.52	1.07	2.37	1.15	
Pc of variance	36.0	15.3	33.9	16.5	

Perception of Cultural Differences (Table 11–5)

For both M + I and PR, perception of cultural differences between religious and secular Jews does not share any common component with perceptions of differences among the class and ethnic categories. Two factors are necessary to explain the interrelations of variables among M + I. The first factor represents differences among ethnic groups, and the second factor represents differences among religious people from the ethnic groups. Hence, both factors might be interpreted as ethnic factors. Three factors are needed for the explanation of the interrelations of variables among PR. The first two factors are quite similar to the M + I factors. Only one variable appears to have substantial loading on the third factor—the difference between religious and secular Jews. Thus it appears that perceptions of cultural differences between religious and nonreligious Jews are differentiated from the perceptions of other kinds of cultural differences.

Table 11-6 Perceptions of social distance among categories.
Factor loadings (based on principal factor with varimax rotation)

SOCIAL CATEGORIES	MOROCCANS + IRAQIS		POLES + RUMANIANS		
	Factor 1	Factor 2	Factor 1	Factor 2	Factor 3
Various *edot ha'Mizrah*	.29	.62	.15	.21	.584
Ashkenazim from various countries of origin	–.01	.60	.13	.07	.572
Edot ha'Mizrah and Ashkenazim	.86	.12	.81	.24	.222
R's country of origin and the apposite broad ethnic category	.91	.06	.80	.18	
Workers and owners	.60	.10	.27	.61	.20
Religious vs. nonreligious	.35	.19	.06	.56	.09
Eigenvalue	2.65	1.23	2.48	1.03	1.01
Pc of variance	44.1	20.4	41.4	17.1	16.8

Perception of Social Distances (Table 11-6)

Among M + I, perceptions of social amalgamation or distance between religious and secular are differentiated from the perceptions of distance among ethnic and class categories. Here again we have a two-factor solution: the first factor represents the distance between Ashkenazim and *Mizrahim* as well as between social class. Because the respondents who perceive substantial social distance between Ashkenazim and *Mizrahim* are likely to perceive substantial distance between classes, the question arises as to whether these respondents see these as overlapping, divisions, or as two significant but separate divisions in Israeli society. The answer appears to be that that they are seen as overlapping because when respondents were asked to name the largest class among Ashkenazim and *edot ha'Mizrah*, the largest class among *edot ha'Mizrah* named most frequently was 'workers' or 'wage-earners', and the largest class among Ashkenazim that was named most frequently was 'employers', 'middle class', or 'wealthy'.

The second factor among M + I represents amalgamation among various groups of origin belonging to the same broad ethnic category. Among PR, we have three factors. Here again, the first factor represents perceptions of distance between *edot ha'Mizrah* and Ashkenazim. The variables highly loaded on the second factor are religious-secular and social classes. We can only speculate here that many Poles and Rumanians perceive a correspondence between lower class position and greater religiosity. The third factor is similar to the second factor in the M + I analysis.

Table 11-7 Perceptions of conflict among categories.
Factor loadings (based on principal factor with varimax rotation)

SOCIAL CATEGORIES	MOROCCANS + IRAQIS	POLES + RUMANIANS
	Factor 1	Factor 1
Edot ha'Mizrah and Askenazim	.66	.54
Affluent and economically weak	.65	.53
R's economic class and other classes	.59	.62
Religious and nonreligious	.30	.29
R's country of origin and the apposite broad ethnic category	.65	.71
R's country of origin and his broad ethnic category	.42	.56
Eigenvalue	2.53	2.51

Table 11-7 (Continued)

SOCIAL CATEGORIES	MOROCCANS + IRAQIS	POLES + RUMANIANS
	Factor 1	Factor 1
Pc of variance	42.2	41.9

Perceptions of Conflict (Table 11-7)

One factor suffices to explain the interrelations among the variables for M + I and PR. In both cases, perceptions of conflict between religious and secular Jews constitute the only viable having no significant loading on the factor. Differently stated, it appears that different types of ethnic conflict as well as conflict between social classes have a common component. This component, however, is not responsible for the formation of perceptions of conflict between religious and secular Jews, which appears to constitute a different dimension.

Table 11-8 Level of pride in identities according to country of origin and level of religiosity.
Factor loadings (based on principal factor with varimax rotation)
Low Religiosity (0–3 mitzvot)

TYPES OF IDENTITIES	MOROCCANS + IRAQIS		POLES + RUMANIANS	
	Factor 1	Factor 2	Factor 1	Factor 2
Jewish	.45	.36	.20	.74
Israeli	.36	.25	.04	.77
Broad ethnic	.65	.18	.70	.15
Specific ethnic	.92	.09	.80	.05
Class	.06	.62	.32	.22

Table 11-8   (Continued)

TYPES OF IDENTITIES	MOROCCANS + IRAQIS		POLES + RUMANIANS	
	Factor 1	Factor 2	Factor 1	Factor 2
Religious	.21	.42	.23	.30
Eigenvalue	2.44	1.07	2.39	1.26
Pc of variance	40.6	17.8	38.1	1.26

HIGH RELIGIOSITY (4–5 MITZVOT)				
TYPES OF	MOROCCANS + IRAQIS		POLES + RUMANIANS		IDENTITIES
	Factor 1	Factor 2	Factor 1	Factor 2	Factor 3
Jewish	.04	.68	.18	.66	.12
Israeli	.10	.44	.27	.33	.70
Broad ethnic	.76	.18	.68	.07	.19
Specific ethnic	.99	.07	.84	-.02	-.27
Class	.46	.17	.03	-.03	-.13
Religious	.26	.44	-.23	.51	-.15
Eigenvalue	2.43	1.26	1.83	1.42	1.04
Pc of variance	40.6	17.8	30.6	23.6	17.4

Identification (Table 11–8)

Our analysis revealed that pattern of pride in the various identifications differed according to level of religiosity. We present, therefore, separate factor analyses for those in the category of zero to three observances and those who observe four or all five mitzvot. In the low religiosity M + I category, the factor is loaded by both the subethnic identifications and the Jewish identification. The dominant variables in the second factor are pride in one's social class and in one's position on religion. In the high religiosity M + I category, the pattern is quite different, especially as to the second factor. The first factor can be interpreted as ethnic, but for this category the Jewish identification, which appears to have a substantial loading among the less religious, is replaced by the class identification. The Jewish identification in the dominant component of the second factor, together with pride in religious position and the Israeli identification. It appears that in the low religiosity category the Jewish identification is related to the ethnic identifications, whereas in the high religiosity category it is related to the religious identification.

A different picture emerges among Poles and Rumanians. In the low religiosity category, the picture is quite straightforward; the first factor represents the broad and specific subethnic identifications, and the second factor represents the more general Jewish and Israeli identifications. The religious position is not significant in either factor. A different pattern is revealed in the high religiosity P + R category. Here we have a three-factor solution. The first factor is parallel to the first factor found among their less religious counterparts. The second factor is loaded mainly by the Jewish and religious identifications, but the only variable significantly loaded on the third factor is pride in the Israeli identification. It appears that among respondents with high levels of religiosity, of whatever origin, pride in Jewish identification is related to pride in their identification as religious Jews. However, whereas among Moroccans and Iraqis both Jewish and religious identification, among Poles and Rumanians the Israeli identification constitutes a separate factor.

Table 11-9 Relative deprivation in political power.
Factor loadings (based on principal factor with varimax rotation)

SOCIAL CATEGORY	MOROCCANS + IRAQIS		POLES + RUMANIANS	
	Factor 1	Factor 2	Factor 1	Factor 2
Ashkenazim	−.09	.14	.03	.53

Table 11-9   (Continued)

SOCIAL CATEGORY	MOROCCANS + IRAQIS		POLES + RUMANIANS	
	Factor 1	Factor 2	Factor 1	Factor 2
Edot ha'Mizrah	.80	–.24	.19	.00
R's country of origin	.71	–.26	.46	.45
R's economic class	–.25	.76	–.48	– .08
R's religious group	–.08	.33	–.19	– .07
Eigenvalue	2.07	1.00	1.48	1.03
Pct of variance	41.4	20.0	29.5	20.6

Relative Deprivation in Political Power (Table 11-9)

With regard to feelings of injustice or relative deprivation in the distribution of political power, the centrality of feelings that relate to ethnic and class memberships is obvious. In both M + I and P + R, variables that pertain to ethnicity and social class are highly loaded on the factors. Feelings of relative deprivation in the political power of respondents' religious or secular allegiance seem to belong to a different domain.

Table 11-10   Support for political organization on the basis of ethnicity, class, and religious position. Product-moment correlation coefficients.

	MOROCCANS %	IRAQIS %	POLES %	RUMANIANS %	TOTAL %
Edot and broad ethnic category	.59	.44	*	*	.56

Table 11-10   (Continued)

	MOROCCANS %	IRAQIS %	POLES %	RUMANIANS %	TOTAL %
Broad ethnic category and class	.40	.38	*	*	.33
Broad ethnic category and religious position	.38	.48	*	*	.30
Class and religious position	.35	.49	.26	.22	.33

*Almost no Poles or Rumanians support political organization on the basis of ethnicity

Support for Political Organization (Table 11-10)

Factor analysis was not used in the analysis of this dimension because support for political organization constitutes only four variables. We present the correlations of support for political organization on a religious basis, on an ethnic basis, and on a class basis. Among Moroccans and Iraqis, there are moderate positive correlations among religious, ethnic, and class bases of political organization. However, even among Moroccans and Iraqis, only a small minority supported political organization on any of these bases. Within that minority, there is a tendency to respond positively to questions on support for political organization on more than one basis, but the meanings, if any, of these overlaps are not clear, and because only small numbers are involved, they appear to have little significance.

CONCLUSIONS

Our findings may be summarized as follows:
1. Among the Israeli Jewish population, there is a considerable overlap of religiosity with ethnic origin and with class. However, within each ethnic group, there is some overlap of religiosity with class, and this convergence crosscuts the religiosity differences among some of the ethnic groups.

2. The cultural differences, social distance, and conflict between religious and secular Jews are perceived by the majority to be greater than those among ethnic groups or classes.

3. Pride in identification with respect to religion (religious, traditional, secular) is less pronounced than pride in ethnic and class identifications among Moroccans and Iraqis, and less pronounced than pride in class identification among Poles and Rumanians.

4. There is little relative deprivation regarding religious position among the majority. Among Moroccans and Iraqis, it is much less than ethnic relative deprivation.

5. Only those with a high level of religiosity, who are disproportionately Moroccan, support political organization on a religious basis. Otherwise, support for this kind of political organization is on par with support for ethnic or class political organizations, a minority in all cases.

6. Most of the factor analyses show that the distribution of the religious images, identifications, and evaluations crosscut rather than converge with the distribution of the ethnic and class subjective dimensions, which do converge at a number of important points (perceived social distance, perceived conflict, feelings of deprivation.) There was no convergence of the religious and ethnic dimensions, and when there was some convergence of the religious and class dimensions, this applied only to one ethnic category and appears to be of minor significance.

7. In most of the factor analyses, the solution for M + I required fewer factors than the solution for PR. This seems to indicate that the subjective dimensions of P + R are more differentiated than those of M + I. This conclusion obtains further support from the fact that in most of the analyses the most important first factor pertaining to M + I explains a higher portion of the variance than the parallel factor among PR. Apparently, M + I reveal a greater tendency to base their various perceptions on common components.

These findings are hardly indicative of a religious-secular division that threatens Israeli society. Respondents might perceive that division to be of greater magnitude than ethnic and class divisions. Nonetheless, the greater weight of the religious factor in the cognitive dimension is not paralleled in the affective and evaluative dimensions, and the implications of the religious-secular division are blunted in all three subjective components (cognitive, affective, evaluative) by the crosscutting of important ethnic and class divisions.

Our sample includes religious Jews, but not haredim, the ultra-Orthodox, who are rare in Beersheba. It can be argued that the significant conflict in Israeli society is not between religious and secular Jews but between haredim and other Jews. But although there are signs of polarization, as some sections of the secular population, including some from edot ha'Mizrah, become 'haredized' or ultra-Orthodox, and some from traditional backgrounds become secular, the traditional section of the population is still by far the largest among edot ha'Mizrah, and it is far from insignificant among Ashkenazim.

If there is an increasing conflict between religious and secular Jews, the organization of the opposing groups is by no means symmetrical. The religious political parties and movements do not face political parties that focus their resources and policies on secularist issues, nor strong secularist voluntary movements. The historical relationship between the Jewish religion and the Jewish people, the importance of a religiously conveyed history in the legitimation of the Israeli state, and the problems of expressing Jewishness without the use of symbols anchored in the Jewish religion have proved obstacles to the development of strong secularist movements in Israel. Secular Jews tend to form ad hoc groups in order to oppose religious Jews or haredim over various issues, but these groups have not developed into widely supported secularist movements. Without such organization, conflict is likely to be confined to short affrays.

REFERENCES

Ayalon, H., E. Ben-Rafael, and S. Sharot. 1985. Variations in ethnic identification among Israeli Jews. *Ethnic and Racial Studies* 8:389-407.

_____. 1986. Secularization and the diminishing decline of religion. *Review of Religious Researh* 27:193-297.

_____. 1988. Class consciousness in Israel. *International Journal of Comparative Sociology*, forthcoming.

Ben-Meir, Y. and P. Kedem. 1979. Index of religiosity of the Jewish population of Israel. *Megamot* (Hebrew) 14:353-62.

Ben-Rafael, E. 1982. *The emergence of ethnicity: Cultural groups and social conflict in Israel.* Wwstport, Conn.: Greenwood Press.

Ben-Rafael, E. and S. Sharot. 1987. Ethnic pluralism and religious congregations: A comparison of neighborhoods in Israel. *Ethnic Groups* 7:65–83.

Coser, L. 1956. *The Functions of Social Conflict.* New York: Free Press.

Deshen, S. and M. Shokeid. 1974. *The predicament of homecoming: Cultural and social life of North African immigrants in Israel.* Ithaca, N.Y.: Cornell University Press.

Goldscheider, C. and D. Friedlander. 1983. Religiosity patterns in Israel. *American Jewish Year Book* 83:3–39.

Kim, J. and C. W. Mueller. 1982a. *Introduction to factor analysis.* Paper No. 13. Sage University.

————. 1982b. *Factor analysis: Statistical methods and practical issues. Paper No. 14. Sage University.*

Kraus, V. 1983. Ethnic origin as a hierarchical dimension of social status, and its correlates. *Sociology and Social Research* 66:452–66.
————. 1984. Social segregation in Israel as a function of objective and subjective attributes of the ethnic group. *Sociology and Social Research* 69:50–71.

Nahon, Y. 1984. *Trends in the occupational status—The ethnic dimension.* Jerusalem: The Jerusalem Institute for Israel Studies.

Shokeid, M., and S. Deshen. 1982. *Distant relations: Ethnicity and politics among Arabs and North African Jews in Israel.* New York: Praeger.

Simmel, G. 1955. *Conflict and the web of group affiliations (1908).* New York: Free Press.

Smooha, S. 1978. *Israel: Pluralism and conflict.* London: Routledge and Kegan Paul.

Swirski, S. 1981. *Lo Nehkshalim Ela Menukshalim (Orientals and Ashkenazim in Israel: The ethnic division of labor).* Hiafa: Mahbarot Le'Mehkar U'Lebikoret (Hebrew).

About the Contributors

Henry Abramovitch is an anthropologist and Jungian analyst who teaches at the Tel Aviv University Medical School. He has done fieldwork on death customs in Madagascar and Jerusalem. His forthcoming work includes a study of the impact of Martin Buber on contemporary psychotherapy.

Hanna Ayalon is lecturer at the School of Education and Department of Sociology and Anthropology, Tel Aviv University. Her areas of interest include sociology of education, social inequality, and quantitative research methods.

Mordecai Bar-Lev is senior lecturer in the School of Education of Bar-Ilan University. He is also head of the undergraduate program on informal education, chair of the graduate program in educational sociology, and since 1987 director of the Sociological Institute for Community Studies, Bar-Ilan University. His areas of interest includes sociology of education and youth, social history of education and youth, and sociology and history of the kibbutz.

Benjamin Beit-Hallahmi is associate professor of psychology at the University of Haifa. He has authored *Psychoanalysis and Religion: A Bibliography* (1978). *Prolegomena to the Psychological Study of Religion* (1989), co-authored *The Social Psychology of Religion* (with Michael Argyle 1975), *Twenty Years Later: Kibbutz Children Grown Up* (with A. I. Rabin 1982), and *The Kibbutz Bibliography* (with S. Shur, J. R. Blasi, and A. I. Rabin 1981), and edited *Research in Religious Behavior* (1973).

Eliezer Ben-Rafael is associate professor of sociology in the Department of Sociology and Anthropology, Tel-Aviv University. His research interests are in ethnicity, terrorism, the kibbutz, and language. He is the author of *The Emergence of Ethnicity: Cultural Groups and Social Conflict in Israel* (1982), *Israel-Palestine: A Guerrilla Conflict in International Politics* (1987), and *Status, Power and Conflict in the Kibbutz*, (1988).

Yoram Bilu Holds a joint appointment as senior lecturer in psychology and in sociology and anthropology at the Hebrew University. His research interests include Jewish ethnopsychiatry, folk religion, dreams and culture, and Moroccan Jews in Israel. In 1985, he was the first recipient of the L. Bryce Boyer Award in psychoanalytic anthropology.

Peri Kedem is lecturer in the Psychology Department and School of Social Work at Bar-Ilan University. She serves also as the head statistical consultant of the Psychology Department, of the Institute for the Advancement of Social Integration in Schools, and of the Male Infertility Laboratory of the Life Science Department. Her fields of interest are methodology, attitudes, ideology, and group identification, with a special interest in psychology and religion.

William Shaffir is professor of sociology at McMaster University in Hamilton, Ontario, Canada. His chief areas of interest include the sociology of religious transformation, professional socialization, and field research methods. His current research includes studies of Montreal's Hassidic community, and the migration and return migration of Canadian Jews to and from Israel.

Stephen Sharot is associate professor of sociology in the Department of Behavioral Sciences, Ben-Gurion University of the Negev. His research interests are in the sociology of religion, ethnicity, class, and historical sociology. He is author of *Judaism: A Sociology* (1976), and *Messianism, Mysticism, and Magic: A Sociological Analysis of Jewish Religious Movements* (1982).

Zvi Sobel has taught sociology at Miami University (Ohio), Brandeis University, and for the past 20 years at the University of Haifa. He is the author of *Hebrew Christianity: The 13th Tribe* (1974) and *Migrants from the Promised Land* (1986).

Leonard Weller is professor of sociology at Bar-Ilan University. While his main interests are social psychology and the family, he has researched many areas in sociology and psychology, including biofeedback, mental retardation, ethnicity, religiosity, group dymanics, and delinquency.

Ephraim Tabory is senior lecturer and chair of the Department of Sociology and Anthropology at Bar-Ilan University. His main research interests are in religion and religious movements in Israel.

Index